Gypsy Feast

THE HIPPOCRENE COOKBOOK LIBRARY

Gypsy Feast

**Recipes and Culinary
Traditions of the Romany People**

Carol Wilson

HIPPOCRENE BOOKS, INC.
NEW YORK

Copyright © 2004 Carol Wilson.

Illustrated by John David Smith.

Book and jacket design by Acme Klong Design, Inc.

For more information, address:
HIPPOCRENE BOOKS, INC.
171 Madison Avenue
New York, NY 10016

ISBN 0-7818-1027-2

Cataloging-in-Publication Data available from the Library of Congress.
Printed in the United States of America.

TABLE OF CONTENTS

The seeds for this book were sown when I was about ten years old and even at that early age, intensely interested in food and cooking and the kinds of food that people ate and why. I was fascinated, too, by the Romany way of life. As a child, growing up in the suburbs of Wakefield in Yorkshire, England, my friends and I watched, enthralled as the Gypsies arrived in their gaily painted horse-drawn and motor caravans to set up camp in a local meadow every summer.

They were and still are often referred to as "Gypsies" but their correct and preferred name is Roma. *Rom* means man in the Romani language and the word to denote people is *Roma*. *Romani* is used when referring to Gypsy groups.

Romany (the Anglicized version of Romani) women in their colorful exotic clothes, bedecked with gleaming gold jewelry, went from door to door selling their wares—"lucky" heather, freshly picked flowers, and wooden clothes pegs, together with the tantalizing offer of reading our mothers' palms and foretelling the future. The meadow is long gone—houses now stand there and Roma no longer call at local homes or work in the farm fields.

To earn money Roma worked at a number of occupations, including seasonal work such as fruit, vegetable, and hop picking. Their labor was an essential part of the local economy and every year large numbers of Roma traveled to the same fields, orchards, and farms for employment. Sometimes they would work on a farm for no payment, but would be allowed to stay on the farmer's land in lieu of wages. Romany men have always been particularly skilled at working with horses. Other occupations included wine-making and fishing, alongside the traditional occupations of making wooden clothes pegs, baskets, and nets; beekeeping; making artificial flowers from grasses; and collecting and selling rags, which were used to make paper. The women sold pegs, baskets, artificial and wild flowers, and also told fortunes, although the latter was reserved for non-Roma, who were known as *Gadje* or *Gorger*. The women often sang or danced at local fairs and horse races, too.

The relentless onslaught of modern technology has had an enormous effect on Romany throughout the world. As the modern world slowly encroaches on their traditional way of life and urban regeneration gradually eradicates large numbers of woods, forests, and meadows, their ancient customs are in decline and in danger of being lost forever. The integration of many Roma into non-Roma (*Gajikane*) cultures has also diluted many traditional values and beliefs. Modern young Roma have largely forgotten the old traditions and culture.

Many Roma are now settled in houses and few if any travel throughout the country in colorful wagons. Machines have largely replaced the traditional seasonal occupations of fruit picking and farm work and cars have taken the place of horses. Convenience foods, modern cooking tools and appliances have ousted the traditional recipes and cooking methods. As the Roma have developed more contact with non-Roma, particularly in cities, their eating habits have become more like those of non-Roma.

This book is my attempt to record the old ways, foods, feast days, marriage customs, funeral rites, and a unique way of life that has almost disappeared forever.

My grateful thanks to my wonderful husband Gordon and my son Ivan for their patience, help, and encouragement to me in writing this book and also for their invaluable help as willing recipe testers.

I would also like to thank John David Smith for his superb illustrations.

My thanks also to those Roma who have generously shared their fond memories of foods and celebrations in times past.

We are all wanderers of this earth,
our hearts are full of wonder and
our souls are full of dreams.

—*Romany saying*

NOTES ON THE RECIPES

Basic Ingredients
As a rule, Roma used the best quality foods they could obtain, e.g. butter in preference to margarine and free-range eggs.

Fats—The fat traditionally used in Romany cooking was lard, dripping, bacon fat, or butter. The use of polyunsaturated oils is a recent innovation, but these oils can often be substituted for hard fats. The flavor and texture of the finished dish, however will differ from the original.

Beurre manié—French for "kneaded butter"—equal parts of softened butter and flour, used to adjust the thickness of sauces and soups.

Buttermilk—the liquid left after cream has been churned into butter. It is used with baking soda for making bread and scones, where it reacts with the soda to produce an aerating gas and distinctive flavor. In some countries it is served as a refreshing summer drink. It is sold alongside fresh milk products in most supermarkets.

Flour—all-purpose flour (plain flour) is made from wheat.

Self-rising flour—all-purpose flour sifted with baking powder.

Wholemeal flour—also called all-purpose wholemeal or wholewheat flour. This is made from the whole grain of the wheat and has no baking powder added.

Strong or *bread flour*—made from hard wheat and contains more gluten than all-purpose flour. It is used to make bread and ensures that the bread holds its risen shape without collapsing.

Glacé cherries—also known as candied cherries.

Jam—also known as preserves or conserve.

Sweeteners—I have used unrefined sugar in the recipes, which was originally cheaper than white sugar, and which we all now know is better for health. Nowadays sugar has fallen into disrepute, particularly refined white sugar. Most refined sugars are chemically processed to produce white sugar as efficiently as possible and some of these processes include the use of animal bones in the de-coloring process, which makes these sugars unacceptable to strict vegetarians.

Brown refined sugars are white refined sugars that have been coated with molasses to give them color and flavor. The difference in flavor is very noticeable: unrefined sugars have a deeper, richer taste and aroma than refined sugars.

Extracted from the crushed cane, the sugar cane juice is naturally clarified and crystallized to produce a range of golden, light, and dark brown sugars which are completely natural, and full of the nutritious goodness of molasses. The darker the sugar, the stronger the flavor, due to the amount of molasses retained in the sugar.

The unrefined natural sugars used in these recipes are widely available throughout the United States. They include:

Milled golden cane sugar is light golden and an everyday, natural alternative to refined white sugar. It is dry and free-flowing. Use it in tea, on cereals and fruit, and for baking.

Demerara sugar has a crunchy texture, distinctive aroma and golden brown color. Use this in coffee. The large sparkling crystals also make it the ideal topping for cakes, cookies, melon, or grapefruit.

Light brown muscovado sugar is the ideal replacement for refined, light brown sugar. It has a glorious fudgy flavor and adds extra depth of flavor to cakes, cookies, toffee, and chocolate.

Dark brown molasses sugar is the ultimate dark brown sugar, sticky, with a rich aroma and extraordinary depth of flavor. It is superb for rich fruitcakes, chocolate-based recipes, and savory marinades and sauces.

Sugar crystals are large golden crystals with a distinctive but subtle flavor that is excellent in coffee. The coarse textured crystals are ideal for crunchy toppings on cakes, cookies, and fruit pies.

Cooking Methods

Much of the Romany cooking was done over the campfire. I have adapted the traditional methods to oven or stovetop cooking. Some of the recipes are suitable for barbecuing and this is stated in the recipe.

INTRODUCTION

It is difficult to establish with any certainty the world population of Roma today, but estimates indicate that there are approximately twelve to fifteen million worldwide. Around ten million Roma live in Europe, with an estimated one hundred thousand living in the United Kingdom.

Most Roma today live in Romania, Bulgaria, Spain, and Hungary. Since the demise of Communist regimes in Eastern Europe, there has been an increase in Roma cultural and ethnic unity. Nowadays the word *Roma* is gradually replacing the word *Gypsy*, but there are also groups of Gypsies who do not call themselves Roma, such as the Sinti and the Calé. The Sinti hail from central Europe (mostly Germany), while the Calé are from Spain.

A nomadic people, their gradual migration or *aresajipe* from India in the fourteenth century, led them to become scattered throughout the world. The reasons for their exodus are unknown, but their migration took them through Persia, Armenia, and eventually into Europe. As they traveled they absorbed many aspects of new foreign cultures, traditions, and language into their own culture. Romany are believed to have arrived in the United Kingdom in the fifteenth century, when their appearance certainly caused something of a stir—their burnished copper colored skin, glossy black hair, flamboyant colorful clothes, obscure language, and almost magical knowledge of herbs and plants, led to them being greeted with suspicion, even hostility wherever they traveled. Their swarthy looks resulted in a general belief that they were from Turkey or Egypt and they became known as Egyptians or Gyptians, which later became Gypsies.

The first record of Gypsies in Britain was in the accounts of the Lord High Treasurer for Scotland, dated April, 22, 1505: "Item to the Egyptians by the Kinges command vii lib," a payment of £7 for something that is not recorded. In July of the same year, King James IV wrote to his uncle the king of Denmark: "Anthony Gagino, a lord of Little Egypt" had arrived with his retinue in Scotland "during a pilgrimage through the Christian world undertaken at the command of the Apostolic See." The earliest recorded mention of Gypsies in England was in "A *Dyalog of Syr Thomas More, Knight*" in 1529.

Gypsies danced and entertained James V at Holyrood House in Edinburgh in 1530, but in the mid-sixteenth century suspicion of foreigners combined with a fear of vagrants, led Henry VIII to make it an offence merely to be a Gypsy. In 1530 he ordered their departure within forty days unless they chose to abandon their "naughty, idle and ungodly life." However, by the time of Elizabeth I there was estimated to be around ten thousand Gypsies in England and although their presence was not exactly welcomed they were accepted as part of the community.

The first Gypsies arrived in North America after having been deported from England in the seventeenth century. The earliest evidence of their residence is a 1695 court record in Henrico County, Virginia. Their presence was also mentioned in colonial newspapers as a "Gypsy problem." French Emperor Napoleon I was responsible for the transportation of hundreds of Gypsies (mostly men) to Louisiana between 1801 and 1803.

Dutch Gypsies arrived in America in early colonial times, as did a number of German Gypsies who settled in Pennsylvania. Smaller numbers of Gypsies traveled to America from Hungary, Romania, Syria, and Turkey, while Spain and Portugal also banished their unwanted Gypsies to America.

More Gypsies arrived in the United States from Serbia, Russia, Austria, and Hungary toward the end of the nineteenth century, and as part of a larger wave of immigration from southern and eastern Europe in the early twentieth century. Primary immigration ended, for the most part, in 1914 with the onset of the World War I when immigration laws became stricter. A subgroup of the Russian Rom, the Kalderash (Coppersmith) specialized in work that involved mainly the repair and re-panning of industrial equipment used in bakeries, laundries, confectioneries, and other businesses. They also developed fortune-telling businesses in urban areas. Another group identified as "Russian Gypsies" were the Rusniakuria, ("Ruthenians") who were known in New York as musicians and singers.

The Romnichels, or English Gypsies, began to arrive in America in 1850 and worked mostly as horse-traders, but with the rapid decline of the horse trade after World War I, the majority had to rely on occupations such as basket-making, furniture-making, and fortune-telling.

The Ludar, or Romanian Gypsies, also came to the United States during the great immigration from southern and eastern Europe between 1880 and 1914, with most coming from northwestern Bosnia. They worked as animal trainers and showpeople, including monkeys and bears as part of their entourage. The Ludar created a "vil-lage" of homemade shacks in Maspeth, a section of the borough of Queens in New York City, which existed from about 1925 to 1939, when it was razed. Another sim-ilar settlement was erected in the Chicago suburbs during the same period.

A small number of Gypsies arrived in the United States from Germany and were sometimes referred to as the "Black Dutch." In the early days there was some con-tact between Native Americans and Gypsies and there were still a few of these *Chikeners* in 1929. Most of the Gypsies living in the United States today, howev-er, are descended from immigrants of the Eastern European Diaspora in the late nineteenth and early twentieth centuries. Following the restrictive immigration laws of 1924, Gypsy immigration to the United States continued on a reduced scale, through indirect Latin American routes. The Gypsies of North America, like those of Europe, lived and worked in extended family groups called *kumpania*. Each group was governed by a hereditary chief, *Rom Baro*, who was responsible for upholding the traditional laws. These communities still exist and usually prefer to be self-employed. A common occupation for the men is buying and selling used cars and trucks, while the most common occupation for the women is fortune-telling. American Gypsies like Gypsies throughout the world have their own legal system and a tribunal of elders known as the *Kris*, which hears and decides cases. As there are no Gypsy lawyers, complainants always represent themselves; the ultimate punishment is banishment and exile from one's community.

In 1911, in the first week of September, the British press and the residents of south London were treated to a fascinating spectacle, when a group of more than a hundred Austrian Galician Gypsies made their home in a field by the side of a house in Garratt Lane, Wandsworth. This group of Gypsies was only one of a number of large contingents of foreign Gypsies who traveled through Britain in the 1900s, causing quite a stir among the locals. The *Zingari*, as these Austrian Galician Gypsies were known, were highly skilled coppersmiths and performers and had left Galicia fifteen years before to wander through Europe. The band was divided into three national groups—Russian, Hungarian, and Polish. These Gypsies, who were multilingual (speaking German, Polish, Russian, French, Spanish, Romany, and English), announced that they intended to stay in England for a year or so before moving on to South America.

The Austrian Galicians were hoping to get an engagement for a troupe of singers at one of the many London music halls. Their elderly leader, Maria Petrovna—described as "garishly dressed and loaded with coins and barbaric jewelry"—gave an interview to the *Daily Express* newspaper in Russian through an interpreter, in which she described her band as coppersmiths skilled in the manufacture of pots and pans. She also commented: "There is nothing we want; we are just like fishes in the water. Only I do not like the English meat, the beef and mutton are so stiff that I will not buy them and so we must eat chicken and pork every day."

Romanian and Russian Coppersmiths arrived in Liverpool in 1911. They, too, were highly skilled in the repair and renovation of copper vessels, which were much used in the sugar, jam, and pickle factories in this region of England.

True Roma are descended from the ancient warrior classes of northern India. Their blood groups are related to those found in northwest India and the surrounding areas. Intriguingly, there is an ancient legend among some Roma that they came from Israel and had Jewish origins. According to this, the patriarch Abraham was accompanied and protected by Gypsies on his journey from Ur, and many Gypsies prayed to him for protection.

The Romany language, known as *Romani* or *Romanes*, is rooted in ancient Punjabi or Hindi. Stefan Valyi, a Hungarian theological student working at the University of Leiden in the Netherlands, is believed to have discovered the true origins of the Gypsies in 1763, when he met some Indian students on the Malabar Coast and was struck by the similarity of the students' language to that of the Hungarian Gypsies. When he returned to Hungary, Valyi spoke some Indian words to the Gypsies, who understood almost all of them. Romani also contains many

Persian words and some now believe that its grammar is closer to the Dom of eastern Bengal than Punjabi.

Most Roma speak some form of Romany (which is essentially a spoken, rather than a written language) while others speak dialects of local languages with extensive borrowings from Romany. Romany culture and traditions have always been passed on orally—there are no written records as there is no way to write the language, except phonetically, and some sounds defy our alphabet. Their spoken language is very old and is a mixture of whatever country the Roma live in, combined with Romany and some slang. Some Romany words have been absorbed into English; for example, *pal* comes from *phral* meaning "brother," the English slang word *kushti* means "good," and the English *cosh* comes from *krash*, the Romany word for a heavy stick.

Another unifying force apart from language was the *patrin*, a secret code developed by the Roma as a means of communication amongst themselves, in which signs were left by one group to inform others passing that way. A seemingly insignificant bunch of grass by the side of the road, a notch on a tree trunk, a cross marked on the ground, or a sign left on a village wall or farm gate informed other Roma which direction the group had taken, how many were in their group, and more importantly, if the villagers or farmer were friendly or hostile.

Roma have become widely dispersed throughout the world and their culture and social organization vary accordingly. The largest concentrations are found in the Balkan peninsula, in central Europe, and in Russia and the other successor republics of the USSR. Smaller numbers are scattered throughout the Middle East, North Africa, and the Americas. The Spanish Gypsy population is thought to be around half a million. These are divided into two major groups: the *gitanos* (in old Spanish, gitano was a way of saying "Egyptian") and the *hungaros* (Hungarians emigrating from central Europe), who now live predominantly in southern Spain. The *hungaros* were poorer than the *gitanos* and lived an exclusively nomadic lifestyle, usually in tents or shacks (*casitas*) on the outskirts of the larger cities. Many *gitanos* denied the *hungaros* the status of being in their same ethnic group, but outsiders still tend to label them collectively as Gypsies.

The Roma are divided into groups sometimes referred to as nations or tribes. These divisions generally reflect historical patterns of settlement in different geographical areas. The European tribes include the Calé of Spain, Finland, and Wales; the Sinti of Germany and central Europe; the Manouche of France; the Romanichals of the United Kingdom; the Boyash of Romania; and the Roma, a subgroup of the larger Roma population of Eastern Europe and the Balkans. Although historically the Roma are wanderers, nowadays most Roma live in settled communities.

Today there is no single Roma culture, just as there is no general agreement as to who qualifies to be called Roma. Romany groups around the world hold different traditions, customs, and beliefs. Some of these are very old and are still adhered to, while others have died out and become obsolete. It is difficult to say exactly when a particular custom or tradition became obsolete or among which group, as Romany people are so widely scattered and even in the same county one group's customs are different from those of another group. Groups that settled in one location generally absorbed some of the *gajikané* (non-Roma) local culture. But one important characteristic of all Roma is a strong sense of their unique identity. Romany culture stresses the importance of its own traditions and its people are extremely conscious of their uniqueness and are careful to emphasize the differences between themselves and others. Contact with non-Roma is regarded as potentially polluting, a belief probably inherited from the religious beliefs of their Hindu ancestors. Several Romany traditions are still observed and many Roma have not give up *romipen* (the Gypsy way of life) completely—for instance many Roma still place a red string around a newborn baby's neck, as an acknowledgment from the father that the child is his.

The International Gypsy Committee organized the first World Romani Congress in 1971, held in London, England, at which representatives from India and about twenty other countries were in attendance. The Congress approved a Romany flag embellished with the red sixteen-spoked chakra that is respected by Roma throughout the world. This was one of the proposals at the *Uniunea Generala a Romilor din Romania* (General Assembly of Roma in Romania) led by Gheorghe Nicolescu in 1933 in Bucharest, along with a library, hospital and university for Roma, plus the creation of a national holiday marking the end of Romany slavery. The top of the flag is blue to represent the heavens and green below, to represent the earth. In the center the chakra, symbolizes movement and progress and also recognizes the Indian origins of the Roma.

GOOD AND BAD LUCK

Te xav ka ta biav
(May I eat at your wedding.)
(Blessing said to young Gypsies to wish them the best of luck)

The image of Gypsies as unclean couldn't be further from the truth. In reality they have always been very clean and have followed strict rules relating to food hygiene. Roma were frequently suspicious of non-Roma people and often regarded *them* as unclean and as a possible source of infection. A man who did not keep his person or belongings clean was called "*chickly*" (dirty) and was despised.

Roma society relies on distinctions between behavior that is pure (*vujo* or *wuzho*) and that which is polluted (*marimé*). The term *marimé* (or *moxadó* in England and Wales) means defiled, polluted, or unclean. Other terms for *marimé* are *melali*, *mageradó, mokadi, kulaló, limaló, prastló, palecidó, pekelimé, gonimé*, or *bolimé*. The term indicates impurity or uncleanliness, which may be physical, ritual, or moral and also refers to the sentence of expulsion imposed for violating purity rules, or indeed for any disruptive behavior. The Roma have never imposed the death sentence, but a punishment considered worse than death was the *marimé* punishment, whereby a person was banished from the community, and had no social contact with other members of the tribe. The punishment included not only the offender, but usually his or her family as well and the length of banishment could last for days or even years.

Food prepared by *Gaje* (non-Roma) was *marimé* and thus was avoided. This was not always possible when, for instance a Roma person was in the hospital, but was to be avoided as much as possible by eating food brought by relatives, drinking from cartons or bottles, and using disposable cutlery. It was perfectly permissible for Roma to eat with their hands to avoid using possibly unclean utensils. It was also deemed necessary to take precautions when *Gaje* entered Roma space; for example tableware and cutlery were set aside for *Gaje* and were washed separately.

Dogs and cats were regarded as *mochardi*, unclean in the ceremonial sense because they lick themselves all over. Menstruating women were banned from cooking or touching food for someone else. Likewise Roma would not eat or drink anything a woman had stepped over—this was given to the dogs. These practices were due to the belief that a woman's body was divided into two parts—above the waist and below the waist. A woman was clean from the waist up and "polluted" from the waist down. There was no shame associated with the upper part of the body but the lower part was an object of shame due to its association with menstruation. The fact that blood flowed without injury was regarded as proof of a bodily impurity. This concept of *marimé* as applied to women is one explanation why many Roma women wore long skirts and the fact that the bottom of those skirts must not touch a man other than the woman's husband.

Food was carefully prepared to avoid any *marimé* contact. Dishes and crockery were never washed in the same sink or bowl used for washing clothes or hands, but in a bowl kept solely for that purpose. A special bowl was used for washing the face and body, and towels for washing the body were used for nothing else. Many households kept special soap for washing food-related items. Tables and eating surfaces were kept spotless. A sick person had their own crockery and utensils and when they recovered or died, these were all destroyed.

There were rigid rules for drawing water from streams and rivers. The water at the farthest point upstream was the purest and used for cooking and drinking; water from farther downstream was used to wash dishes and for bathing; the water farthest downstream was used for washing or watering horses.

Roma have always had a great love of animals, particularly horses and dogs. No pets were allowed into the wagon though, but were always kept outdoors. Cruelty to animals was strictly prohibited and animals were killed only for food. The horse was essential to the survival and mobility of the Roma and is treated with great respect. Eating horsemeat was taboo and a very serious offence as horses were sacred to the Roma and it was believed that anyone who ate horseflesh would become insane. Like the Native Americans, Roma preferred colored horses and every *Rom* aspired to own a black and white horse.

Cats, rats, and foxes were also *marimé*. Owls were regarded as a portent of death and to hear an owl's hoot was considered very bad luck or *bibaxt*. The cry of the screech owl or *mulenger tschirklo* (the death bird) was a portent of imminent death and for that reason owls were avoided as food and pets. Different *Romany* had particular taboos that were unique to them. The Coppersmiths, who arrived in England in the early 1900s from Russia, would not eat hare because they believed the creature to be a vampire. They also believed that a leg of fowl must not be given to children or they would become liars.

Wuzho is the opposite of *marimé* and means pure and untainted. Some animals are revered as *wuzho* including hedgehogs, horses, and all scavengers (who are honored for recycling that which has died), as well as some people, including most Roma.

Spirits and ghosts were regarded as *wuzho* and *marimé*, respectively. Children were believed to be closer to the realm of spirits, which commanded both respect and fear. *Detlene* was the name given to the wandering souls of stillborn or aborted children.

Foods could also be lucky; garlic, salt, pepper, and vinegar, for instance, were believed to encourage good health. Among Swedish Roma, there was an ancient and obscure belief that while it was acceptable to borrow some food, it was forbidden to borrow salt, pepper, and bread and although these could be given as gifts, strictly speaking they should not be given away. By lending these foods they believed they were giving away good luck.

Roma did not have a specific religion of their own, but usually adopted the faiths of the countries in which they lived (although this was frequently supplemented by traditional Roma beliefs). Romany groups around the world hold different traditions, customs and beliefs. Among the Romany today can be found Roman Catholics, Eastern Orthodox, Muslims, Protestants, and Pagans, who all adhere to the dietary beliefs of their religion, e.g. Muslim Roma don't eat pork.

Although many became Christian in recent times, due to contact with missionaries, public education and people outside the Roma group, formal religion was frequently supplemented by faith in the supernatural, omens, and curses. Superstitions varied among different Roma groups, but played an important role in everyday life. The Gypsy religion also bore some striking similarities to Judaism: Roma were monotheistic, believing in one male deity called *Del* and the devil or *Beng* but never made images of their god. They also practiced circumcision and adhered to strict anticruelty laws. However there were also similarities with Hinduism, as they frequently practiced numerology. Religion and faith were a way of life; much like keeping *dharma* is for people in India, in that it determines how a person should act their whole lives. The aim of Hindu Dharma is "to reach peace of spirit and harmony in the material life." Roma call this set of requirements and prohibitions *romipen*—that which gives life order. Good luck charms, amulets, and talismans are common among Gypsies, and one of their most unshakeable and fundamental beliefs is in the existence of vampires, spirits, and ghosts.

Good luck charms, amulets, and talismans were common among all Romany and were carried to prevent bad luck or heal sickness. Some Roma considered horseshoes good luck in the same way as non-Roma. Some carried bread in their pockets as protection against bad luck (*bibaxt*) and supernatural spirits or ghosts (*muló*). One of the most unshakeable and fundamental beliefs, was the existence of spirits and ghosts. Roma almost never traveled at midday or at night, out of respect and fear for these restless spirits of the dead, who had the ability to possess people. Roma believed absolutely in the power of *muló*, as demonstrated by their use of curses, called *amria*, and healing rituals. They practiced fortune-telling only for the benefit of gullibe *Gadje* (non-Roma) and as a means of earning a living, but almost never among themselves.

While not all Roma followed all of the magical ways, the *Shuvani* or "wise woman" practiced magic. She was the keeper of the tribe's magic, rites, and superstitions and used the forces of nature to bless, curse, or heal. The powers of the Shuvani were rooted in a belief in the spirits of the earth, water, air, forest, and fields.

Since Roma considered illness to be an unnatural condition, called *prikaza*, there were many supernatural ways in which they believed disease could be prevented or cured. A fever could be eased by shaking a young tree for instance, or by drinking powdered potions of certain animals dissolved in spirits, to the accompaniment of a chant. Carrying a mole's foot was a cure for rheumatism, and carrying a hedge-hog's foot would prevent toothache.

Prikaza or "bad luck" was the result of coming into contact with *marimé* objects, creatures, or people—it followed any who were tainted (although there were means of undoing it). Actions that caused *prikaza* included bringing a dog into a wagon or *vardo*, coming into contact with a cat, becoming too close to the *Gaje*, and above all mentioning any bodily fluids or functions—a strict taboo. The color red was also very *prikaza* to some Romany and amongst these, primary red almost never appears in their clothing, and their wagons or *vardos* were never painted with that color.

Roma were true to their word and deals were sealed with a handshake, which was as binding as an oath. When selling horses, cars, or indeed anything, "luck money" was an important part of any sale and had to be given back to the buyer to ensure that his purchase brought him luck.

Kon khal but, khal peski bakht
(He who eats much eats away his own luck)

Traditionally, eating habits of the Roma were dictated by their nomadic way of life. Their diet consisted largely of whatever was readily available and in season, such as wild fruits, berries, leafy plants, herbs, flowers, fish and shellfish, game and small mammals, which were free for the taking in lanes, fields, hedgerows, woods, meadows, rivers, and streams. Foods were also often traded along the road. Boys as well as girls were taught to cook, so they would always be able to look after themselves in the wild. The value of wild foods to the Roma is difficult for us to appreciate nowadays, as we are used to easily accessible shops and stores which offer a great variety of foods.

Wild foods were vital for their survival and the Roma developed a phenomenal knowledge of these—which were edible, which were poisonous (even deadly), and where to find them. Since ancient times, people the world over have practiced healing and the healer, man or woman, was usually an elder of the group. Before the advent of modern medicine, people depended on nature in both health and sickness and were led by instinct, taste and experience to use wild plants to treat illness. Evidence of herbal remedies has been discovered in Stone Age excavations and herbs certainly played an important role in Ayurvedic medicine in India two thousand years ago. In the past, wild foods were much more abundant; the decline began with the industrial revolution and the development of built-up areas, when many meadows, woods, and pastures were destroyed in the name of progress.

As the Roma gradually came into greater contact with people of towns and cities, their eating habits became more and more like those of the non-Roma. As time passed, wild foods once greatly appreciated by the Roma eventually came to form an insignificant and almost nonexistent part of their diet.

There is no "Romany cuisine" as such. Their gastronomy used ingredients indigenous to wherever they traveled. Among the Romany people throughout the world there were enormous differences in the types of food eaten according to the country in which they lived and the tribes and families to which they belonged. Eastern European Roma for instance had plentiful supplies of buckwheat, potatoes, and sour cream, while in Spain rice, olive oil and hot sweet peppers were part of the everyday diet. But it was an unspoken rule that the eldest person present, whether a man or woman, was always served first, as the Roma admired old age for the wisdom and knowledge acquired with the passing years and accorded it due respect.

Eating together at feasts and when visiting was an expression of trust and solidarity as was sharing food and meals. Giving hospitability was considered of vital importance. All Roma rituals involved sharing food, and families or the group always ate together. Sharing food with others demonstrated friendship, respect, and an acknowledgement of their cleanliness. Refusing to share food was a serious insult; one of the most serious punishments the Roma as a group could impose on a person was to refuse to eat with him or her, which was regarded as social death.

At the beginning of the twentieth century, there were still Roma in tents and wagons in the English countryside and on the outskirts of towns and in the suburbs. The caravan, or *keir vardo* (wagon-house) as the Roma called it, was drawn by a horse or perhaps a couple of donkeys and later by car. The outside of the *vardo* was usually beautifully painted and some were elaborately gilded with gold leaf. The women of the family ensured that the interior of the wagon was made comfortable and attractive. Roma women favored pretty china and lace and these were much in evidence.

Roma traveled in their wagons and would make camp in a suitable place. The place they chose first had to undergo a ritual carried out by the *Shuvani*. Using a broom called a *besom* (made from the twigs of a birch tree) she would walk all around the camp brushing outward, away from the *vardos* to sweep away any uncleanness. The most remarkable object inside the *vardo* was the stove, or *bo*, which was usually just inside the door and gave out much heat. It had a metal chimney that went through the roof. Food was left to cook on the stove when inclement weather made it impractical and sometimes impossible to cook outdoors.

Every family had a collection of pots, pans, plates, and knives. Each adult possessed a *churi*, or knife, with which to cut food. Originally they had no forks or indeed a word for fork—the term *pasengri* signified a pitchfork. Spoons were called *royis*. The kettle (*kekkauvi*) and boiler (*pirry*) were made of copper and were hung over the fire by means of the *kekkauviskey sastra*, or kettle-iron.

Almost everything was put into the *sastra* (a big iron cooking pot on a tripod) where it would cook slowly over the campfire all day. A thin stew known by some English Roma as "Joe Gray" contained whatever meat could be obtained, such as bacon or a bit of beef, plus perhaps tomatoes, carrots, and onions and starchy vegetables such as potatoes, for energy. No one can remember how this stew acquired its name; perhaps it was a particular favorite of someone of that name, or perhaps he became well known for making this particular dish. Puddings, both sweet and savory, were boiled in a calico cloth and a particular favorite often served for Sunday dinner was a boiled meat or bacon pudding. Early Roma generally did not possess ovens, so local women or a friendly baker usually baked pastry for them for special occasions, such as weddings or baptisms.

When the Roma first left India, pepper was the spice widely used to impart heat to food (the chili had not yet arrived from the Americas) and this was an early and essential ingredient of most of their dishes.

Soups (*zumin*) were the basis of Romany menus and were made from whatever was readily available, such as offal (there are various ways of preparing entrails as they have always been the most available meal for a number of Romany families, due to the fact that they could be obtained for free or very cheaply, as most non-Roma people didn't want them), bones, meats, pulses, and vegetables.

Other treats came from the seashore. Shellfish, such as crabs, were caught from amongst the rocks. Seaweeds could be collected from beaches and cliffs. Wild duck eggs could be found near rivers and ponds and were fried on an old shovel over the fire.

Milk wasn't much appreciated by some Roma, as it was generally considered to be a drink for children, but butter (almost never margarine) was a staple. Other fats included meat drippings and fat skimmed off broth, which were spread on bread and sprinkled with salt to make a tasty snack. At one time Roma used to bake their own bread, but as time passed it became more usual to buy loaves from a baker. Roma were thrifty shoppers, too. They bought whatever food was left in the shops in the evening just before they closed when prices were reduced.

Coffee, drunk very strong, black, and sweet, was another staple for many Roma and was drunk freely throughout the day. Dandelion coffee, regarded as a tonic and a nerve builder was made by drying dandelion roots in the sun, then cutting them up and roasting them in a pan over the hot embers of the fire. The roasted roots were then pounded with heavy stones, sieved, and stored for winter.

Honey was much used as a sweetener before sugar was affordable and many Roma kept beehives. One of the most sought-after types of honey (which is prized by connoisseurs today) was heather honey. Rich reddish-brown in color with a dense, almost gelatinous texture, heather honey has a superb distinctive flavor that is not too sweet, with a hint of bitter caramel.

Ingenious recipes for sweet dishes such as puddings, cookies, and cakes were also devised. Gypsy Petulengro in *A Romany Life* (Methuen and Co., London, 1955) describes "potato sweet," an inspired creation made by making a hole through the center of a potato. The hole was filled with jam and the end piece of potato replaced to form a plug, after which the potato was baked in the hot embers of the campfire. Children especially, enjoyed these jam-impregnated potatoes. The same author had fond memories of *buni-manricli* or honey cake and honey biscuits, which were made with plenty of fat, particularly the much esteemed hedgehog oil.

A typical day began early with a breakfast of tea, bread, butter, and cheese. After breakfast the men went off to work while the women went out fortune-telling or selling flowers and the children took the horses or donkeys to lanes and commons to graze. Sometimes the children returned with *hotchiwitches* (hedgehogs) they had found. Lunch wasn't usually eaten, as the adults were out working all day and children learnt from an early age how to fend for themselves. Dinner was served at sunset and usually consisted of a thick fatty soup or stew accompanied by seasonal vegetables and potatoes, rice, or pasta.

Meat or game was broiled or cooked on a spit over the fire. Wild garlic and other herbs were used to flavor soups and stews when in season. In spring Roma sometimes made a kind of tea or soup of the young tender leaves of nettles. This was known as *dandrimengreskie zimmen* (the broth of the stinging thing) and was greatly enjoyed.

In the journal of the *Gypsy Lore Society* (published by The Society, founded in May 1888 and based at the University of Liverpool Library until 1974, when it was dissolved) of 1912 to 1913, Eric Otto Winstedt describes a tribe of Gypsies—the Coppersmiths (who had arrived in Liverpool on their way to America). When the men returned from whatever work they had been able to find, they returned to the camp for a meal of red herrings, tea, bread, and butter, followed by rice pudding. Red herrings salted and smoked until they became hard and dry and reddish in color, were the food of the period for most poor people, although it was reported at the time that eating them caused a terrible thirst. Winstedt wrote: "Their diet appeared to consist almost exclusively of fowl. Once I saw two loins of mutton, a goose and three fowls all waiting together in one pan to be cooked."

He and a friend were invited to join these Gypsies for a meal "consisting of stewed meat, besides a fowl, vegetables and stewed pears. Adults ate with their fingers and the children ate the broth in which the meat or fowl were cooked."

Food was usually boiled, stewed, or fried and was also left to cook over the campfire or on the stove all afternoon (there were few if any ovens) so anyone who was hungry could help himself or herself.

Romany knowledge of food and their skill in preparing and cooking it was remarked on by Mrs. Ernest Stewart Roberts, widow of the Master of Caius College Cambridge in her book *Sherborne, Oxford and Cambridge* (London, 1934, p. 131). She relates how she and her husband spent part of their honeymoon with her husband's aunt, who was married to Doctor John Mawer of Bucarest in 1886. She remarks that the cook in the doctor's household "like all the best Roumanian cooks was a Gypsy."

FRUITS AND BERRIES

May kali i muri may gugli avela
(The darker the berry, the sweeter it is).

Wild fruits and berries were once plentiful throughout the countryside and could be eaten raw or made into desserts and puddings. **Elderberries** (*Sambucus nigra*), the fruit of the elder tree, were prolific along the waysides and were picked when the clusters of the dark purple berries hung heavily over the hedgerows—usually in November. They must never be eaten raw and so were always cooked. The berries were also used frequently in cures for various ailments and made into a purple dye.

Glossy juicy **blackberries**, among late summer's most delicious fruits, are Britain's most common wild fruit and once grew in abundance in the hedgerows. The fruit's botanical name is *Rubus fruticosus*, which is in fact a collective name for a large group of fruits in the same genus—there are said to be more than two thousand varieties of blackberry including cultivars and hybrids. Roma and country people used to gather the berries and sell them, as their inky juices were used for dyes. Black silk that had developed a green hue for instance was dipped in blackberry juice mixed with ivy leaves to give a dense black. Ribbons and other fabrics were also dyed various hues of blue and black with blackberry juice.

Hordes of Romany used to descend on the Yorkshire moors to pick purplish blue **bilberries** (*Vaccinium myrtillus*), an exhausting back-breaking process as the plants grew only about a foot high. The small tart berries with their faint dusty "bloom" were made into tarts, puddings, and pies. The berries also had many medicinal uses.

Blackcurrants (*Ribes nigrum*) grew so profusely in some hedgerows that it was possible to gather basketloads. Blackcurrants are delicious eaten raw and when ripe, they combined excellently with other berries in summer puddings. Redcurrants, also found in the wild, were used in the same way.

Green, yellow, and red **gooseberries** (*Ribes grossularia*) were eaten with custard and made into tarts, pies, and boiled puddings. When yellow, the berries are rich and sweet. The acrid green berries are very sour, but some people prefer these and consider them to have the best flavor. Gooseberries were often used to stuff oily fish such as mackerel before cooking, to counteract the richness of the fish.

Great numbers of **mulberry** (*Morus nigra*) trees were planted in England in the seventeenth century to feed the silkworms—destined to supply a new silk industry. Unfortunately, the wrong type of tree was planted and was unsuitable for silkworms.

Consequently, the delicious dark juicy crimson fruits were there for the taking when the ripe mulberries tumbled from the trees. Their vivid juices stained clothes and skin but the fragile fruit could be eaten alone or used to make a steamed pudding. Mulberries were also served hot, their dark purple juices streaming from the fruit.

Wild **strawberries** (*Fragaria vesca*) and **raspberries** (*Rubus idaeus*) were once plentiful but are now scarce. The small berries have a magnificent flavor, quite different than that of today's cultivated berries. The fragrant scented berries were eaten alone or with cream. The fruit was also employed to whiten teeth and remove tartar—a juicy strawberry was rubbed over the teeth and gums and left for five minutes before rinsing well with warm water. Roma women and children went early in the morning or on a cool day when the fruit was in peak condition and as fresh as possible and collected only the firm, plump, scarlet berries that had very few green or white patches.

The sweet mealy textured berries of the **hawthorn** (*Crataegus monogyna*) were enjoyed raw and the young leaves were also eaten raw in the spring. The green buds that appeared in springtime were eaten with bread and butter or even layered with meat in a suet crust to make a tasty steamed savory pudding.

The **wild cherry** or **gean** (*Prunus aviums*), common throughout Europe, was ready to eat around June and varied widely from harsh, acidic, almost inedible little fruits to succulent plump, and sweet. They were put into fruit pies and puddings.

Apples and pears were eaten just as they were or made into a variety of cakes, pies, and tarts. They were also baked in the ashes of the campfire, sometimes filled with sugar, honey, and dried fruits and spices if these were available.

Medlars (*Mespilus germanica*) grew wild in the British countryside. In the fall when the leaves turned deep red, the green-brown fruits fell from the trees. They were ready to eat in late fall when overripe or "bletted," i.e. allowed to soften until almost rotten, to break down the acids and tannins. The bletted fruit turned a deeper brown and became wrinkled. If gathered before this stage they had to be kept for several weeks until they became soft and bletted. They were eaten raw or baked with a little butter.

Bullaces (*Prunus insititia*) or **damsons**, a type of wild plum, much smaller than cultivated varieties, with a strong tart flavor are indigestible when raw, but the sharp tasting fruit is transformed when cooked. Both the wild and cultivated fruits made excellent puddings and pies.

From May to September Britain's farm fields were full of fresh **rhubarb**, the stems a deep dark red and the leaves dark green. No doubt many Roma helped with the picking and took back a few bundles of the tart-tasting stems to transform into tasty puddings. The leaves of the rhubarb plant contain oxalic acid and are highly poisonous and so were never eaten.

Quince (*Pyrus cydonia*) trees flourish in Britain's cooler climate; the long growing season results in fruit with an intense flavor and deep pink flesh. The trees bear sweetly scented pale pink blossoms in the spring, with the fruit ripening from October to mid-November, when the skin turns yellow-gold and the fruit has an unmistakable scent. Quinces are covered in a soft down that must be washed off before cooking and are easily bruised, so needed careful handling. Raw quinces are inedible as the grainy flesh is rock-hard and mouth puckeringly acrid, but cooking them with sugar transforms the unpromising fruit into amber-colored softness with a sublime perfume. Just a few slices added to apple or pear dishes before cooking impart an ambrosial fragrance. A single fruit will scent an entire room with its wonderful perfume.

Sweet plump **figs** were enjoyed by Spanish Roma and Gypsies who made a "cake" of the pressed fruit, which was easy to carry and provided instant nourishment. Figs were also baked.

Dried Fig Cake   PAN DE HIGOS

MAKES 6 TO 8 SERVINGS

This cake would traditionally have been wrapped in fresh fig or vine leaves.

2 pounds dried figs, sliced or chopped
1 cup chopped unblanched almonds, hazelnuts, or walnuts
4 teaspoons dried fennel seeds or toasted sesame seeds
1 teaspoon ground cinnamon (optional)
1 teaspoon grated orange peel (optional)
2 tablespoons honey or unrefined milled golden cane sugar

Mix all the ingredients together and press into a shallow cake pan lined with nonstick baking parchment. Cover with a circle of nonstick baking parchment and place a heavy weight on top. Leave in a cool place for a few days, and then remove the weight and paper. Wrap well and store in an airtight pan until required, up to a week.

Baked Figs

The instructions for this dish are per fig. You can make as many or as few as you like.

Dip each fig in water and roll in about 1 tablespoon sugar. Put into a baking dish and cook for about 20 minutes at 425°F, by which time the sugar will have mingled with the juices and formed a rich brown syrup at the bottom of the dish. Serve warm or cold.

Berry Sweet with Nuts

MAKES 4 SERVINGS

4 medium slices wholemeal bread
1 cup milk
4 tablespoons butter
2 eggs, separated
1/4 cup unrefined milled golden cane sugar or honey
3/4 cup ground nuts, e.g. hazelnuts
2 cups berries, e.g. blueberries, blackberries

Soak the bread in the milk. Cream the butter with the egg yolks and sugar until smooth. Stir in the soaked bread (there's no need to squeeze the bread) and nuts, then add the berries. Whip the egg whites until stiff but not dry and gently fold into the mixture. Pour into a greased 4- to 5-cup pudding basin and cover securely. Place an overturned plate in the bottom of a large pan. Set the pudding basin on top of the plate and pour boiling water into the pan to come about ¾ of the way up the pudding basin. Cover the pan and bring to simmering and simmer steadily for 1 hour, topping up with boiling water as necessary.

MAKES 4 SERVINGS

This pudding is cooked in a floured pudding cloth (you can use a large clean tea towel) or you can steam it in a greased pudding basin for the same amount of time.

1 pound fresh cherries
2 cups self-rising flour, plus extra for sprinkling
Pinch of salt
6 tablespoons shortening or butter
6 tablespoons unrefined milled golden cane sugar
$^{1}/_{2}$ cup milk

Mix all the ingredients together. Wring out a large tea towel in boiling water. Spread the cloth out and sprinkle generously with flour. Place the pudding mixture in the center and gather up the ends of the cloth and tie tightly with string, leaving room for the pudding to expand during cooking. Alternatively put the mixture into a greased 5-cup pudding basin. Place an overturned plate in the bottom of a large pan. Set the pudding on top of the plate and pour boiling water into the pan to come about ¾ of the way up the pudding. Bring to simmering and simmer steadily for 2 hours, topping up with boiling water as necessary. Dip the pudding in cold water (this stops the "skin" from sticking to the cloth) and untie the cloth.

Tea and Fruit Pudding

This pudding can safely be left simmering for up to 3 hours, but will be cooked after 2 to 2½ hours.

1½ cups cold black tea
1 teaspoon baking soda
½ cup unrefined milled golden cane sugar
Pinch of salt
2 cups flour
1 cup grated shortening or butter
1½ cups dried fruit
1 teaspoon ground mixed/pumpkin spices (optional)

Mix all the ingredients and put into a floured pudding cloth (see Cherry Pudding, page 19) or a greased 5-cup pudding basin. Place an overturned plate in the bottom of a large pan. Set the pudding on top of the plate and pour boiling water into the pan to come about ¾ of the way up the pudding. Bring to simmering and simmer steadily for 2 to 3 hours, topping up with boiling water as necessary. Dip the pudding in cold water (this stops the "skin" from sticking to the cloth) and untie the cloth.

Bread and Fruit Pudding

2 cups stale bread
$1/2$ cup flour
$1/2$ cup unrefined milled golden cane sugar
1 tablespoon butter or lard
1 cup dried fruit
1 teaspoon baking soda
$1/4$ cup milk

Soak the bread in 1 cup water, and then press dry. Mix the soaked bread with the rest of the ingredients and put into a floured pudding cloth (see Cherry Pudding, page 19) or a greased 4- to 5-cup pudding basin. Place an overturned plate in the bottom of a large pan. Set the pudding on top of the plate and pour boiling water into the pan to come about $3/4$ of the way up the pudding. Bring to simmering and simmer steadily for 3 hours, topping up with boiling water as necessary. Dip the pudding in cold water (this stops the "skin" from sticking to the cloth) and untie the cloth.

Rhubarb Ginger Crisp

2 pounds rhubarb
1 cup ginger cookies, crushed
Grated peel and juice of 1 orange
$3/4$ cup unrefined light brown muscovado sugar

Preheat the oven to 325°F. Trim the rhubarb and cut into 1-inch lengths. Put the pieces into a bowl, cover with boiling water, and let stand for 10 minutes; drain (this reduces the acidity). Put the rhubarb into a buttered 4-cup baking dish and cover evenly with the cookie crumbs and orange peel. Pour on the orange juice and sprinkle the sugar on top. Bake for 30 to 40 minutes until the rhubarb is just tender, but not a soft mush. Serve hot with custard or cream.

Damson Cobbler

Damsons are a variety of plum, much smaller than cultivated plums, with a tart strong flavor. They are blackish purple in color and when ripe have a powdery bloom of natural yeast, which gives the fruit a bluish hue. The fruits ripen in September and are sold from roadside stalls and in local shops and markets in England. Damsons are indigestible when raw, but the sharp tasting fruit is transformed when cooked. Small tart plums can be used instead.

2 pounds damson plums
Scant 1/2 cup unrefined light brown muscovado sugar

Topping
2 cups flour
1/4 cup unrefined milled golden cane sugar
1/2 teaspoon salt
1 tablespoon baking powder
1 stick butter
3/4 cup milk
2 tablespoons unrefined demerara sugar

Preheat the oven to 400°F. Place the fruit in a buttered 5-cup baking dish about 2 1/2 inches deep and sprinkle with the muscovado sugar. For the topping: Sift the flour, cane sugar, salt, and baking powder into a mixing bowl and rub in the butter until the mixture resembles fine bread crumbs. Add the milk to make a thick sticky dough. Spoon tablespoonfuls of the mixture on top of the damsons. Sprinkle with the demerara sugar and cook for about 30 minutes, until golden brown. Serve warm with cream, custard, or ice cream.

The light brown sugar and cider (or apple juice) form a delectable syrup as the apples cook.

6 large green cooking apples
1 stick butter
Scant 1 cup golden raisins
3/4 cup walnuts, chopped
1/2 cup unrefined light brown muscovado sugar
1 teaspoon ground cinnamon (optional)
1 cup cider or apple juice

Butter 6 squares of foil each large enough to wrap an apple. Peel and core the apples and place each one on a piece of foil. Cream 2/3 of the butter until soft and stir in the golden raisins and walnuts. Spoon the mixture into the center of each apple. Dot with the remaining butter and sprinkle with sugar and the cinnamon, if using. Lift the foil around each apple to form a bowl. Pour the cider or apple juice carefully over and around the apples. Loosely wrap the foil around each apple to form a parcel and seal the edges well. Place around the edge of the preheated barbecue and leave until the apples are soft, about 30 to 40 minutes.

Caramel Apples

6 large green cooking apples
2 tablespoons golden raisins
2 tablespoons chopped blanched almonds
4 tablespoons butter
I cup apple juice or cider
$^3/_4$ cup unrefined milled golden cane sugar

Preheat the oven to 350°F. Peel and core the apples and leave them whole. Place in a buttered baking dish and fill each apple with I teaspoon golden raisins and I teaspoon of chopped almonds. With a sharp knife, make a circle around each apple, to penetrate the skin but not the apple flesh. This helps to prevent the apples from bursting during cooking. Divide the butter into 6 equal pieces and place a piece inside each apple. Pour the juice or cider into the dish and cook for 30 to 50 minutes, until the apples are tender, basting frequently with the juices during cooking. Remove from the oven and pour the cooking juices into a pan. Add 3 tablespoons water and the sugar and place over a medium heat. Stir until the sugar has dissolved completely then let the mixture bubble until syrupy. Pour over the apples and serve at once.

Apple Bread Pudding

MAKES 4 SERVINGS

I pound apples (3 large)
$^1/_4$ cup unrefined milled golden cane sugar
6 to 8 slices of bread

Peel and core the apples and cut into pieces. Put them into a pan with 2 cups water and the sugar and cook gently until soft. Butter a 4-cup pudding basin and line it with some slices of bread. Spoon some of the apple mixture on top. Continue alternating layers of bread and apple finishing with a layer of bread. Put a plate on top that just fits inside the rim of the basin. Place a heavy weight on top and let it stand overnight in the refrigerator. Turn out and serve with cream.

MAKES 4 SERVINGS

Strawberries and raspberries are delicate and very perishable so should be rinsed very gently just before using. Strawberries should be hulled after washing to avoid making them soggy—the hull acts as a plug. This can be made with a mixture of summer berries if preferred.

2¹/₂ cups raspberries or strawberries
2 cups redcurrants
1 cup unrefined milled golden cane sugar
Butter
6 to 8 slices of bread

Put the berries and currants in a pan with a little water. Cook gently until soft, then push the mixture through a sieve and stir in the sugar. Butter the bread slices and line a buttered 4-cup pudding basin. Warm the fruit puree and fill the basin with alternate layers of fruit and buttered bread, ending with bread. Put a plate on top that just fits inside the rim of the basin. Place a heavy weight on top and leave in a cold place overnight. Turn out and serve with cream.

Frying Pan Blackberry Tart

Cultivated blackberries are widely available nowadays and although they don't have the same depth of flavor as wild berries they're still very good to eat and also have the advantage of having less pips than the wild variety. This can be made with any fruit in season, such as apples, gooseberries, or rhubarb.

8 ounces pie pastry
1 to 2 cups blackberries
Unrefined demerara sugar
2 tablespoons butter

Roll out the pastry into a circle to fit your frying pan or griddle. Cover half the pastry with the fruit. Sprinkle with sugar and fold over the pastry, sealing the edges well. Heat 1 tablespoon of the butter in the frying pan and when hot lift the pastry onto it. Cook over a medium heat for about 5 minutes. Add the remaining 1 tablespoon butter to the pan, turn the pastry over and cook for 5 more minutes or until the fruit is soft and the pastry is cooked through.

Blackberry Butter

This beautiful deep purple-colored spread is delicious with scones and cream or used as a filling for a plain sponge cake.

2¹/₂ cups blackberries
6 medium green cooking apples
Grated peel and juice of 2 lemons
1¹/₂ cups unrefined milled golden cane sugar for every 1 pound fruit pulp

Wash the fruit and chop the apples roughly—there's no need to core and peel them. Place the fruit in a pan with the lemon peel and juice and simmer gently for about 15 minutes until very soft. Push through a sieve and weigh the pulp. Stir in the required amount of sugar and heat gently until the sugar has dissolved completely. Bring to the boil and cook gently until the mixture is thick and creamy, stirring all the time, about 20 minutes depending on the ripeness of the fruit. Pour into warm sterilized jars and cover with plastic or metal lids. Keep in the refrigerator for up to 3 months and use within 2 weeks of opening.

Plum Dumplings

3^1/$_2$ cups all-purpose flour
1 teaspoon salt
1 stick butter
2 eggs, beaten
1 to 2 tablespoons milk
^{1}/$_4$ cup unrefined milled golden cane sugar
1 teaspoon ground cinnamon
16 plums, stones removed

Sift the flour and salt together. Cream half the butter until soft, and then gradually beat in the eggs, mixing well. Stir in the flour mixture, and then add sufficient milk to make a stiff dough. Turn the dough onto a lightly floured surface and roll out ^{1}/$_4$-inch-thick. Cut into 32 rounds using a 3^1/$_2$-inch cookie cutter. Combine the sugar and cinnamon together in a small bowl.

Place a plum on 16 of the dough circles and sprinkle with spiced sugar. Cover with the remaining rounds of dough, dampen the edges, and seal well. Drop into a pan of salted boiling water, cover, and simmer for 12 minutes. Remove the dumplings to a serving dish with a slotted spoon and dot with the remaining butter and any remaining spiced sugar. Serve hot or cold.

Honeyed Pears

³/₄ cup clear honey
2 tablespoons lemon juice
6 firm pears

Place the honey, 2¹/₂ cups water, and the lemon juice in a deep
saucepan and heat gently until the honey has dissolved. Peel the
pears carefully, keeping them whole and leaving the stems on.
Stand them upright in the honey syrup, then cover and simmer
for 10 to 15 minutes until the pears are just tender. Remove the
pears, drain well, and place on paper towels.

  Boil the syrup for about 25 minutes until it is reduced to about
¹/₂ cup. Replace pears in the syrup and continue to boil, allowing
syrup to bubble high around the pears, basting them frequently.
Continue to boil until the syrup thickens and coats the pears. As
soon as the syrup darkens, remove from the heat. Lift the pears
out carefully by the stems, and place on a serving dish. Quickly
spoon any remaining syrup over the pears. Serve hot or cold with
cream or ice cream.

Elderberry Sauce

This is delicious with fish.

8 cups elderberries
1 small onion, chopped
2 teaspoons salt
1 cup red wine vinegar
3 cups unrefined milled golden cane sugar

Put all the ingredients into a pan and heat gently until the fruit is
broken down and the onion is tender. Press the mixture through a
sieve and return to the pan. Simmer until the sauce has thickened,
with no excess vinegar remaining. Leave to cool, then cover and
refrigerate until needed. It will keep in the refrigerator for up to 2
weeks.

Rhubarb and Apple Sauce

This is delicious with rich fatty meats and poultry, such as pork and duck.

4 stems rhubarb, chopped
1 eating apple, peeled, cored, and chopped
Unrefined milled golden cane sugar
2 tablespoons butter

Put the rhubarb and apple in a pan with sugar to taste and the butter. Cover and cook over a low heat until the fruit is soft and tender. Taste and add more sugar if needed. Beat to a smooth pulp and serve.

Rustler
(Flower)

Flowers, now enjoying something of a renaissance as a fashionable ingredient, were sometimes scattered over salads and even added to stews, for their bright color and flavor. The practice of using flowers in cookery is very old. Medieval monks cultivated flowers such as marigolds and lavender in their kitchen gardens, alongside herbs and vegetables, to add variety to the diet and enhance the flavor of many dishes.

The sweet refreshing scent and deep purple flowers of the **lavender** plant have ensured its popularity as a garden shrub for hundreds of years. The therapeutic properties of lavender were well known, but lavender was also used in cooking, where it added both flavor and color to a variety of sweet and savory dishes. A few flowers were crushed lightly to release their volatile oil and scent and added to food before cooking. They imparted a delicate fragrance to the finished dish. Lavender flowers are especially good cooked with apples or rhubarb. To make a scented icing for a plain cake stir a few finely chopped flowers into some sifted confectioners' sugar and a little water (you can add a few drops of blue or red food coloring if you wish). Lavender sugar is delightful—use it instead of ordinary sugar when making cakes or custards. Place 10 flowers in a jar of sugar and seal tightly. Leave for a few days before using.

Savory dishes were also often enhanced by lavender's aromatic, almost spicy scent. Make a delicious aromatic butter by beating 2 teaspoons crushed lavender flowers with 1 stick of butter, one teaspoon fresh thyme, and a few drops of lemon juice—serve with lamb chops, roast chicken, or white fish. Beat a few chopped flowers into soft cream cheese and serve with crisp biscuits. Add a few flowers to stuffings for poultry, pork, beef, and lamb. Lavender has a particular affinity with lamb. Scatter rosemary and a few lavender flowers over a leg of lamb before roasting to impart an intriguing flavor. Lavender is good for the digestion, too, as it aids the flow of bile.

In spring, the hedgerows and verges were awash with the creamy foam of lacy **elderflower** blossoms, their sweet Muscat scent wafted on the light breeze. The cream-colored flowers have a heady perfume and were picked early in the morning as soon as the dew had dried. Dipping the flowers into a light batter and frying them until crisp, made frugal but exquisite fritters. The berries and flowers were also made into wine and refreshing nonalcoholic drinks. Elderflowers have a wonderful affinity with both rhubarb and gooseberries which, when cooked with a few elderflowers, develop a lovely Muscat flavor. The creamy blossoms were beaten into the batter of cakes and muffins, to which they not only imparted their subtle sweet scent, but also produced a cake with a lighter, more delicate texture. They were also boiled in gruel as a fever-drink, and could be added to the posset of the baptism feast. Elderflower cordial was a refreshing thirst quenching summer drink with the concentrated scent of the sweet flowers.

Daisy flowers and leaves could also be eaten from March to October. The vivid blue of cornflowers and the delicate mauve of chive flowers added a splash of vibrant color to several dishes. The spicy flowers of gillyflowers (clove-scented pinks) were added to stews. Cowslip leaves and flowers were used with herbs in stuffings for meat. Sunflower buds were cooked as a vegetable. Violet petals were sometimes scattered over green salads and were reputed to particularly complement the flavor of beef.

Young tender **dandelion** leaves sprinkled with a little salt, a squeeze of lemon juice, and pepper made delicious sandwiches. The leaves should always be torn to pieces, rather than cut, in order to keep the flavor. In some parts of England the flowers were used to make dandelion wine. This was made by pouring an equal volume of boiling water over the bright yellow flowers and stirring well. Then it was covered with a blanket and allowed to stand for three days, stirring at intervals. The liquid was then strained and sugar, ginger, orange, and lemon rinds were added. It was boiled and left until cold, when a little yeast was placed in it on a piece of toast causing the mixture to ferment. It was covered and left to stand for two days until it had ceased "working." The mixture was poured into a wooden cask, well bunged down, and kept for two months before drinking. The wine was reputed to be an excellent tonic and very good for the blood.

Roma also used many flowers for their medicinal properties, for instance **marigolds** were much valued as a healing herb and were used as a cheaper substitute for expensive saffron (hence, the flower was known as "poor man's saffron"). The beautiful golden orange color (*calendulin*) is soluble in fat and was used extensively to color soups. In Shakespeare's time the dried flowers were put into broths as they were believed to possess recuperative powers and there was a common belief that marigolds raised the spirits and cheered the heart. Because of this, the bright orange petals were added to salads and were also used to flavor vinegar. Use only the Pot Marigolds (*Calendula officinalis*), not the African or French varieties.

Scented **rose** petals were often scattered over cherries in pies before the top crust was added. The petals were also usually included in dishes containing almonds, as they helped prevent the nuts from "oiling." In the seventeenth century, rose petals were an ingredient in medicinal skin ointments used to treat smallpox. Roma made rosehip tea by cutting open rosehips, placing them in a cup, and pouring boiling water over them. This was left until cold, strained, and sweetened with a little honey. Picking rosehips was once a source of employment for Britain's Roma. The collected rosehips were sent to factories to be made into rosehip syrup. Rosehips are rich in vitamin C and rosehip tea has a powerful healing effect on the body and strengthens the immune system. It can also be drunk hot, to ease the symptoms of colds and flu and spices, such as a pinch of cloves or a piece of cinnamon stick may be added. Wild rose leaves were dried and infused in boiling water to make a pleasant tasting tea.

Cowslips possess sedative properties and were made into wines and syrups, which were sipped before bedtime to ensure a good night's sleep.

Lime blossoms, gathered in July and lightly dried, were infused in boiling water to make a pale-colored fragrant refreshing tea. The young soft leaves were also eaten with bread and butter.

Primrose petals were believed to have a soothing effect on a "diseased mind" and were often added to tea leaves to make a calming drink. Primrose pie is a very old English country recipe.

If you want to use flowers in cooking there are three essential rules:

1. Avoid picking flowers close to roads or sprayed fields.

2. The flowers must be free from chemicals and pesticides (those bought from a florist won't be suitable) and should be shaken to dislodge any small insects, then quickly but gently washed under cold running water. The exception is elderflowers, which lose much of their fragrance if washed; just give them a good shake before using.

3. Rose petals should have the white part at the base removed, as this has a bitter flavor. Use only heavily scented varieties.

Elderflower Cordial

MAKES ABOUT 6 CUPS

3 1/2 cups unrefined milled golden cane sugar
Grated zest and juice of 1 lemon
20 freshly picked elderflowers, stalks removed

Put the sugar and lemon zest into a pan with 2 1/2 cups water. Heat slowly until the sugar has dissolved completely, then increase the heat and bring to the boil. Add the elderflower blossoms to the pan, pushing them well down into the liquid. Bring back to the boil, and then remove from the heat. Cover and let stand until cold. Stir the lemon juice into the syrup. Strain

---

through a damp muslin-lined sieve twice into sterilized bottles. Seal tightly and store in the refrigerator for up to 14 days. To serve, dilute with chilled sparkling water to taste and decorate with a stem of flowers and a slice of lemon.

Primrose Pie

MAKES 4 SERVINGS

12 ounces pastry for double pie crust
2 large cooking apples, peeled, cored, and sliced
1/2 cup unrefined milled golden cane sugar
1 cup primrose petals

Preheat the oven to 350°F. Line a 7-inch pie dish with pie pastry. Cover with the apples and sprinkle with sugar to taste. Add a generous layer of primrose petals and sugar and cover with more pastry. Bake for 20 to 30 minutes, until the apples are tender and the pastry is cooked.

Rose Petal Honey

MAKES ABOUT 3 CUPS

2 1/2 cups clear mild flavored honey (e.g. acacia honey)
2 1/2 cups scented rose petals
5 rose leaves

Place the honey in a saucepan and bring slowly to the boil. Add the petals and leaves and simmer for a few minutes. Remove from the heat, cover, and let stand for a few hours for the flavor to develop. Bring to the boil again and strain back into the empty honey jar. Store in the refrigerator for up to 14 days. This is delicious with scones and excellent used in any sweet recipe that calls for honey.

NUTS

Nuts, rich in protein, fat, and minerals, were one of the most valuable and nutritious wild foods and were found throughout the countryside. They were added to soups and savory dishes and used in sweet puddings and cakes.

Acorns, the fruit of the oak (*Quercus robur*), although having a very bitter flavor due to their tannic acid content, contain a high percentage of starch and oil and could be eaten in times of dire need. Acorns were collected around October and were peeled, chopped, and roasted or boiled to get rid of the bitterness before they could be eaten. They could be ground into flour for making bread and cakes or added to wheat flour to extend the supply. Although extremely bitter, when peeled, roasted, and ground they could be used as a substitute for coffee. Acorn coffee was made in Germany in much the same way as dandelion coffee was made in England. The rind, bark, and leaves of the oak tree were also used medicininally and in the making of dyes.

a. Almond
b. Hazel
c. Walnuts

The fruit of the **almond** tree (*Prunus amygdalus*), found in all the Mediterranean countries, has always been in great demand. Almonds contain protein of a higher value than any other nut. When ground and added to water, the resulting almond milk or almond cream was a valuable addition to the diet, as a substitute for animal milk, and made a cooling, pleasant drink. The nuts could be eaten raw or roasted and were invaluable in cooking where they were often used in dishes for special occasions. Sugared almonds and almond sweetmeats are traditional wedding fare in several European countries, most notably Spain.

Beechnuts or beechmast, the fruits of the beech tree (*Fagus sylvatica*), appear only every third or fourth year. The triangular-shaped nuts (there are four in each pod) are enclosed in a greenish four-sided case and fall easily out of the husk like seedpods when ripe. They had to be peeled of their hairy down before the sweet white kernels could be eaten raw, roasted, or baked. However eating large quantities of uncooked beechnuts sometimes caused headaches and dizziness. This is due to the fact that the nuts are very mildly toxic, as they contain Saponic glycoside, although this is broken down when the nut is roasted or otherwise processed. Beechnuts are one of the most delicious of all wild nuts and are particularly valuable due to the kernel's high (nearly 50 percent) oil content. The nuts could be pressed to yield their oil, which could be used for cooking and which was reputed to keep much longer than most other oils. The peeled nuts were scalded and added to a cake mixture (up to half the weight of the mixture) to make a rich cake with a delicious nutty flavor. Beechnuts were also used as a coffee substitute. The kernels were roasted until golden brown and quite hard, then pulverized and steeped in boiling water before use. In some parts of Europe the very young leaves were cooked like spinach and eaten as a vegetable. Beech leaves were also applied to blisters and swellings and chewed to relieve painful gums and chapped lips.

The sweet **chestnut** (*Castanea sativa*) is a relative of the oak and beech and although similar in appearance, is entirely unrelated to the horse chestnut (*Aesculus hippocastanum*), which is inedible. In the past, sweet chestnuts were abundant in forests, woods, and hedgerows, as well as English parks and large gardens, where they were grown more for their ornamental beauty than their fruit. John Gerard wrote in his 1597 *Herball* (which appeared at a time of splendid exploration, when Europeans were discovering new lands, plants and animals; it is the most famous English herbal) that the trees were "a stately adornment of some well kept English parks." Slender flowers with a powerful aroma appear in the summer, while the glossy dark green leaves turn to rich gold in the fall. The seeds grow into spiky green husks, which each contain between two and five closely packed nuts with a dark brown skin. The green protective covering splits into four in October when the seeds fall to the ground and a lining of silky soft down protects the skin of the fruits. The nuts were gathered and spread out to dry.

Fresh chestnuts, due to the amount of tannic acid they contain, must never be eaten raw and are always cooked before use. Slit the shells (to prevent them from exploding in the oven), place on a baking tray or in a roasting pan and put into a 400°F oven for 15 to 20 minutes. Alternatively, place the slit nuts on a plate, 6 at a time and microwave for 30 to 60 seconds. Peel the nuts while hot to ensure removal of the inner brown furry skin, which is bitter.

Roast chestnuts, sprinkled lightly with salt and eaten piping hot, were a favorite winter treat. They were roasted in the embers of the fire. The unshelled nuts were dropped into a bowl of cold water—any that floated to the top were moldy and were discarded.

Chestnuts are the least oily nut and have a higher starch content than any other nut, making them easy to digest and very versatile. They were boiled, roasted, or fried; added to soups, stews, and casseroles; combined with vegetables such as cabbage or brussels sprouts; and served as a vegetable on their own. They have a natural affinity with poultry and game. Their starchy sweetness also meant they were excellent in sweet puddings, desserts, and cakes.

In France and Italy, dried chestnuts were ground into chestnut flour that was made into bread, pastries, cakes, fritters, and pancakes and also used as a thickener for soups and stews. Chestnut flour is pale brown and has an unusual but pleasant smoky flavor. Polenta has become a fashionable food item, which is nowadays made from maize, but was, in fact, originally made with chestnut flour and was a staple peasant dish in the past.

The chestnut season is short, but whole peeled chestnuts either canned or vacuum packed are available from major supermarkets. Dried chestnuts are also available from health food stores, but must be soaked in water overnight then simmered for 5 minutes before use. One pound of fresh chestnuts (weighed in their shells) is equivalent to about 12 ounces peeled, 6 ounces dried, reconstituted chestnuts or 12 ounces canned nuts. Canned chestnut puree (plain or sweetened) saves hours of preparation.

Hazelnuts (*Corylus avellana*) were once very common throughout the English countryside and thrived in hedgerows and woods, their glossy brown nuts ripening in September or October. Cultivated hazels, sometimes known as cobnuts or filberts, have been grown in Britain since at least the sixteenth century. When freshly picked at the beginning of the season, the husks were green, the kernels particularly juicy, and the raw nuts had a delicate, pleasant flavor and were a useful supplement to the diet. Roasting the nuts brought out their full flavor. Nuts harvested later in the year had brown shells and husks, and developed a fuller flavor. They could keep for a long time if gathered at the correct time of year and packed and stored properly. Roma used the twigs and shoots for weaving into baskets, as the wood bends easily without breaking.

English **walnut** trees (*Juglans regia*) found in parks and old gardens yielded rich, crisp-textured nuts with crinkled surfaces and perhaps the best flavor of any nut. When fresh and milky, they were more flavorful and had a better texture than the rather woody and sometimes rancid specimens we get today in the shops. Walnuts, like other nuts, are valuable source of protein, but are acid forming and should be eaten sparingly. American black walnuts have a stronger flavor than English walnuts. The boiled green husks of the fruit made a good yellow dye and the leaves yielded a brown dye, which Roma used to stain their skin. Interestingly, no insects will touch the leaves of the walnut tree.

Ingenious Gypsy women made pipes from walnut shells. The end of the nut was sawn off and the kernel removed. A hole was drilled in the hollow shell, into which a drinking straw was inserted. The pipe was painted and left to dry. Then the hollow bowl was filled with tobacco and lit, ready to be smoked by the maker.

Chestnut Soup

2 tablespoons oil
1 small onion, chopped
1 carrot, chopped
1 pound fresh chestnuts, peeled weight
5 cups vegetable stock
1 potato, sliced
1 bay leaf
Pinch of paprika
Salt and pepper

Heat the oil in a large pan and cook the onion and carrot for 5 minutes. Add the peeled chestnuts, stock, potato, bay leaf, and paprika. Bring to the boil, cover, and simmer gently for 30 minutes or until the vegetables are tender. Cool and puree in a blender or push through a sieve. Season with salt and pepper to taste. Reheat and serve.

Stewed Chestnuts

2 tablespoons butter
1 tablespoon unrefined milled golden cane sugar
2^1/$_4$ cups vegetable stock
1 pound chestnuts, peeled weight
Salt

Melt the butter in a pan and sprinkle in the sugar. Cook until browned then pour in the vegetable stock. Add the peeled chestnuts and cook until tender but still whole and all the stock has been absorbed. Season with salt to taste before serving.

Chestnut and Cabbage Pudding

MAKES 3 TO 4 SERVINGS

1 large cabbage
4 tablespoons shortening or butter
1 tablespoon flour
1 1/4 cups stock or broth
1 cup bread crumbs
2 pounds chestnuts, peeled and cooked
1 onion, chopped

Reserve a few large cabbage leaves and finely chop the rest. Heat half the shortening and when melted, stir in the flour. Cook for 1 minute, then add the stock and stir until smooth. Add the chopped cabbage leaves and cook for a few minutes until tender. Scald the whole cabbage leaves in boiling water and drain well. Line a large buttered pudding basin with the bread crumbs, then line with the whole cabbage leaves, so that part of the leaves stand above the rim. Reserve some cabbage leaves for the top. Fill with alternate layers of chestnuts, chopped onion and the cabbage mixture. Melt the remaining fat and pour over the top layer. Cover with the reserved cabbage leaves. Steam for 1 hour.

Chestnut Preserve

MAKES 4 TO 5 JARS

2 pounds fresh chestnuts, shelled while warm
3 cups unrefined milled golden cane sugar
1 vanilla pod

Place the chestnuts in a pan and cover with cold water. Bring to the boil and cook for 30 to 40 minutes until tender. Drain and rub through a sieve and weigh the mixture. Add the sugar to the warm puree and place in a pan with 3 tablespoons water per pound of sweetened puree. Add the vanilla pod and place over a low heat, stirring all the time. Cook until the mixture is stiff and comes away from the base of the pan. This will take 15 to 25 minutes, depending on the size of the pan. Remove from the heat and take out the vanilla pod. Spoon the mixture into hot sterilized jars and cover with waxed discs and lids. Store in a cool dry place for up to 4 weeks.

Chestnut Cake

Chestnut flour can be found in delicatessens and gourmet food stores. It has a brief shelf life, but it can be frozen if well wrapped.

1 1/2 sticks butter
3 eggs
3/4 cup unrefined milled golden cane sugar
5 tablespoons brandy
1 1/4 cups chestnut flour

Preheat the oven to 375°F. Melt the butter and cool. Put the eggs and sugar into a heatproof bowl over a pan of simmering, not boiling water and whisk until the mixture is thick and mousse-like and has doubled in volume. Remove the bowl from the heat and whisk until cool. If you use an electric mixer there is no need to whisk over hot water. Gently fold in the brandy, followed by the butter. Sift the chestnut flour over the surface and fold in lightly with a spoon. Pour into a 9-inch round cake pan lined with non-stick baking paper and bake for 35 minutes until the cake springs back when pressed lightly. Cool in the pan for 5 minutes then turn out onto a rack and cool completely.

Hazelnut Butter

MAKES 1 1/2 CUPS

1 1/2 cups hazelnuts
3 tablespoons vegetable oil

Place the hazelnuts on a baking tray and roast in a hot oven (400°F) for 5 to 10 minutes until the papery skins can be removed easily when rubbed with a cloth. Do not allow to cool but place in a food processor and grind them to a fine paste. Add the oil and pulse until well combined. This can be made 1 week ahead and kept covered in the refrigerator.

Walnut Cookies

1 1/2 sticks butter
3/4 cup unrefined milled golden cane sugar
3 cups flour
2 cups chopped walnuts

Preheat the oven to 350°F. Cream the butter and sugar until light then add the flour and walnuts. Roll the mixture into small balls and place on greased baking trays, well apart, as the cookies spread during baking. Flatten each ball slightly with a fork. Bake for about 15 minutes until golden brown. Cool on a wire rack. Store the cookies in an airtight tin, where they will keep for up to a week.

HONEY

goodlo *"sweet"*
góodlokénner *"beehive"*

Roma have long known and appreciated the energy boosting qualities of honey. Fructose and glucose, natural sugars present in honey, are easily digested and rapidly absorbed into the bloodstream to provide energy. Vitamins B1, B2, B3, B6, and folic acid are present in honey, together with a high amount of vitamin C. Minerals such as iron, copper, manganese, calcium, magnesium, potassium, and phosphorus are also present, plus traces of pollen and wax, and several enzymes; the amounts of these vary and depend on which flowers the bees visit. Heather honey, for instance, is particularly rich in the minerals calcium, potassium, magnesium, and phosphorus.

Honey was used for all kinds of ailments. Honey is hygroscopic (it draws out water) and is a natural antiseptic. During World War I, honey was used to dress wounds, as it drew the water from bacteria cells causing them to die. Long before this, Roma had applied honey to cuts, sores, and burns, which then healed quickly and prevented further infection.

Sore throats and irritating coughs were soothed with a honey mixture: mix 2 tablespoons honey, 2 tablespoons chopped sage leaves (fresh or dried), and 2 tablespoons cider vinegar with a little hot water. An old cure for insomnia was 2 teaspoons of honey stirred into a cup or mug of hot milk. An old Roma bedtime drink uses the juice of oranges and lemons mixed with honey and hot water.

The flavor, color, and texture of honey varies enormously from pale, thick, and creamy, to golden amber, to the richly aromatic, almost black, liquid honeys. Each honey has its own unique flavor, depending on which flowers the bees visit to gather the nectar from which they manufacture honey. **Acacia honey** for instance, is clear, pale, and very sweet with a heavily scented flavor and a runny consistency, while honey made from rape is a "set" honey with a thick texture and a creamy taste with oily overtones. **Greek mountain honey** is dark, with a rich, almost resinous taste, redolent of Mediterranean herbs, flowers, and pine trees. **Lavender honey** from Provence is pale gold with a delicate hint of lavender, and **sunflower honey** is a rich yellow color, very thick and creamy with an oily, waxy (but not unpleasant) flavor.

One of the most sought after types, much prized by connoisseurs, is **heather honey**. Rich reddish-brown in color, with a dense, almost gelatinous texture, heather honey has a superb distinctive flavor that is not too sweet, with a hint of bitter caramel. Heather honey is usually made from the common bell heather (*Erica cinerea*), but is also produced from the less common ling heather (*Calluna* *vulgaris*) and this type of honey is very special indeed, having a strong floral scent and a deep powerful flavor. It is usually labeled "Ling Honey" and is easily recognizable, being dark and thick and containing air bubbles.

Commercially produced blended honey comes from mixed flower honeys from around the world and has a uniform, bland, sweet flavor intended to appeal to a mass market.

Single flower honey must legally contain a minimum of 75 percent nectar from a particular type of flower. Beekeepers must ensure that the bees gather nectar predominantly from a specific type of flower, which is achieved by transporting the hives to wherever that flower is plentiful. The hives are left until the flowering season has finished, after which the beekeeper quickly removes the honey from the hives.

When bees gather nectar, they also collect microscopic granules of pollen from the stamens of flowers, which they moisten with nectar and tuck into pouches on their hind legs. The minute grains stick together to form yellow, orange, red, white, and black pellets, which the bees take back to the hive to nourish the brood. Pollen is a mixture of proteins, amino acids, minerals, and vitamins and is praised by many people who swear by its stimulating and restorative powers.

Before the discovery of sugar and its subsequent widespread availability and usage, honey's main use was to sweeten foods and it was also an important ingredient in cooking and brewing. Honey beer and mead were the staple drinks throughout Britain in ancient times and honey has been used in cookery for thousands of years; honey cakes were found in a five-thousand-year-old Egyptian tomb! Cakes made with honey are moist and keep remarkably well. Molded, spiced honey cakes were made in monasteries and convents throughout Europe to celebrate saints' days and other religious feasts, as honey cakes retained their shape and the carved detail of the molds well. The unique flavor and smooth texture of honey blends easily with other ingredients to produce many delectable sweet and savory dishes.

It is best to buy organic honey, or a good quality honey that hasn't been filtered or heat-treated, as these processes remove valuable enzymes and nutrients. Feeding the bees on a sugar and water solution placed near the hives is a method used to produce cheaper honeys, but this shortcut means that the enzyme action doesn't occur. Health food shops, small local beekeepers, honey farms, local markets, and farm shops are the best sources of good quality honey. Keep the jar tightly sealed in a dry place. Honey will keep indefinitely, although it will crystallize during long storage or if it becomes too cold. If this happens just place the jar in hot water for a few minutes and the honey will become liquid again.

Try using different types of honey to subtly change the flavor of this deliciously moist cake.

1 1/4 cups heather honey
6 tablespoons butter
1 1/2 cups wholemeal flour
2 teaspoons ground mixed/pumpkin spices
1 teaspoon baking soda
1/2 cup finely chopped candied orange peel
3 eggs
3 tablespoons milk
Finely grated peel of 1 orange

Preheat the oven to 325°F. Place 1 cup of the honey in a small pan with the butter and heat gently until just melted; cool. Sift the flour, spices, and baking soda into a large bowl and stir in the candied orange peel. Beat the eggs, milk, and orange peel and add to the dry ingredients with the cooled honey mixture. Beat until well mixed and pour into a greased, baking paper-lined 8-inch square pan or a 7-inch round cake pan. Bake for about 1 hour and 15 minutes, until cooked through. Cool in the pan for 5 minutes, and then turn out onto a wire rack. Prick the top of the cake with a skewer or fork and brush with the remaining 1/4 cup honey while the cake is still warm. When cold, wrap in greaseproof paper or nonstick baking paper and keep in an airtight pan. Keep for at least a few days (up to a week) before eating to allow the flavors to develop.

Honey Raisin and Walnut Loaf

4 tablespoons butter, melted
^{1}/2 cup clear honey
^{1}/2 cup unrefined light brown muscovado sugar
2^1/4 cups all-purpose flour
Pinch of salt
1 teaspoon baking soda
1 teaspoon ground mixed/pumpkin spices
1 teaspoon ground cinnamon
1 cup chopped walnuts
4 tablespoons raisins
1 egg
^{1}/2 cup milk

Preheat the oven to 350ºF. Stir together the melted butter, honey, and sugar, mixing well. Sift the flour, salt, baking soda, and spices into a mixing bowl and stir in the walnuts and raisins. Beat the egg with the milk and beat into the honey mixture. Pour this into the flour mixture and beat well until smooth. Pour into a greased 9 x 5-inch loaf pan and bake for 1 to 1^1/4 hours until a toothpick inserted into the center comes out clean. Cool in the pan for 5 minutes then turn out onto a wire rack to cool. Serve sliced with butter.

Honey Fruitcake

^{1}/2 cup dried figs
^{1}/2 cup dates, chopped
1 cup dried apricots, chopped
1 cup raisins and golden raisins, mixed
^{2}/3 cup whole candied peel, chopped
^{1}/4 cup glacé cherries, quartered
1^1/2 sticks unsalted butter
1 cup milk
5 tablespoons honey, lavender if possible
3 tablespoons whiskey
2 cups all-purpose flour

1 teaspoon ground mixed/pumpkin spice
2 large eggs
$^1/_2$ teaspoon baking soda
Unrefined demerara sugar to decorate

Place all the fruits in a saucepan with the butter, milk, and honey and heat gently until the butter has melted. Simmer over low heat for 5 minutes, stirring, and then pour into a mixing bowl. Leave to cool. When completely cool (at least 40 minutes later) stir in the whiskey. Preheat the oven to 300°F. Sift the flour and mixed/pumpkin spice into the honey and fruit mixture. Beat the eggs with the baking soda and add to the mixture, mixing well until thoroughly combined. Put into a greased lined 8-inch round cake pan and make a small hollow in the center with the back of a spoon. Bake for 1$^3/_4$ to 2 hours until a toothpick inserted into the center comes out clean. Sprinkle the top with the demerara sugar while still hot and leave to cool in the pan. Remove the lining paper when cold and store in an airtight tin for up to 3 weeks.

Cranachan

MAKES 4 TO 5 SERVINGS

This rich Scottish dessert was eaten on very special occasions and is very rich and alcoholic! The raspberries aren't traditional, but they make this sweet extra special.

6 tablespoons coarse oatmeal
1 cup heavy cream
3 tablespoons honey (heather honey is traditional)
Scant half cup whisky
1 to 1$^1/_2$ cups raspberries (optional)

Toast the oatmeal in a dry frying pan over high heat until lightly browned. Cool. Whip the cream until thickened but not stiff (the oatmeal will thicken the cream even more) and stir in the oatmeal and honey. Slowly stir in the whiskey and raspberries and spoon into small serving glasses. Chill until ready to serve.

Beef, Honey and Beer Casserole

The sweetness of the honey combines with the bitter beer to make a rich tasty stew.

2 tablespoons flour
$^1/_2$ teaspoon each of salt and pepper
3 pounds stewing beef, cut into 1-inch pieces
1 tablespoon oil
2 large onions, chopped
2 bay leaves
4 tablespoons honey
2 cups dark beer or stout
2 cups beef stock

Mix the flour with the salt and pepper and toss the pieces of beef in this to coat. Heat the oil in an ovenproof casserole, add the meat and fry quickly until brown on all sides. Remove the meat and add the chopped onion to the pan and cook until lightly browned. Preheat the oven to 325°F. Add the bay leaves, honey, beer and stock to the pan and bring to the boil, stirring. Add the meat and cover the casserole. Transfer to the oven and cook for 2 to 3 hours until the meat is tender. Serve with boiled potatoes and green vegetables.

These fruity, lightly spiced meatballs can be made with ground pork, lamb, or beef.

¹/₂ cup dried apricots, finely chopped
1 ¹/₂ pounds ground pork
2 cloves garlic, finely chopped
1 teaspoon ground cinnamon
Salt and pepper
2 tablespoons oil
1 tablespoon honey
1 tablespoon white wine vinegar
2 tablespoons tomato puree

Mix the apricots, pork, garlic, cinnamon, and salt and pepper to taste and roll into small balls with wet hands. Heat the oil in a frying pan and fry the meatballs for about 15 minutes over a medium heat, turning them until browned on all sides. Remove from the pan and drain the meatballs on paper towels. Pour off the fat from the pan, reserving the juices and add the honey, vinegar, and tomato puree to the pan with 5 tablespoons water. Cook gently until the glaze is thickened and glossy. Place the meatballs in a container and spoon the glaze over them. Cover when cold and keep in the refrigerator. They should be eaten the same day.

VEGETABLES AND HERBS

Chitries
(Greens, herbs, vegetables)

Wild plants were eaten as vegetables in their own right or used to impart extra flavor to soups and stews. Aromatic herbs picked while young and fresh added flavor and variety to many dishes. Fish and meat, particularly lamb, was often cooked on a bed of fennel or rosemary twigs and as it cooked, the fragrance permeated the meat and at the same time exuded a glorious aroma. Green leafy wild plants such as nettles were cooked like spinach and their flavor is very similar.

Potatoes, turnips, and onions were the most commonly used vegetables, and were not usually peeled as Roma believed (correctly, as it was later discovered) that the peel was good for them, although they had no idea why. We now know that valuable vitamins and minerals lie just underneath the peel.

Root vegetables, mainstays of cold winter months, were surprisingly versatile and were also included in many sweet dishes, where their inherent natural sweetness and moist texture made them successful ingredients of delicious cakes and puddings. Cakes made with carrots, parsnips, and beets are beautifully moist and keep well.

Carrots and parsnips belong to the *umbellifer* family and are especially delicious when eaten with their herbal relatives—fennel, parsley, chervil, and dill. Parsnips are among the few vegetables that are improved by frost; this is because when the living root is frozen, some of the starch is converted into sugar. In country areas of Britain, parsnips were credited with curing toothaches, stomachaches, and dysentery.

Parsnips have a distinctive flavor that is enhanced by the addition of sugar and/or butter, cream, and a sprinkling of cinnamon, nutmeg, or herbs. Small parsnips were baked or roasted whole.

Potato picking was a seasonal source of employment for most British Roma and potatoes could also usually be bought cheaply from a friendly local farmer. They were cooked by baking in the hot ashes or boiled and mashed. Unlikely as it may seem, using cold mashed potatoes in cake, bread, and scone recipes makes them light and moist. The bland, neutral taste of potato absorbs the flavors of the other ingredients and is undetectable in the finished item. Potato flour or *fécule*, as it is sometimes known, is made by grinding potatoes and soaking their pulp in water to create pure potato starch. The resultant snow-white gluten free flour is very fine and was much used by Eastern European Roma. Indeed potato flour is still very much used in that part of the world to make light delicate cakes and biscuits and as a thickener for sauces. It can be found in major supermarkets and delicatessens.

Asparagus or "sparrow grass," now an expensive food item, was once grown in and around London. Battersea in south London was famous for its "Battersea bundles," and the city of London was ringed with asparagus growers, particularly in Deptford, Fulham, Isleworth, and Mortlake. By the eighteenth century, its cultivation was widespread as other areas followed London's lead and asparagus-producing market gardens quickly sprang up. The Vale of Evesham in particular was a noted asparagus-growing region and these areas were a welcome source of seasonal employment for Roma, who picked and packed the crop. In the past, asparagus was sent to market in bundles of 60 or 120 spears tied with osier twigs in traditional patterns to keep them firmly together.

Beets or **beetroot** were baked, a method that preserved more of the valuable minerals and vitamins. Scrub the beetroot well and wrap in foil. Cook for about 2 hours in a 350°F oven (the actual cooking time will depend on the size). Alternatively, grate the raw beetroot, brush lightly with oil, and bake for about 20 minutes in a moderate oven until tender.

Bracken (*Pteris aquiline*) grew profusely on English moors and hillsides, where it flourished luxuriantly. The young fronds were gathered when still tightly curled and cooked like asparagus. Long ago, when it was difficult to find other fresh vegetables, bracken fronds were sold in bundles like asparagus. When cooked, it was said to have a distinctive smoky flavor.

Cabbage was a favorite staple of thick nourishing soups—the fattier the soup, the better—and was usually cooked with pork if available. Sauerkraut (literally "sour cabbage") was a favorite way of eating cabbage in Eastern Europe. Finely shredded white cabbage was packed in layers with salt in a large jar and left for two to three weeks until it had fermented in the brine formed from the salt and cabbage juices.

Chervil (*Anthriscus cerefolium*), a member of the carrot family, was used with watercress and dandelion in spring tonics to provide a powerful combination of vitamins and minerals after the cold, dark days of winter. Only the young tender green leaves were used; as the plant matures, the older leaves lose their pungent flavor. The flavor is also lost if chervil is overheated, so it was added it at the end of cooking or served raw scattered over soups and stews. Its powerful flavor is excellent with eggs, fish, and chicken and in herb butters, sauces, and dressings.

Chickweed (*Stellaria media*), found growing wild in the United States, as well as Britain, has smooth delicate stems and tiny star-shaped white flowers. Both leaves and flowers were eaten—the flowers in salads and the leaves in omelets or cooked similarly to nettles and served as a vegetable. The cooked leaves have a flavor reminiscent of pea pods.

Dandelion (*Taraxacum officinale*) roots were made into coffee, although it has to be said that this doesn't taste anything like coffee! The roots were dug up in the fall and washed thoroughly—often by placing them in a net before turning and shaking under a waterfall. The roots were spread out and left to dry in the sun then roasted slightly to bring out the flavor. They were then ground and used like coffee. Similarly, in Belgium, chicory was and is sometimes today used as a drink on its own. The root is sliced, kiln-dried, roasted, and then ground. **Chicory** has properties similar to those of dandelion, being tonic, laxative, and diuretic. In France and Belgium, chicory roots are sliced, dried, roasted and ground, then added to coffee to impart a slightly bitter taste and dark color. Enormous quantities of chicory are cultivated in continental Europe, to satisfy the demand for ground chicory as an additive to coffee. French food writers say it has a calming effect and serves to correct the excitation caused by the principles of coffee.

Fennel (*Foeniculum vulgare*), an umbelliferous herb with yellow flowers and feathery leaves, was enormously useful as every part of the plant could be utilized. The seeds are fragrant, with a warm, sweet aromatic flavor. The leaves were especially good cooked with fish and the tender stems were added to soups.

Garlic mustard (*Alliaria petiolata*) was and is a very common and very useful wild green plant, although few people today are aware of this flavorsome wild herb. The young heart-shaped leaves appeared in spring (with a second crop appearing in the fall) and gave off a strong aroma of garlic when crushed between the fingers. The young leaves were eaten raw and older leaves added to other greens and cooked dishes to give a delicate garlic-mustard flavor.

Jack-by-the-hedge (*Alliaria officinalis*) peeps out from the bottom of garden and country hedges. It was also called onion nettle, due to the onion flavor of the raw leaves, and "sauce-alone" and was used as a salad vegetable by country people because of its mild garlic taste. A tall soft green herb with small white flowers, its leaves were shredded and used in stuffing or eaten raw with bread and cheese as the onion aroma was lost if cooked. Nowadays, the plant is usually left for the birds to enjoy its seeds and pods.

Lovage (*Levisticum officinale*), another member of the carrot family with small, pale yellow flowers, appears in summer, when a pleasant aromatic perfume pervades the whole plant. The young stems, leaves, and seeds were used in soups, stews, and salads. To reduce your salt intake, use lovage instead of salt to flavor food. A little goes a long way.

Wild marjoram (*Origanum vulgare*) is wonderfully aromatic and was used in stuffings, where its strong, slightly spicy flavor permeated the meat. In its native Mediterranean areas, the herb was used to season pasta and breads.

Sorrel (*Rumex acetosa*), a member of the dock family, appeared in the spring. The leaves contain oxalate of potash, which gives them an acrid taste and also accounts for its alternative name of "sour grass." Sharp-flavored sorrel leaves, well washed and scalded with boiling water to remove their acid, were added to stews and soups. The prepared leaves have a refreshing citrus taste and were chopped and sprinkled into egg dishes or cooked and pureed to eat with duck or pork.

The dark green arrow-shaped leaves of **Good King Henry** (*Chenopodiumbonus-henricus*), a British plant that grows about three feet high, were gathered when young and tender and cooked like spinach, or could be tied in bundles, simmered for a few minutes, and served with melted butter. The leaves were also boiled with pork or other meats. Its flavor is similar to that of spinach, but is less pronounced. The young tender shoots were cut, peeled, boiled, and eaten like asparagus and had a mild laxative effect.

The steamed leaf shoots of **hogweed** (*Heracleum sphondylium*), a plant that appeared in England in early summer, also tasted very much like asparagus. Roma were very careful not to confuse this with the giant hogweed (*Heracleum mantegazzianum*), whose sap was known to blister the skin.

Hops (*Humulus lupulus*) have been grown in Kent for centuries for the brewing industry to preserve and clarify beer. Their bitter flavor was much appreciated by drinkers of British beers. A hop is a type of vine that produces new shoots each spring. The shoots are trained up a framework of poles and strings and may grow up to twenty-five feet. Hop stringing is a skilled art, originally undertaken by balancing on stilts, but is now done from a type of chair lift fixed to a tractor. Until World War II, hop picking was an annual event each September when Roma, along with whole families from London's East End and others in search of casual work, descended on Kent for the harvesting season. It was laborious backbreaking work, but nowadays there are machines to remove the drudgery. Hops were also eaten as a vegetable. Hop shoots were gathered in early spring (never later than May), soaked in cold salted water, and washed well. After being tied in bundles like asparagus, they were cooked in boiling water until tender and served with melted butter. The leaves and flower heads were also used to produce a fine brown dye.

Horseradish (*Armoracia rusticana*) growing in the wild has more flavor than the cultivated variety, and Roma added it to dishes to impart a fiery bite. Eaten with oily fish or rich meat, either by itself or steeped in vinegar, or in a plain sauce, it acted as an excellent stimulant to the digestive organs, and an aid to complete digestion.

The refreshing fragrance and flavor of **mint** (*Labiatae*) was aptly described more than a thousand years ago by Pliny as "a scent that awakens the spirit and flavor that stimulates the appetite." There are many varieties of mint: peppermint, spearmint, apple mint, and pineapple mint, to name just a few. Freshly chopped mint was sprinkled over fresh fruit, salad vegetables, buttery new potatoes, carrots, and cabbage, but used in moderation, as it quickly overpowers other flavors.

The humble **stinging nettle** (*Urticanceae*), usually regarded as a troublesome weed, was highly esteemed by the Roma. Nettles were boiled with pork, put into soups, or served plain. Young nettle leaves can be cooked in the same way as spinach: wash well and place in a pan with just the water clinging to the leaves. Cook over a low heat for 7 to 10 minutes, chopping them as they cook in the pan and add butter, salt, and pepper to taste. The flavor is remarkably similar to spinach. Nettles were also boiled with pork to make a delicious thick soup. The stinging acid in the leaves is instantly destroyed by heat and the leaves are an excellent source of iron.

Parsley (*Carum petroselinum*) has a strong taste and is full of valuable nutrients, particularly iron and calcium. The leaves were added to fish dishes, snails, omelets, and all kinds of vegetable dishes.

Rosemary (*Rosmarinus officinalis*), an intensely aromatic plant with lovely blue or pink flowers, is a wonderfully useful herb. Only a little is needed to add flavor to stuffings, stews, marinades, and rice and pasta dishes.

Sage (*Salvia officinalis*) has a strong odor and a warm, slightly bitter flavor due to the volatile oil contained in the tissues of the plant. Sage leaves were made into a tea and also eaten with bread and butter. Its penetrating distinctive flavor is particularly well matched with pork, poultry, and cheese dishes and aids in the digestion of these rich foods.

Summer or **garden savory** (*Satureia hortensis*) and **winter savory** (*Satureia montana*) have a distinctive taste, similar to that of marjoram. The herb was used to flavor poultry, veal, or fish and added to stuffings and sausages (particularly salamis). Stems were boiled with broad beans and peas, and in pea soup.

Cicely (*Myrris odorate*) leaves were added to rhubarb as it cooked; their slightly sweet anise flavor enhanced the vegetable and less sugar was needed to sweeten the sour rhubarb. A stem of the sweetly fragrant plant was added to sharp-tasting greens such as sorrel or dandelion as they cooked, then removed before serving. The anise-scented leaves were also added to salads and the seeds were eaten with cheese. The root was boiled and eaten hot or cold.

Tansy (*Tanacetum vulgare*) has a bitter flavor and was used very sparingly when the leaves were young. It was traditional to eat the herb at Easter time, when it was added to puddings and cakes. Tansy cakes were made from the young leaves of the plant mixed with eggs, and were thought to purify the blood after the limited fare of winter. It was also eaten with fish, especially mackerel. Curiously, cows and sheep will eat tansy, but horses, goats, and pigs will not go near the plant. Meat was rubbed with tansy leaves to keep flies away.

Tarragon (*Artemisia dracunculus*) is highly perfumed and has a pungent, yet delicate flavor, reminiscent of aniseed, which was well matched with chicken and fish dishes, vegetables, and cheese.

Thyme (*Thymus vulgaris*) has a highly aromatic scent and a warm pungent taste. The fragrant leaves were used in stuffings, sauces, stews, soups, jugged hare, and roast lamb.

Wild celery (*Apium graveolens*) flourishes in wet places and has a stronger flavor than cultivated celery. The whole plant was eaten raw or cooked. The stalks, which are not as thick as the cultivated variety, were eaten raw, particularly with cheese, in salads, braised with butter, or included in soups and stews.

Watercress (*Nasturtium officinale*) once grew wild in streams throughout Britain and Roma valued it highly, particularly in the winter months when it was the only green leafy vegetable available. Its hot peppery flavor comes from the mustard oil contained in the leaves, which is released when they are crushed. Watercress was eaten mostly by the working classes in England, usually with bread but often just on its own by those who were too poor to afford even a loaf. For this reason, watercress became known as "poor man's bread." It was sold in Covent Garden by London's street sellers, who tied it into bunches and buyers ate them from their hands, as we would eat an ice cream cone. Watercress was cut by hand and its harvest provided seasonal employment for many Roma.

All the soups presented here can be frozen. Remember to allow room for expansion as the soup freezes, and keep seasoning to a minimum—this can be adjusted when reheating. Cream, milk and garlic are best added just before serving. You may need to dilute the soup with extra liquid just before serving.

Asparagus Soup

MAKES 4 SERVINGS

This is made with the trimmings from the stems, together with leftover cooking liquor.

1 to 2 tablespoons oil
1 small onion, finely chopped
2¹/₂ cups vegetable stock
1 potato, peeled and chopped
1 pound asparagus stems, sliced
1 cup heavy cream
Salt and pepper

Heat the oil in a large pan and cook the onion until soft but not browned. Add the stock and potato, bring to the boil, and cook for 10 minutes. Add the asparagus stems and cook for about 7 minutes or until tender. Puree the soup in a blender or food processor and strain through a sieve back into the pan. Stir in the cream and season to taste with salt and pepper. If the soup is too thick add some water. Serve hot or cold.

Nettle Soup

Pick young tender leaves (wear gloves!) from an unpolluted spot, well away from roadside exhaust fumes and roaming dogs. Wash leaves well before using.

1 tablespoon oil
1 onion, finely chopped
1 pound potatoes, peeled and diced
8 ounces tender nettle leaves
Salt and pepper
Grated nutmeg

Heat the oil in a large saucepan and add the onion and potatoes. Cook gently over a low heat until soft but not browned (about 5 minutes), then add the nettles, cover, and cook for another 5 minutes. Add 5¾ cups water and bring to the boil. Simmer for 15 to 20 minutes until the vegetables are cooked. Place in a food processor or blender or push through a sieve until smooth. Season to taste with salt, pepper, and nutmeg and reheat just before serving.

Pea Soup

1 tablespoon butter
2 ounces slab bacon, derinded and chopped
1 onion, chopped
1 stalk celery, diced
1 carrot, chopped
1 pound dried split peas
10 cups ham or vegetable stock (or use stock cubes)
Salt and pepper

Melt the butter in a large saucepan. Add the bacon, onion, celery, and carrot and cook for 10 to 15 minutes until the vegetables begin to soften. Stir in the peas and stock and bring to the boil. Cover and simmer for about 1 hour until the peas are soft. Cool slightly, then puree in a blender or press through a sieve until smooth. Return to the pan, season to taste with the salt and pepper, and reheat until piping hot.

Cauliflower and Ham Soup

This thick, satisfying soup makes a filling meal. If you have boiled a piece of ham use the stock to make this soup; if not use a good quality ready-made ham or vegetable stock.

4 cups stock
1 large cauliflower, broken into florets
2 onions, thinly sliced
1 bay leaf
Salt and pepper
2 tablespoons butter
1 tablespoon flour
1/2 cup milk
4 ounces cooked ham, chopped

In a large pan heat the stock until boiling then add the cauliflower florets, onions, and bay leaf and season to taste with salt and pepper. If the ham is salty you may not need to add any salt. Cover and simmer for 20 minutes, then remove the bay leaf. Place the mixture in a blender or food processor and blend until smooth. Melt the butter in a small pan, then stir in the flour and cook for 1 minute, stirring constantly. Remove from the heat and whisk in the milk. Return to the heat and bring to the boil, stirring constantly. Simmer for 1 minute then add to the cauliflower stock and pour into a large pan. Bring to the boil and simmer for a minute or two. Just before serving, add the ham to the soup and stir well.

Thick Vegetable Soup

2 tablespoons oil
2 tablespoons butter
2 to 3 carrots, thinly sliced
2 onions, finely chopped
8 ounces rutabaga, chopped
8 ounces parsnips, chopped
1/4 cup pearl barley
6 cups water
1 teaspoon salt

Pepper
2 bay leaves
2 stems fresh thyme
1 tablespoon Worcestershire sauce (optional)
2 leeks, sliced thinly

Heat the oil and butter in a large pan and fry the carrots and onions until the onion is soft, then add the rest of the ingredients, except the leeks. Bring to the boil, then reduce the heat and simmer gently for 1 hour. Add the leeks and simmer for another 30 minutes. Discard the bay leaves and thyme and adjust the seasoning if necessary.

Creamy Onion Soup

MAKES 4 SERVINGS

Unlike the French brown onion soup, this British soup is thick, white, and creamy.

2 tablespoons butter
1 1/2 pounds (about 5 medium) onions, sliced thinly
1 large potato, peeled and diced
Salt and pepper
Freshly grated nutmeg
1/2 cup cream

Heat 1 tablespoon of the butter in a large pan and cook half the onion and all the potato for about 10 minutes until soft but not browned. Add 4 1/2 cups water, bring to the boil, and simmer for 15 minutes. Heat the remaining 1 tablespoon butter in another pan and cook the rest of the onion over a very low heat for about 15 minutes until very soft but not browned. Puree the soup mixture in a blender, and then add the onion. Season to taste with the salt, pepper, and nutmeg. Reheat the soup and stir in the cream just before serving.

Red Lentil and Split Pea Soup

MAKES 4 SERVINGS

This slightly spicy warming soup is delicious as it is, or you can add 4 ounces chopped, cooked bacon or ham to the finished soup.

2 tablespoons butter
I onion, finely chopped
I clove garlic, finely chopped
I teaspoon ground cumin (optional)
$^3/_4$ cup red lentils, rinsed well
$^1/_2$ cup split peas, rinsed well
2 tablespoons tomato puree
6 cups unsalted stock
2 carrots, finely diced
Salt and pepper
I tablespoon chopped fresh parsley

Melt the butter in a pan and cook the onion and garlic for 2 to 3 minutes, until softened but not browned. Add the cumin (if using), lentils, split peas, and tomato puree and cook for a few minutes, stirring constantly. Pour in the stock, bring to the boil, and then simmer for 20 to 25 minutes until the pulses are soft. Put the mixture into a food processor or blender and process until smooth, and then return to the pan. Add the diced carrots and simmer for about 15 minutes until the carrots are tender. Season to taste with salt and pepper. Stir in the parsley and serve.

Cabbage Soup with Bacon

This soup is hearty and filling.

2 tablespoons butter
2 large onions, finely chopped
8 ounces slab bacon, finely chopped
1 small cabbage, shredded
3 potatoes
Salt and pepper
4½ cups vegetable stock

Melt the butter in a large pan and cook the onions and bacon for 2 minutes. Add the cabbage and potatoes and season to taste with salt and pepper—you may not need salt if the bacon is salty. Add the stock, bring to the boil, then reduce the heat and simmer for about 30 minutes until the vegetables are tender.

Roast Asparagus

12 spears asparagus, trimmed
3 tablespoons oil
Salt

Preheat the oven to 450°F. Place the asparagus in a bowl and toss in the oil and salt. Lay the asparagus on a baking tray or in a shallow baking dish. Cook for 12 to 15 minutes, turning once, until tender.

Parsnip Fritters

4 parsnips, peeled and thickly sliced
Salt and pepper
4 tablespoons butter
¹/4 cup all-purpose flour
Oil for frying

Put the parsnips in a pan with just enough cold water to cover.
Bring to the boil, cover the pan, and cook until tender. Drain well
and mash the parsnips until smooth. Season well with salt and
pepper and beat in the butter. Stir in enough flour to make a
moderately firm mixture. Drop spoonfuls of the mixture into hot
oil and cook until crisp.

Lancashire Potato Cakes

MAKES 4 SERVINGS

Potato cakes were always served hot and made a tasty accompaniment to bacon, or were eaten on their own with lots of butter
and sprinkled lightly with salt.

1 pound (about 3 medium) potatoes, peeled
2 tablespoons butter
¹/2 teaspoon salt
1 egg
1 cup all-purpose flour
1 teaspoon baking powder

Boil the potatoes until tender. Drain them and mash with the
butter and salt. Add the egg, flour, and baking powder to form a
soft but not sticky dough and roll out to ¹/2-inch thickness and
cut into 3-inch rounds. Cook for about 15 minutes on a hot
greased griddle or well-greased frying pan, turning halfway
through the cooking time. Serve at once with plenty of butter.

Potato Flour Pancakes

6 eggs
I cup potato flour
Pinch of salt
Oil for cooking

Beat the eggs until frothy and gradually whisk in the potato flour, salt, and ¾ cup water until the mixture is pale yellow and foamy. Cover and leave to stand for 30 minutes, then beat again before cooking. Heat a little oil in a frying pan and when very hot pour in sufficient batter to cover the base of the pan. Cook for a few minutes on each side until crisp and golden. Serve with lemon and sugar, honey, or maple syrup.

Vegetable Frittata

This thick solid omelet looks impressive cut into wedges and accompanied by a crisp green salad.

I pound new potatoes, scrubbed
I onion, chopped
I red bell pepper, chopped
5 tablespoons oil
I (10-ounce) pack frozen spinach, thawed and drained
6 eggs
Salt and pepper

Cook the potatoes in boiling salted water until tender. Cool and slice thickly. Cook the onion and pepper in the oil for 5 minutes, then add the potatoes and cook until lightly browned. Stir in the spinach and cook for I minute. Whisk the eggs and salt and pepper to taste and pour into the pan, stirring. Cook gently for 10 minutes until set. Place the pan under a broiler for a few minutes until the top is browned. Let it stand for 10 minutes, then turn out and cool. Serve cold cut into wedges with a green salad.

Watercress Butter

1 bunch or 1 (3- to 4-ounce) bag washed watercress
4 tablespoons butter
1 teaspoon lemon juice
Pinch of sugar
Salt and pepper

Pick all the leaves from the stalks and discard the stalks (or save for soup). Put the leaves into a blender or food processor with the rest of the ingredients and blend until well mixed. Shape into a roll and wrap in plastic wrap. Chill until firm. Serve with chops, steaks, chicken, or fish.

Spring Herb Pudding

Use freshly picked young leaves such as nettles, hawthorn, wild garlic, tansy, watercress, lettuce, dandelion, strawberry, or raspberry.

1 pound mixed fresh young green leaves, finely chopped
1 onion, finely chopped
1/2 cup pearl barley
1 generous cup oatmeal
1/2 teaspoon salt
2 to 3 eggs, beaten
4 tablespoons butter
Salt and pepper
Oil for frying

Mix together the leaves, onion, barley, oatmeal, and salt. Put into a buttered 4- to 5-cup pudding basin and cover with a tight-fitting lid, foil, or greaseproof paper tied securely. Boil or steam for 2 hours. Turn out into a large mixing bowl and beat in the eggs, butter, and salt and pepper to taste. Shape into a flat cake. Heat the oil in a skillet until hot then fry the cake about 10 minutes or until browned on both sides, turning halfway. Serve immediately with roast lamb, or bacon and eggs.

Creamed Sorrel

This recipe doesn't contain cream; the name comes from the texture of the finished dish.

1 pound sorrel leaves, coarsely chopped
3 to 4 tablespoons butter
Salt and pepper

Place the sorrel leaves in a pan with very little water. Cook for 7 minutes over a medium heat until tender. Drain well and toss in the pan with the butter and salt and pepper to taste.

Rosemary Sandwich Cake

1 1/2 sticks butter
3/4 cup unrefined milled golden cane sugar
3 eggs, separated
1 generous cup self-rising flour
3 tablespoons cornstarch
1 tablespoon chopped fresh rosemary, plus a few stems to decorate

Preheat the oven to 325°F. Cream the butter with 1/2 cup of the sugar until light and creamy. Whisk in the egg yolks. Sift together the flour and cornstarch and fold into the butter mixture. In a separate bowl, whip the egg whites until they form soft peaks and whisk in the remaining 1/4 cup sugar. Gently fold half the meringue into the cake mixture until incorporated, and then fold in the other half with the chopped rosemary. Spoon into a greased and floured 8-inch round cake pan and bake for about 1 hour, or until a skewer inserted in the center comes out clean. Cool in the pan for 15 minutes then turn out onto a wire rack until completely cooled.

Sweet Parsnip Pie

8 ounces pie or puff pastry
1 1/2 cups cooked mashed parsnips
3/4 cup unrefined light brown muscovado sugar
1 cup milk
1 teaspoon vanilla extract
2 eggs

Preheat the oven to 350°F. Roll out the pastry and line a 9-inch round dish or pan. Combine the mashed parsnips, brown sugar, milk, and vanilla, mixing well to combine. Beat the eggs and stir into the mixture. Pour into the pastry shell and bake for 35 to 45 minutes until cooked through.

FUNGI

Kesali
(Forest spirit)

Mushrooms and fungi flourish in damp woods and grassy meadows. All Roma knew that many fungi were poisonous and accordingly were very careful. Edible fungi were recognized by their pleasant mushroom odor, mealy aroma, a faint anise-like scent, or sometimes no particular odor at all. Poisonous fungi were distinguishable by their foul smell and also by breaking off a small piece, which when placed on the tongue tasted bitter or caused it to tingle, or if the fungus quickly turned deep blue or developed a greenish tinge.

Mushrooms were often fried in hedgehog fat or included in savory puddings and pies. Roma would never put a knife to a mushroom, as they believed this would "bleed its heart." Late summer, fall, and early winter were the best times for finding fungi, although there were also some spring species to look out for. Beech woods and pine forests were a very rich habitat for all types of fungi. In the past, foraging for mushrooms was a necessary part of life for Roma in order to feed their families. Mushrooms were also preserved by drying and storing for the winter.

The flavor of wild mushrooms is incomparable and much superior to cultivated varieties, with each variety having its own unique flavor. Cultivated mushrooms lack the delicacy, aroma, and full flavor of wild mushrooms.

Many fine **cépes** (*Boletus edulis*) with the wonderful aroma of the woods and rich, earthy flavor can still be found in woods and forests. When very fresh and firm these were eaten raw, thinly sliced and simply dressed with lemon and oil, although many Roma thought that they were at their best when subjected to long slow cooking to bring out their deep flavor. Mushroom caps were also roasted directly on the dying embers of a fire.

The **button mushroom** (*Marasmius oreades*), sometimes known as the fairy ring mushroom, has a fine flavor. These sprout abundantly during the warm months, especially after rain and their excellent flavor and aroma are out of all proportion to their small size. Added to soups, ragouts, and stews, they impart a distinctive, somewhat sweet taste.

Chanterelles (*Cantharellus cibarius*) are distinguished by their beautiful golden yellow color, fleshy cap, and curly edges. They flourish in large groups during summer and fall in woods, especially those of beech and oak. These fragrant mushrooms have the aroma of apricots and although they can be dried they do not retain their flavor as well as some other types of mushroom. Tasty chanterelles have a special affinity with potatoes and eggs and are delicious in cream sauces, although they are often reputed to be difficult to digest.

Morels (*Morchella esculenta* and *Morchella vulgaris*) rate among the finest wild mushrooms and appear in orchards and forests (before most other edible mushrooms) in the spring. Because of its honeycombed appearance, the morel is sometimes called the "sponge mushroom." Small, fleshy-capped morels are so esteemed today that devotees will travel hundreds of miles in their pursuit. Morels come in various colors: reddish, gray, black, or brown, and have a wonderful meaty, slightly nutty flavor that is enhanced even more by cooking them in butter. Morels are never eaten raw, as they are likely to cause upset stomachs.

Oronges de Cesars (*Amanita caesarea*) or "Caesar's Mushroom" was the most highly prized mushroom of ancient Rome—hence its name. It grows in deciduous woods in summer and early fall and has a vivid orange cap (which can be up to six inches across) that fades to yellow with age. It has a pleasant flavor and is particular good gently fried in olive oil with shallots and crushed garlic.

The **oyster mushroom** (*Pleurotus ostreatus*) can be found in clumps on rotting logs, stumps, and trees, from spring until late fall. The cap and gills are white, with a firm flesh and good flavor. In warm humid weather these mushrooms decay very quickly and decayed specimens must never be eaten.

The common **field mushroom** (*Psalliota campestria*) is pink and white when young, but becomes brown and almost black as it ages. Small and unopened the mushrooms have a delicate flavor, while older specimens have a more pronounced flavor.

Puffballs (*Lycoperdon* and *Calvatia*), range in diameter from less than an inch to more than a foot and are among the best of the edible mushrooms. When young, they are moderately firm and are delicious sliced and fried or broiled. As they mature and the interior turns yellow, this is a sign that they are no longer worth eating. The pear-shaped puffball grows on rotting logs and stumps, and most puffballs come up in late summer and fall. The **giant puffball** (*Lycoperdon giganteum*), common in summer and early fall in grassy areas and meadows, is fried or if very young eaten raw. In its dry state, its woolly interior mass was used to staunch wounds and bleeding.

Other types of mushrooms included **horse mushrooms** (*Psalliota arvensis*); spectacularly large **parasol mushrooms** (*Macrolepiota procera*), which appeared in the stubble of ploughed fields after the harvest in late August; and the pale, creamy **St. George's mushroom** (*Tricholoma gambosum*) found in pastures. The latter is very good to eat with a delicious nutty flavor and mealy aroma. It can be fried or boiled but is excellent when stewed. The golden yellow **"chicken of the woods" mushroom** (*Laetiporus sulphurous*) grows on tree trunks and has a firm texture and a distinctive flavor. The thick soft flesh has the texture of cooked chicken—hence its name. It was eaten fried in a little fat or could be simmered in chicken stock to make mock chicken. The young rosettes and the tender edges of mature clusters are more palatable than the older, tougher specimens. Chicken of the woods should not be eaten raw. The **wood blewit** (*Pimpinella morada*) is strongly flavored and is particularly good when young, but again, must never be eaten raw.

There are two kinds of toothed mushrooms that are tasty and unmistakable. *Hydnum repandum*, sometimes called the **hedgehog mushroom**, is reddish brown or gold and grows on the ground in forests and on the edges of woods and gets its name from its spine-like gills. It has a deliciously nutty flavor and crunchy texture. The other type is any of several species of the genus *Hericium*, often called the **bear's head**, or **lion's mane**. They appear as a white mass in late summer on dead, often standing trees.

The **truffle** most commonly found in Britain is *Tuber aestivum* but truffles from France and Italy are much larger and have a superior flavor. Truffles, although uncommon and difficult to find, could be discovered in woods under elm trees and were a popular delicacy. Their unique taste and aroma are unforgettable. Like other fungi, they were eaten while very fresh and often cooked in the embers of the campfire.

Finally, *a word of warning*: don't be tempted to pick wild mushrooms, unless you're an expert. Some deadly poisonous mushrooms look remarkably similar to edible varieties.

**I pound fresh mushrooms =
6 cups sliced fresh mushrooms =
3 ounces dried mushrooms**

Creamed Mushrooms

This is a delicious starter or an appetizing snack served on toast.

Juice of 1 small lemon
1 pound small button mushrooms
2 tablespoons butter
1 tablespoon oil
1 small onion, finely chopped
Salt and pepper
1/2 cup cream
1 tablespoon chopped fresh parsley

Sprinkle a little of the lemon juice over the mushrooms. Heat the butter and oil in a frying pan and cook the onion for 1 minute. Add the mushrooms, shaking the pan so they don't stick. Season to taste with salt and pepper, then stir in the cream and remaining lemon juice. Heat until hot but don't allow it to boil. Sprinkle with parsley and serve at once.

Mushrooms with Snails

1 teaspoon salt
A few peppercorns
3 to 4 dozen snails, cleaned and rinsed
2 tablespoons cooking oil
4 to 6 ounces bacon, chopped
1 onion, finely chopped
A few cloves garlic, chopped
8 ounces wild mushrooms, chopped
2 cups stock or water

Boil 4 cups water in a large pan with the salt and peppercorns. Add the snails and simmer for 30 minutes. Drain the snails and put to one side. Heat the oil in a skillet and cook the bacon, onion, and garlic until soft. Add the mushrooms and cook for a few minutes until the juices run. Stir in the stock and snails. Cook gently for about 10 minutes until the mushrooms are tender and the dish is piping hot.

This recipe is from Slovenia, where Boletus mushrooms grow freely in the forests. Slovenians love Boletus for their flavoring qualities. They are used fresh, pickled, salted and dried.

4 ounces fresh mushrooms
2 tablespoons finely chopped onion
1 tablespoon butter
2 cloves garlic, crushed
1 tablespoon chopped fresh parsley
Salt and pepper
1 teaspoon flour
3 tablespoons milk or stock

Slice the mushrooms and sauté them with the onion in the butter. Add the garlic, parsley, and salt and pepper to taste. Simmer until all the water has evaporated. Sprinkle with the flour and pour in the milk or stock. Simmer gently for 1 minute then serve immediately.

EGGS

Yaras
(Eggs)

Although hens' eggs were by far the most popular, duck, goose and even seagull eggs were also enjoyed. It's also likely that the eggs of swans and other wild fowl were eaten if they were available. A good method of preserving eggs was to butter them. A freshly laid, still warm egg was rolled in butter in the palms of the hand. As the egg cooled, it developed a seal that kept it fresh inside.

Duck eggs are larger than hen eggs, and the thick white or speckled shells have a bluish tinge. They have a richer, more distinctive flavor and contain less water than hen eggs, so the whites are more gelatinous and the yolks a brighter orange-yellow. Ducks lay their eggs in muddy places by the waterside and as a result they often carry bacteria; the shells must be scrubbed well and the eggs need to be cooked thoroughly—hard boiled for a minimum of 10 minutes—and shouldn't be used for any dish that is cooked at a low temperature or for a short time. Duck eggs were also enjoyed scrambled, poached, or fried, sometimes on a shovel. They were also used in cakes and puddings. Wild duck eggs taste very fishy and so were not used for cakes or sweet puddings. One duck egg equals two hen eggs in baking.

Goose eggs are very large and the whites and yolks are less firm than those of hen eggs. They have a delicate flavor (milder than duck eggs) and could be cooked by any of the methods used for hen eggs, as well as in cakes and puddings. Soft boiling them takes 7 to 8 minutes. They are also good scrambled or made into a large omelet. One goose egg will serve four people. Another good way to cook them is by baking. Break the egg into a buttered ovenproof dish and cover with grated cheese or cream. Bake for 25 minutes at 400°F.

Seagull eggs were collected from seaside rock faces and must have had a pronounced fishy flavor.

Moorhen eggs were also made into omelets, as were the eggs of partridges and pheasants.

Eggs were one of the most useful and versatile foods and could be baked in the ashes of the campfire, fried, poached, and boiled. Fritters made with eggs, flour, and milk mixed with fruit or meat and fried were cheap, filling, and tasty.

This is a simple Spanish gitane meal of eggs baked in small dishes with vegetables. Chorizo is often included.

1 onion, chopped
2 tablespoons olive oil
3 cloves garlic, crushed
1/2 cup green peas
1/2 cup canned garbanzo beans
1/2 cup diced carrots
1/4 cup tomato sauce
Salt and pepper
4 slices ham
4 chorizo sausage links, sliced
8 eggs

Preheat the oven to 375°F. Sauté the onion in the oil over medium heat until soft. Add the crushed garlic, peas, garbanzo beans, and carrots. Continue to sauté for a few minutes, stirring occasionally to prevent scorching. Add the tomato sauce and simmer on low for 15 minutes. Add salt and pepper to taste. Lightly oil 4 custard cups and divide the vegetable mixture equally between them. Top each with 1 slice of ham and several slices of chorizo. Gently break 2 eggs into each dish so that the eggs float on top. Place the dishes in the oven and bake for 15 to 20 minutes, until the whites are set and the yolks are slightly runny. Serve immediately.

Eggs with Green Sauce

8 hard-boiled eggs
2 generous cups mayonnaise
I tablespoon melted butter
Pinch cayenne pepper
Salt and pepper
4 bunches (or packets of ready washed) watercress, 3 to 4 ounces
4 tablespoons French or oil and vinegar dressing
Chopped parsley to garnish

Cut the eggs lengthways. Remove the yolks and press them through a sieve. Mix them with 4 teaspoons of mayonnaise, the melted butter, cayenne pepper and salt and pepper to taste. Spoon the mixture back into the whites. Place half the watercress in a pan with a little salted water and boil gently until limp and soft. Process or blend until smooth. Leave to cool. Chop the rest of the watercress finely and toss in the French dressing. Cover a serving dish with the watercress and place the stuffed eggs on top. Combine the cold watercress puree with the rest of the mayonnaise and pour over the eggs. Sprinkle with chopped parsley just before serving.

Baked Cheese Omelet

A tasty dish flavored with herbs and cheese, which is baked in the oven.

2 tablespoons butter, melted
6 eggs
Salt and pepper
2 ounces cheese, grated
1 teaspoon chopped fresh parsley
1 teaspoon chopped fresh chives
2 tomatoes, sliced

Brush an ovenproof dish with the melted butter and place in the oven set at 400°F, to become hot. Beat the eggs lightly and stir in the salt and pepper, cheese and herbs. Arrange the tomatoes in the heated dish and pour in the egg mixture. Bake for about 15 minutes until set. Serve immediately.

Baked Eggs

A delectable dish of eggs, cheese and breadcrumbs baked in cream.

1 1/2 cups fresh breadcrumbs
4 eggs
2 tablespoons butter
Salt and pepper
4 ounces cheese, grated
1 cup heavy cream

Preheat the oven to 375°F. Scatter half the breadcrumbs over the base of a buttered 4-cup ovenproof dish. Break the eggs into the dish and scatter with more breadcrumbs. Dot with the butter and season to taste. Sprinkle with the cheese and the rest of the breadcrumbs. Pour over the cream and bake for 15 to 20 minutes until bubbling.

Gypsy Toast

MAKES 2 SERVINGS

2 eggs
Pinch each of salt and pepper
1 tablespoon milk
2 slices bread
2 tablespoons oil, butter, or lard for frying

Beat the eggs lightly and season with salt and pepper. Add the milk. Soak the bread slices in the mixture. Heat the oil in a frying pan and when hot add the soaked bread. Fry until crisp, turning occasionally.

Egg Custard Flan

MAKES 4 SERVINGS

6 ounces pie pastry
2 eggs
2 tablespoons unrefined milled golden cane sugar
1 1/4 cups milk
Grated nutmeg (optional)

Preheat the oven to 425°F. Roll out the pastry and line a 7-inch round pan about 1-inch-deep. Whisk the eggs lightly with the sugar. Heat the milk until warm and pour onto the eggs, whisking lightly. Strain into the pan and sprinkle with nutmeg if using. Bake in the center of the oven for 10 minutes, then reduce the heat to 350°F and bake for another 20 to 25 minutes, until the custard is set.

MEAT, POULTRY, AND GAME

O shoshoy kaste si feri yek khiv sigo athadjol
(The rabbit that has only one hole soon is caught)

Wild animals and game were invaluable in the Romany diet and boys were taught to hunt from a young age. Every Roma knew that an injured or slowly killed animal, such as one caught terrified in a trap for a long time would make bad food, so they made sure that their intended food was killed as swiftly and painlessly as possible. Fear and pain do in fact cause definite reactions that can be smelled.

Most people think of **hedgehog** when asked about Romany food and although this gradually fell from favor over the years, some old Roma people still have fond memories of this delicacy called *hotchi-witchi* (an ancient Romany name). Curiously the same word is used for both hedgehog and porcupine in Sanskrit. In the *Journal of the Gypsy Lore Society* (Volume VII, Number I), J.W.S. Mackie notes that porcupine was "a great favorite for a meal with the lower castes" in India.

Roma considered hedgehogs to be clean animals, as they ate no filth and had clean habits. The hedgehog is common in parks, gardens, and farmland throughout mainland Britain and the spiny creatures prefer woodland edges, hedgerows, and suburban habitats where there is plenty of food for them. Welsh Roma called the month of October *Mis Draenog* (the month of the hedgehog), as by late October hedgehogs were preparing to hibernate and had fattened themselves up for the winter months ahead.

The meat, which was said to be sweet and tender, was served at celebrations. One old Roma man I talked to remembered eating hedgehog and potatoes for his Christmas dinner as a child. Among the Coppersmiths, hedgehog was eaten only at ceremonies or as a medicine. An ancient Romany belief was that cows never lay down if there were hedgehogs around for fear that the hedgehogs would drink from their udders leaving the cow dry. A plump hedgehog could be cooked in various ways—unskinned, rolled in wet clay, and baked *en croute* in the embers of a campfire. When cooked, the clay was broken and with it came the bristles and skin. Some Roma preferred to remove the spines by running a red-hot poker over the dead creature, then skinning and roasting it. Another method was to lay the dead hedgehog on its back on the embers of the fire—if laid on its stomach the creature would burst. The spines were then easily removed. The hedgehog was cleaned, its intestines removed, then rinsed well and cooked. It was important to rinse the hedgehog well to get rid of the copious amount of blood it contained. The skinned animal was put into a frying pan with cold water, heated to boiling, and the water discarded. This was repeated twice more, once in cold water and once in tepid water.

Roast hedgehog was said to be rich and succulent with a flavor similar to that of pork or goose. The hedgehog was often flavored with garlic and placed, still in its skin, over hot coals or stones to cook in its own juices. When it was judged to be cooked, its prickles were shaved or picked off, the skin peeled back, and the meat was served alone or wrapped in aromatic leaves. The Roma also enjoyed fried hedgehog. The meat was cut into slices and fried in a frying pan or the pieces roasted on a spit over a fire. Chicken and other fowl were also cooked this way.

Hedgehog fat was highly esteemed and was one of the oldest Romany cures. It was rubbed into the skin as a treatment for sciatica, put into the ears to treat earache or temporary deafness, and was also applied to hair to keep it dark and lustrous.

Some Roma, who enjoyed eating a roasted hedgehog, would under no circumstances taste a roasted **squirrel**, although others considered the creature to be delicious and wholesome as it lived on pure nutritious food gathered from fields and woods.

Birds such as **sparrows**, **rooks**, and **pigeons** were plucked and cleaned and put into the cooking pot with vegetables and herbs. Sparrows were also strung between two forked sticks and cooked over the campfire. The fat skimmed off broth was used to cook snails.

When buying fowl Roma preferred to buy them while still alive, so that they could check that the birds were in prime condition. Birds were chosen for their size rather than tenderness. **Geese** were farmed extensively, particularly in eastern England and autumn goose fairs were popular events, the most famous being held at Nottingham in England, which still survives today as a funfair. After the harvest, the geese were sent into the fields of stubble to graze on the grain left lying around and so were called "stubble geese."

A favorite method of cooking an older bird was to stew it. *Goos in a Hogepotte* is a medieval recipe in which the goose was cut up and put into a pot with water, spices, bread, ale, wine, and onions and cooked slowly. Pieces of rabbit were often added to the pot to stretch the dish to feed more. The dry rabbit meat absorbed the flavor of the goose and was served to the children so there was more goose for the hungry men.

Goose fat and feathers were highly prized. Goose fat is very soft and was usually known as goose grease. A hot poultice of the grease was placed on the chest to ease the suffering of bronchitis or a cough. Skin troubles were treated with a yellow ointment made from melted goose grease combined with broom and gorse flowers;

a green version was also made using watercress juice. Goose grease was also mixed with the juice of coltsfoot leaves, honeysuckle berries, and pellitory-of-the wall (a humble plant belonging to the same group as the stinging nettle and the hop) to make an ointment for ulcers and hemorrhoids.

A mixture of melted goose fat, horseradish juice, mustard, and turpentine, shaken until white and creamy, was applied to stiff and rheumatic joints. Warm goose grease was smeared onto babies and children's heads, lips, and noses, to protect them before going out into the winter cold. Goose grease was rubbed into leather harnesses, straps, and other equipment to soften them. It was also rubbed into the cracked hooves of horses and used to polish beaks, legs, hooves, and trotters of animals going on show. Goose feathers provided quills, fishing floats, and down for mattresses, pillows, and eiderdowns. The large wings were used as brushes and dusters.

Before cooking birds and fowl, Roma made sure that the creatures were free from disease by inspecting the liver; if it was spotted it was sign of disease, so the animal was thrown away. Birds (complete with feathers) were wrapped in clay and cooked in the fire. The clay and the burnt feathers were removed; the bird cut open and the insides removed before eating.

All sorts of wild game were available, and Roma had their secret ways of ensnaring these. All game, with the exception of pigeons were hung, unplucked, unskinned, and ungutted for up to a week (depending on the weather) in a cool place, to make them tender and bring out the flavor. Game birds were ready when the feathers just above the tail could be removed easily. Game was frequently cooked with the foods it lived on while alive, such as rabbit with wild thyme and mushrooms, which ensured excellent flavor. Any leftover game was made into tasty soups and broths.

Moorhen, waterfowl living by lakes and ponds, were known as *parni-cannie* and were a much sought-after winter dish. They were easy to catch and were roasted with herbs such as fennel, wild thyme, and garlic. The strongly flavored dark, dry flesh tends to have a rather "muddy" flavor, but aromatic herbs counteract it.

Wild ducks were in season from September to February. Their flesh often tasted fishy owing to their diet of fish. They were usually roasted or sometimes salted— a large duck was rubbed inside and out with salt and hung for one to three days in a cool place. It was rinsed well and put in a pot, covered with water or stock, and cooked slowly for a few hours.

Grouse were in season from August to December and only young birds were roasted. They were often stuffed with rowanberries or even tiny raspberries, which grew wild on the moors inhabited by grouse. Older birds were cooked slowly in water or stock.

Partridges, in season from September to February, were casseroled or roasted, sometimes stuffed with an onion or with wild mushrooms.

Pheasants, though in season from October to February, are at their best in November and December, as they have much more flavor after the first frosts. They were broiled, roasted, or "jugged" in the same way as hare and were also good stuffed with apples. If cooked without first hanging, their flavor was similar to that of chicken.

Pigeons, in season year-round, needed no hanging and were also jugged or casseroled sometimes wrapped in the vine leaves that grew in the gardens of southern England. Wood pigeons were plentiful in corn-growing regions of England, especially at harvest time.

Woodcock, a migratory bird, arrived in Britain in the winter and was in season from September to February. After hanging, it developed a rich gamy flavor and was usually roasted.

Rabbits and hares were prolific in the countryside, but some Roma believed that killing a hare caused bad luck and refused to do so. Hares were found from August to the end of February but were at their best in the fall. Young hares could be jointed and broiled with fat, while old hares were treated like game and hung for several days to tenderize the meat and develop the flavor. Hare was stuffed with agrimony, sorrel, and other herbs to impart a delicate flavor to the rather dry flesh and crab apple jelly was a favorite accompaniment. The skin was used to make belts and hats.

Hare entrails were cleaned and treated, then twisted to make strings for Gypsy violins and banjos. The famous Hungarian and Magyar Gypsies, who are reputed to be the best fiddlers in the world, used this "Gypsy catgut" which they believed to be far superior to the more commonly used sheep catgut.

Trotters and **pigs' tails** could be bought cheaply from a local butcher and were boiled. **Kidneys** and **tripe** were well cleaned and fried. Bones were very cheap and were used to make soups and stock.

Snails were popular with Roma and could be gathered easily. Many Roma would use only those that lived near hawthorn hedges, but never near ivy. Snails could also be fattened by keeping them in a covered tub and feeding them on herbs, lettuce and fruit and vegetable peelings. They were frequently flavored with garlic, boiled in salted water, stuffed with fat, and baked. It was also believed that snail spittle would remove warts.

Although there is no record of Roma eating **badgers**, food writer Waverley Root wrote in his famous book, *Food* (Simon and Schuster, 1980) that eighteenth-century English peasants ate them, so it is possible that Roma also caught and ate these nocturnal animals. A written record from the eighteenth century stated that "The badger is one of the cleanest creatures, in its food of any in the world and one may suppose that the flesh of this creature is not unwholesome. It eats like the finest pork and is much sweeter than pork." (The Country Lady's Director Richard Bradley, 6th Edition, 1736). Lilli Gore in *Game Cooking* (Weidenfeld & Nicholson, 1974) commented that what she though to be "delicious sucking pig was in fact a badger." The meat was reported to be dark and succulent with a strong flavor.

Henry Smith, in his *Master Book of Poultry and Game* (Spring Books, n.d.c. 1950), gave instructions for baking a badger ham, making the meat from the forequarters into a pie and roasting the legs. He also suggested making gravy from the feet and tail.

Game Soup

MAKES 3 TO 4 SERVINGS

1 pound leftovers of any type of game
2 carrots, chopped
1 onion, chopped
Water or stock to cover
3 cloves
2 bay leaves
2 tablespoons chopped fresh parsley
Pinch of ground mace
Black pepper
Salt and pepper to taste

Put all the ingredients into a large pot and bring to the boil. Cover and simmer for 2 hours. A little wine can be added to the soup if you wish.

Old Fowl

MAKES 3 TO 4 SERVINGS

To ensure an old fowl will be tender and white, place a whole lemon inside the bird. Tie or skewer the neck opening and back opening and boil the bird as usual, according to size and age—a very old fowl can take up to 4 hours. Remove the lemon before serving.

Rabbit in the Pot

The amount of onions and the weights of the rabbit don't really matter here. Most rabbits on sale are young and ready to cook. In the wild, they would have been paunched and skinned, then soaked in cold water for several hours before cooking. The cooking time can be 45 to 65 minutes, depending on the size and tenderness of the rabbit joints.

Place some sliced onions in the base of a large pan or flameproof casserole. Cut up the rabbit and place the pieces in the dish. Season to taste with salt and pepper. Strew some herbs of your choice over the meat (include some fresh marjoram buds if you can). Cover with water, wine, or beer and bring to the boil. Skim the surface then cover and simmer for about 45 minutes or until the rabbit is tender. Serve with boiled or baked potatoes.

Stuffed Baked Rabbit

MAKES 4 SERVINGS

1 rabbit, jointed
Salt
1 onion, chopped
1 generous cup bread crumbs
2 to 3 stems fresh thyme
Pepper
2 to 4 slices fat bacon
1 cup milk or water

Preheat the oven to 350°F. Soak the rabbit joints in salted water for an hour, then dry well. Mix together the onion and bread crumbs. Place a layer of rabbit in the bottom of a casserole or baking dish and sprinkle half the onion mixture over it. Lay 1 to 2 stems of thyme on top, season with salt and pepper, and add the rest of the rabbit joints. Season with salt and pepper and sprinkle the rest of the stuffing mixture over the rabbit and add a stem of thyme. Lay the slices of bacon on top and pour the milk or water over all. Cover and cook for 2 hours until the rabbit is tender.

Rabbit or Chicken with Mushrooms

MAKES 4 SERVINGS

2 tablespoons flour
Salt and pepper
1 young rabbit or chicken, jointed and bones removed
1 tablespoon oil or fat
1 tablespoon butter
1 small onion, finely chopped
1 to 2 cloves garlic, finely chopped or crushed
4 ounces field mushrooms, sliced
4 ounces button mushrooms, sliced
1 cup ale, cider, or white wine
2 tablespoons chopped fresh parsley

Season the flour with the salt and pepper. Dice the meat and toss in the seasoned flour. Heat the oil and butter in a frying pan or skillet and brown the meat with the onion and garlic. Add the mushrooms, ale, and 1 tablespoon of the parsley and bring to the boil. Simmer for about 40 minutes or until the meat is tender. Remove from the heat, sprinkle with the remaining 1 tablespoon parsley, and serve with baked or boiled potatoes.

Gypsy Dumplings

MAKES 3 TO 4 SERVINGS

These dumplings can be cooked in any of the stews mentioned.

1 cup flour
2 teaspoons baking powder
Pinch of salt
2 eggs, lightly beaten
1 to 2 tablespoons milk

Sift the flour with the baking powder and salt. Beat in the eggs and enough milk to make a stiff batter. Drop in small spoonfuls into boiling stew. Cover and cook for 12 to 15 minutes.

3 pounds rabbit meat, cut into pieces
2 fresh bay leaves
3 stems thyme
2 whole cloves
3 onions, minced
1 tablespoon oil
A few black peppercorns, crushed
Salt
Water and red wine
1 1/2 cups diced carrots
12 small white onions
12 small mushrooms
18 small potatoes
1 tablespoon butter, softened
1 tablespoon flour
1 tablespoon minced fresh parsley

Put rabbit, bay leaves, thyme, cloves, minced onion, oil, pepper-corns, and salt into a large pot. Pour in sufficient water and wine to cover the ingredients in the pan. Bring to the boil, reduce the heat, and simmer gently for 2 hours. Add the carrots, white onions, mushrooms, and potatoes and cook, covered, until vegetables are tender, 25 to 30 minutes. Mix the butter with the flour (to make a *beurre manié*) and stir into the stew until the mixture has thickened. Simmer for 5 minutes. Sprinkle with the parsley just before serving.

Grouse Casserole

$^1/_4$ cup plus I tablespoon flour
Salt and pepper
I brace of grouse, prepared and jointed
4 tablespoons butter or other fat
$2^1/_2$ cups stock or water
I onion, chopped
2 to 3 carrots, chopped
3 tomatoes, peeled and chopped

Season the I tablespoon flour with salt and pepper. Sprinkle the grouse joints with the seasoned flour. Melt the butter or fat in a large casserole and fry the joints until browned. Remove the joints. Add the $^1/_4$ cup flour to the fat in the casserole and stir over the heat until lightly browned. Pour in the stock gradually, stirring well to avoid lumps. Bring to the boil and season to taste with salt and pepper. Add the vegetables and grouse pieces. Cover and simmer gently for about I $^1/_2$ hours until the meat is tender.

Roast Partridge

2 oven-ready partridges
2 slices fat bacon
Butter, melted for basting

Preheat the oven to 425°F. Tie a slice of bacon across the breast of each bird with cotton string. Place in a roasting pan and cook for 20 to 30 minutes, basting them well with butter during the cooking. When the birds are cooked to your liking remove the bacon and serve them with gravy.

Duck with Oranges

1 oven-ready mallard duck, about 3 pounds
1 tablespoon flour
Salt and pepper
1 Seville orange (or 1 ordinary orange and $^1/_2$ lemon), peeled and
sliced thinly
Peel and juice of 2 Seville oranges
1 tablespoon sherry
$^1/_4$ cup flour
2 cups stock

Preheat the oven to 400°F. Rub the bird with flour, salt, and pepper. Put the slices of 1 orange inside the duck and place in a roasting pan. Cook for 20 minutes, then remove from the oven and prick the skin (not the flesh) with a sharp knife—this allows the fat to run out and the skin to crisp up. Return to the oven and reduce the temperature to 325°F and cook for another 20 minutes. Prick the skin again and return to the oven for another 20 minutes, by which time the duck should be cooked and tender, but still slightly pink. Keep hot. Remove the white pith from the orange peel and cut finely. Place in a pan with 1 cup water and boil for 15 minutes. Crush the peel and stir into the sherry. Pour off the fat from the roasting pan and stir in the flour. Add the peel, sherry, stock, and orange juice and cook over a low heat for 2 to 3 minutes. Taste and season. Serve the sauce with the duck.

Jugged Hare

2 tablespoons flour
Salt and pepper
1 hare, jointed
3 1/4 cups strong stock, hot
1 lemon, peeled and sliced
1 onion, stuck with 3 whole cloves
12 black peppercorns
2 tablespoons butter
1/4 cup flour
1 cup red wine

Season the flour with salt and pepper. Dredge the joints with the seasoned flour. Put the hare into a stew jar with the hot stock, lemon, onion, and peppercorns. Cover the jar tightly and stand it in a deep pan of cold water. Bring this to the boil and simmer for 3 to 4 hours (depending on the age of the hare). Remove the hare from the jar and keep hot. Knead the butter and flour together and stir into the stock with the wine. Heat the sauce, stirring until smooth and thick.

Spanish Gypsy–Style Chicken

Grated peel of 1 small lemon
1/2 teaspoon ground cumin
1/2 teaspoon ground mace
1 chicken, quartered or 4 chicken joints
1 tablespoon olive oil
2 cups thinly sliced Spanish onions
1 medium red bell pepper, seeds removed and cut in strips
1 medium yellow bell pepper, seeds removed and cut in strips
1/2 cup sliced pitted Mediterranean black olives
1 tablespoon large capers, drained
1/4 cup dry sherry
Orange slices

Preheat the oven to 400°F. In a small bowl mix together the lemon peel, cumin, and mace. Sprinkle over the chicken, and place the joints, skin side up, on an oiled broiler pan. Bake for 30 to 40 minutes, or until the chicken is cooked through. Heat the oil in a skillet then add the onions and bell peppers. Cook over a medium heat for 5 minutes, and then stir in the olives, capers, and sherry. Bring to the boil and cook for 1 minute. Spoon the mixture onto a large serving plate and top with the chicken. Garnish with orange slices.

Chicken and Vegetable Stew

This was made with an old hen or cockerel. You can of course use chicken instead, but cook the stew for less time.

2 tablespoons butter
2 carrots, chopped
4 to 6 slices bacon, chopped
2 large leeks, chopped
1/4 cup flour
1 1/4 cups water or stock
1 boiling fowl
1 small cabbage, chopped
A few stems mixed fresh herbs
Salt and pepper

Preheat the oven to 350°F. Heat the butter in a large pan or flameproof casserole until melted. Add the carrots, bacon, and leeks and cover the pan. Cook for a few minutes over a low heat to soften but not brown the vegetables. Stir in the flour until lightly colored, then add the water or stock. Add the chicken, cabbage, and herbs and season to taste with salt and pepper. Cover the pan and cook for 2 to 3 hours (depending on the toughness of the bird).

Meat Pudding

A favorite dish among British Roma for Sunday dinner, this can also be made with game, such as venison, grouse, or partridge cut into pieces. Mix the game with half its weight of steak.

2 cups self-rising flour
Pinch of salt
1 stick chilled butter, grated
1 1/4 pounds chuck steak, cut into thin pieces
1 onion, chopped (optional)
4 ounces mushrooms, sliced (optional)
Chopped fresh herbs
Water or beer

Mix together the flour, salt, and grated butter. Add just enough cold water to make a firm dough. Roll out and line a greased 4- to 5-cup pudding basin with three-quarters of the dough. Mix the meat with the onion and mushrooms (if using), and add a sprinkling of herbs. Put the meat into the pastry-lined bowl and add just enough water or beer to cover the meat. Cover with the remaining dough to make a lid. Seal the edges well. Tie on a piece of greased greaseproof paper and kitchen foil—making a pleat in the center of the paper and foil to allow the pudding to rise during cooking. Put into a large pan and add enough boiling water to the larger pan to come halfway up the sides of the bowl. Cover the pan and boil for 4 hours, topping up with boiling water as necessary—be careful not to let the pan boil dry. Serve from the bowl—don't turn the pudding out.

Loin of Lamb with Sweet Herb Stuffing

MAKES 2 SERVINGS

2 tablespoons fresh chopped herbs, e.g. mint, rosemary, thyme, or
coriander
1 cup fine bread crumbs
1 tablespoon unrefined milled golden cane sugar
1 small egg yolk
Salt and ground black pepper
Grated peel of 1 lemon
Grated peel of 1 orange
1 pound loin of lamb

Preheat the oven to 400°F. Mix together the herbs, bread crumbs,
sugar, egg yolk, salt, pepper, lemon and orange peel in a mixing
bowl, until well combined. Lay the loin of lamb flat on a work surface, place the stuffing down the center lengthwise, and then roll
up around the stuffing. Secure with string. Place on a roasting pan.
Bake for 1 hour 20 minutes, until the lamb is tender. Remove from
the oven and cut into thick slices. Serve immediately with new
potatoes.

Tatie Pot

MAKES 4 SERVINGS

"Tatie" is an old English slang word for potato. In times of hardship there would have been more potatoes than meat in this
dish.

2 pounds stewing beef or lamb, cut into pieces
2 large onions, sliced
2 to 3 carrots, sliced
1 bay leaf (optional)
2 sprigs thyme (optional)
12 ounces black pudding, sliced
Salt and pepper
3 to 4 large potatoes, sliced
2½ cups (approximately) stock or water

Preheat the oven to 300°F. Layer the meat, vegetables (except the
potatoes), herbs, and black pudding in a deep ovenproof baking

dish or roasting pan, seasoning each layer with salt and pepper. Cover with a layer of potatoes. Pour in the stock to come almost to the top (the exact amount will depend on the size and depth of your dish or pan). Cover and cook for 2 to 2½ hours until the meat is tender. Remove the lid and increase the oven temperature to 350°F and continue cooking for 35 to 45 minutes until the potatoes are browned.

Bulgarian Stuffed Cabbage Leaves SÄRMI

MAKES 6 SERVINGS

1 pound ground beef or chopped ham
4 tablespoons cooked rice
Salt and black pepper
Small piece of jalapeño (or similar hot pepper), minced
1 egg (optional)
12 medium sized cabbage leaves
2 cups tomato soup

Mix the beef or ham with the cooked rice, salt, black pepper, and jalapeños into a thick paste. Add an egg if it is too thick. Take the cabbage leaves, making sure not to break or tear them, and dip them in boiling water to soften them. Wrap each leaf around some of the filling into a sealed roll. Secure by sewing or simply stick a toothpick through, and simmer for about 1 hour in the tomato soup.

Polish Roasted Plums with Bacon

MAKES 4 SERVINGS

8 large plums
8 shelled almonds
8 slices bacon
Oil or lard

Stone the plums and replace the stones with shelled almonds. Wrap a thin slice of bacon around each plum and secure with a toothpick. Fry in a little oil or lard until the bacon is cooked.

FISH AND SHELLFISH

Matcheneskoe guero
(A fisherman)

There were many Roma fishermen, and Welsh Roma in particular were renowned for their angling skills, and for taking fish by less conventional methods! One method of catching fish at night involved shining a torch in the water, as the light was an irresistible attraction to the fish. When the fish came up to the light, it was scooped up with the free hand.

All types of freshwater fish, such as pike, trout, roach, perch, and carp were enjoyed, as were sea fish. Fish were frequently stuffed with a mixture of herbs and bread crumbs before being baked.

Wild salmon, nowadays much in demand, was once so plentiful in Britain that it was despised by the upper classes (along with lobsters and oysters) but not by the working people and the Roma who ate salmon whenever possible. In the eighteenth century, enormous catches on the rivers Spey, Dee, Don, and Tweed, meant that salmon was cheap and commonly available. The firm deep orange-red flesh is rich and full of flavor.

Wild salmon make the exhausting journey from the North Atlantic Ocean back to the river of their birth for the sole purpose of breeding. Paradoxically, this is also the best time to catch them, as their flavor and texture are at their finest, due to their eating heavily from the rich feeding grounds of the ocean before setting out on their long trip.

Tickling **trout** was the favored Romany way of catching them. Standing downstream the fishermen would feel under the stones until they found a fish, and then rub their fingers gently along its tummy, gradually working up the body with thumb and forefinger until these could be thrust into the gills and the fish could not escape. The fish was then lifted out and killed.

Muddy-bottom fish such as **tench** and **pike** were also appreciated and were skillfully dealt with to take away their rather murky taste. Fish that live on the bottom of streams and ponds require skillful cooking if they are not to taste muddy. Roma knew that all these type of fish have specially arranged overlapping scales, which keep the mud away from the fish's skin while they swim against the stream. When the fish is limp and the scales are disturbed the mud enters the absorbent skin of the fish. Therefore, the fish was not washed and was moved as little as possible. Clay was smoothed over the fish toward the tail and it was baked flat on a grid or on twigs so that the underside would cook slowly. The fish wasn't turned during cooking. When done the clay crust was broken off with the skin attached, to produce a delicious tasting fish with a fine flavor. Sometimes the fish were slit and carefully stuffed with a mixture of bread crumbs, fat, and herbs before cooking.

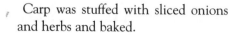

Carp was stuffed with sliced onions and herbs and baked.

In seaside areas, **shellfish** were plentiful. Oysters were laid on heated stones by the fire to roast in their shells. Cockles were gathered from the sand by raking or scratching with a knife and were dropped into baskets. The sand and mud was washed off in the sea and the clean cockles put into sacks. They were rolled in flour and fried in fat until crisp. The shells of **scallops** were scrubbed and given a sharp knock to open them. Another method was to place them in a few inches of boiling water to open. The flat top shell was cut off and the black part (the membrane and thin thread of the intestine) removed leaving just the orange and white flesh. The flesh is creamy white and firm with a mild flavor and the orange coral or roe has a rich flavor and smooth texture. Scallops need only a few minutes cooking time to preserve their delicious unique flavor. It is important not to overcook the sweet white meat as it can easily become tough and rubbery and lose its flavor. Scallops are at their peak in winter as, like most shellfish, they develop their best flavor in cold waters.

To prepare scallops at home, scrub the shells well and place them, curved side down, in an oven set on low for a few minutes. Open the shells with a knife and wash under running cold water, then remove the gray-brown frill and the black thread of the intestine. Soak the flesh in ice-cold water for several hours before using if possible, so the flesh will become firm. Prick the coral with a needle before cooking to prevent it from bursting as it cooks. Scallops can be fried, baked, poached, or steamed and are also very good broiled, wrapped in bacon slices before cooking. Scallops are cooked when they become opaque but remain translucent in the center.

Pearl-bearing freshwater **mussels** provided a livelihood for Scottish Gypsies or *tinklers* in Perthshire. They used large pans with the bases removed (these took the ripple off the surface of the water and acted as water glasses) and waded into rivers when low. The Gypsies looked into the "water glasses" and thrust their arms inside them and removed the mussels from the riverbed. Mussels were cooked by the side of the fire and eaten as soon as the shells opened. They could also be boiled or fried in butter and herbs. As a bonus, their pearls often fetched high prices from the region's jewelers.

Limpets were lifted off rocks when the tide went out and were cooked in the same way as mussels.

Eels were trapped in a basket set with complicated arrangement of sticks, which made it possible for the eels to swim in but not out again. The white flesh is rich and succulent, but not all Roma would eat eels; some thought the slender slippery creatures to be too much like snakes. Those who did like them enjoyed them encased in clay and baked in the ashes of an open fire, fried, roasted, steamed, made into soup, or cooked with buttercup root, which is said to have a similar flavor to truffles.

Shoals of young eels or elvers resembling a mass of jelly streamed into freshwater rivers from March onwards and were caught by scooping them up in buckets and pans (nets would have let the soft slender transparent creatures through). After washing them, the elvers were cooked immediately; their transparent flesh became opaque and firm as soon as it came into contact with heat. Elvers were fried and eaten with a sprinkling of salt and pepper and some chopped herbs.

Whelks were washed thoroughly in seawater to remove the sand then dropped into boiling water—but not allowed to boil or the flesh would harden.

Tasty Baked Fish

MAKES 1 SERVING

You can use fresh herbs such as parsley, tarragon, or chervil in this recipe.

6 ounces any white fish fillet
2 tomatoes, chopped
1 small onion, chopped
3 teaspoons chopped fresh herbs
Grated peel of 1 small lemon
Pinch of salt
2 tablespoons butter

Preheat the oven to 400°F. Place the fish on a large square of greaseproof or nonstick baking paper. In a small bowl mix the tomatoes, onion, herbs, peel, and salt and sprinkle over the fish. Dot with butter and fold the paper to enclose the fish to form a loose parcel. Place on a baking tray or ovenproof plate and cook for 15 minutes until the fish flakes easily when tested with a fork.

This was made from whatever type of fresh fish was available, including damaged fish.

1 pound white fish, cut into pieces
1 onion, sliced
2 tablespoons chopped fresh herbs (optional)
1 1/4 cup mashed potatoes
Salt and pepper

Preheat the oven to 350°F. Grease a deep ovenproof pot or dish with butter. Add the pieces of fish and the onions and herbs, if using. Cover with a tightly fitting lid and bake until the fish is tender. Remove from the oven and discard the skin, bones, and other unwanted parts. Flake the fish with a fork and stir in the mashed potatoes. Return to the oven until browned.

Fish Cakes

1/2 pound white fish
3/4 pound (about 2 medium) potatoes, peeled
1 tablespoon butter
2 tablespoons chopped parsley
Salt and pepper
Beaten egg to bind (optional)
1 egg, beaten to coat
1 cup dry breadcrumbs
Oil or lard for frying

Put the fish in a pan and just cover with water. Bring to the boil and simmer gently for 5 to 10 minutes until the fish is cooked and flakes easily with a fork. Drain well. Boil the potatoes until tender, drain and mash until smooth. Mix in the fish, butter, parsley, and salt and pepper to taste, binding if necessary with a little beaten egg. Form the mixture into a roll on a floured board, cut into 8 slices, and shape into rounds. Coat with egg and crumbs. Heat the oil and fry the fishcakes until crisp and golden on both sides. Drain well and serve.

Stuffed Herrings

¹/2 stick butter
I onion, chopped
I cup fresh breadcrumbs
¹/4 cup chopped walnuts
I tablespoon prepared English mustard
Finely grated peel and juice of I lemon
3 tablespoons chopped fresh thyme
Salt and pepper
4 herrings, cleaned and boned with heads and tails removed

Melt half the butter in a pan and add the onion. Cook gently until softened but not browned, about 5 minutes. Mix together the breadcrumbs, walnuts, mustard, lemon peel, I tablespoon lemon juice, and the thyme. Season to taste and add the onion, mixing well. Open the herrings and lay them skin side down. Press the stuffing mixture evenly over half of each herring. Fold the other half over and slash the skin several times with a sharp knife. Melt the remaining butter in a large frying pan. Fry the fish for about 10 minutes, turning once until browned and tender.

Soused Mackerel

4 mackerel, cleaned
4 bay leaves
Salt and pepper
I ¹/4 cups white wine vinegar
10 peppercorns

Preheat the oven to 300°F. Remove the head and backbone from each fish and roll up, skin side out, ending with the tail end. Secure each roll with a cocktail stick and pack the rolls tightly into a baking dish, so that they fit snugly. Combine the remaining ingredients and pour over the fish. Cover and cook for I hour. Allow the fish to cool in the liquid and chill until required to serve.

Bacon-Wrapped Trout

MAKES 4 SERVINGS

4 trout, cleaned
Salt and pepper
8 thin slices bacon, rind removed

Preheat the oven to 400°F. Season the inside of each fish with salt
and pepper. Wrap 2 bacon slices around each fish and arrange
them in a shallow ovenproof dish. Bake for 15 to 20 minutes until
the fish is cooked through and flakes easily with a fork.

Baked Stuffed Salmon

MAKES 4 TO 6 SERVINGS

1 to 2 stems each fresh rosemary, thyme, marjoram, chives, tarragon,
  finely chopped
1 small onion, finely chopped
1 clove garlic, finely chopped
1 teaspoon ground mace
3- to 4-pound whole salmon, cleaned
1 1/4 cups white wine or water
2 bay leaves
Salt and pepper
3 tablespoons butter

Preheat the oven to 375°F. Mix the chopped herbs, onion, garlic,
and mace and stuff the salmon with the mixture. Put into a large
baking dish or roasting pan and pour in the wine. Add the bay
leaves and season generously with salt and pepper. Dot the fish
with half the butter and cook for 20 to 30 minutes until the fish
flakes easily with a fork. Place the salmon on a heated serving
dish and keep warm. Boil the cooking liquor until reduced, and
then beat in the remaining butter. Pour over the fish and serve.

Baked Whole Salmon

1 stick butter
2 tablespoons chopped fresh parsley
Grated peel and juice of 1 lemon
Salt and pepper
3-pound whole salmon, cleaned
$1/2$ cup white wine or water

Cream the butter with the parsley, lemon peel, and salt and pepper until well blended. Roll into a cylinder in a piece of foil and chill until firm. Place the fish on a large piece of heavy duty foil. Cut the chilled butter into slices and place these inside the fish. Sprinkle the outside of the salmon with salt and pepper, then pour the wine and lemon juice over the fish. Fold the foil over the fish to form a loose parcel, ensuring the edges are sealed so that the juices don't leak out. Place on the grill and cook for 45 minutes. If cooking in the oven, cook for $1 1/4$ to $1 1/2$ hours at 325°F, basting from time to time, until cooked through. Test the middle part of the salmon to check that it is cooked thoroughly.

This is an adaptation of an old Spanish recipe. Since Seville oranges have only a brief season, wine vinegar can be used instead.

4 (8-ounce) salmon steaks
1/2 teaspoon ground white pepper
1 teaspoon salt
1/4 cup Seville orange juice
1/4 cup warm water
2 tablespoons slivered, blanched almonds
2 tablespoons pine nuts
2 tablespoons raisins
2 teaspoons finely chopped fresh marjoram
2 teaspoons finely chopped fresh parsley
2 teaspoons finely chopped fresh mint
Finely grated peel of 1 Seville orange

Place the salmon steaks in a large, shallow frying pan. Mix the pepper, salt, orange juice, and water and sprinkle over the fish. Cover and heat until simmering then leave to simmer for 15 minutes. Turn the salmon steaks over and add the almonds, pine nuts, raisins, herbs and orange peel. Cover the pan and simmer for another 15 minutes until the fish is cooked through. The actual cooking time will depend on the thickness of the fish. Add more water if necessary to keep the pan from drying out.

Fried Eels

MAKES 3 TO 4 SERVINGS

2 medium-size eels
Salt
4 tablespoons butter
3 to 4 teaspoons finely chopped parsley, thyme, and/or sage
1 to 2 shallots, chopped
2 egg yolks
1 cup bread crumbs

Rub the eels well with salt, and then wash them thoroughly. Cut off the heads but leave the skin on. Slit the eels along the belly and take out the bones and guts. Wash well under cold running water. Wipe and dry them and cut into pieces about 3 inches long. Melt the butter in a frying pan and stir in the herbs and shallots. Cook for a few minutes until the shallots are softened. Remove from the heat and cool slightly. Beat in the egg yolks. Dip the eel pieces into the mixture and toss into the bread crumbs to coat. Fry or broil until crisp and brown.

Mussels

MAKES 4 SERVINGS

1 quart fresh mussels
1 onion (optional)
White wine (optional)
Peppercorns (optional)
Fresh herbs (optional)

Scrub mussels under running water; discard any that are open or broken. Scrape off any barnacles and pull off the dark beard. Drop into 2½ cups boiling water. You can add a whole onion, a glass or two of white wine, a few peppercorns, and a bunch of fresh mixed herbs if you wish to flavor the water. Boil briskly for 5 to 6 minutes, shaking the pan from time to time so that all the mussels open.

Crab Pies

8 small crabs, boiled
Salt and pepper
Pinch grated nutmeg
2 cups fresh breadcrumbs
1 stick butter, softened
1 cup vinegar

Preheat the grill. Pick out the meat from the shells and claws and scrub the shells well. Season the crabmeat with salt, pepper and nutmeg and stir in the breadcrumbs and butter. Slowly stir in the vinegar. Spoon the mixture into the shells and brown under a hot broiler.

Crayfish with Lemon

Crayfish were found in streams in August and were traditionally cooked on the campfire and eaten with butter and lemon juice. They resemble small lobsters and were cooked in a similar way. Crayfish are almost extinct in Britain today due to pollution.

2 dozen crayfish
$^3/_4$ stick butter, melted
Lemon juice
Boiling salted water

Plunge the crayfish into a large pan of boiling salted water and boil for 10-15 minutes or until bright red. Rinse in cold water and remove the shells. Place under a broiler set on high to heat through and serve with the melted butter and a sprinkling of lemon juice.

The bori lon pani
(The great salt water, the ocean)

Roma who set up camp near the sea in coastal areas had the added bonus of being able to collect seaweeds. When vegetables were scarce during the winter months, they formed an important part of the diet, as seaweeds are rich in iodine. Edible varieties native to British shores include laver, kelp, and dulse. Possibly the most beneficial effect seaweeds have on the body is cleansing the blood of toxins. Seaweeds make the blood more alkaline and so help to offset the acid-forming effects of eating red meat and sugar, and are also good for cleansing the lymphatic system. It has been claimed that eating seaweed can prevent colds, strengthen nails, and help relieve arthritis (information from the Centre d'étude et de valorisation des algues, 22610 Pleubian, France).

Dulse (*Rhodumenia palmate*) has broad leaves and a strong salty flavor with the tang of iodine. Once sold in city markets by street sellers, it was sometimes given raw to children as a tonic. It is, in fact, a valuable source of vitamins and minerals.

Purple and green **laver** (*Porphyra umbilicalis*) flourishes on the slippery rocks around the west coast of Britain and Ireland. In Ireland this seaweed is called "sloke." It could be gathered from the rocks at low tide at any time of year, but required a great deal of washing to remove all traces of grit and sand. It then needed soaking in fresh water to reduce the salty bitterness. Laver has become a Welsh speciality. In the past, there was a well-organized trade and the seaweed was cured in large, specially built drying houses. Nowadays, fresh laver is washed many times then soaked for several hours before being boiled for five hours to form a dark green-brown puree. This is canned and sold as "laverbread." The Welsh roll the laverbread in oatmeal, shape it into cakes and fry it with bacon. Laver sauce was a traditional accompaniment to Welsh mutton and is also served alongside lobster and other shellfish.

Kelp (*Fucus vesiculosos*) was used in hot water as an embrocation for rheumatism.

Rock tripe (*Umbilicaria pustulata*) is not really a seaweed, but an orange-colored lichen found on rocks and walls in western parts of Britain.

Samphire is also not strictly a seaweed but it grows on tough shingles on rocky coasts and estuaries around the coasts of western or southern England, but rarely in the north. There are two relatively common types—marsh samphire (*Salicornia stricta*) and rock samphire (*Crithmum maritimum*). The latter has a similar flavor to asparagus and for that reason was also known as "sea asparagus." Rock samphire, an umbelliferous plant, grows wild among the rocks on the seacoasts of Europe. It has a curiously distinctive aroma and could be smelled before it was seen. Its long, fleshy, green, glossy leaflets are full of aromatic juice and umbels of tiny, yellowish-green blossoms appear in late summer. The whole plant is aromatic and has a powerful scent. The young leaves were gathered in May, sprinkled with salt, boiled, and covered with vinegar to make an aromatic pickle. It was also eaten as a vegetable, either cooked or raw, usually with fish. London street sellers hawked it as "cress marine." Other plants similar in appearance to samphire were sometimes sold under the same name, but were very inferior in flavor.

Marsh samphire is a member of the beet family and its alternative name of glasswort was due to the fact that it was frequently used in the manufacture of soda glass. It has a saltier flavor than rock samphire and lacks the aromatic flavor of the latter.

Sea holly (*Eryngium maritimum*), a beautiful gray-blue plant, is spiny and prickly like a thistle and grows on sand and shingles near the seashore. The roots were boiled and peeled, then cut up and boiled with the same weight of sugar until thick and syrupy. The roots were then removed and left to cool, by which time they had crystallized.

Seakale (*Crambe maritime*), a native of the coast of Western Europe, is similar to celery in appearance. Its ivory-colored stalks are tinged with purple and are picked when about nine inches long. The flavor is mildly reminiscent of celery. It is now illegal in Britain to harvest wild seakale, as it is a legally protected species, although not an endangered one.

Sloke (Porphyra palmate) is brown when fresh. It was washed well, packed into a pan or cooking pot, and cooked slowly for a long time, turning into a soft green-black pulp. A little butter and a splash of vinegar were added before it was eaten hot.

Major supermarkets and health food stores stock several types of seaweed, usually dried. Seaweed packed in sea salt is available in some larger supermarkets. Before cooking, rinse under cold running water for 2 to 3 minutes to remove the salt. The salt content of seaweed means that usually only pepper is required as a seasoning.

Only a small amount is needed as it expands considerably when reconstituted with water. It can be shredded and eaten raw or simmered gently until tender. Add to salads, stir fries, and soups.

Notice: Seaweed should not be eaten more than once a week by anyone suffering from hyperthyroidism.

Wild Mushroom and Seaweed Risotto

9 cups vegetable stock or water
4 tablespoons butter
2 tablespoons olive oil
1 onion, finely chopped
1½ cups arborio rice
¼ cup finely grated cheese (optional)
8 ounces wild mushrooms, sliced
5 ounces fresh seaweed, washed

In a large pot, heat the vegetable stock until boiling. Lower the heat and simmer gently for 15 minutes. In another large pan, heat 2 tablespoons of the butter with the olive oil in a large pan and sauté the onion until soft, but not brown (about 10 minutes). Add the rice to the onion and cook for a few minutes. Add the hot stock, one ladleful at a time, to the rice. Cook until the rice has absorbed the stock, and then add another ladleful of stock. Repeat this process until all the stock has been used up or the rice is almost cooked, about 20 minutes. Add the grated cheese if using and mix well. In a separate pan, melt the remaining 2 tablespoons butter and sauté the mushrooms for a few minutes. Stir the mushrooms and seaweed into the rice and serve immediately.

Laver and Mashed Potatoes

1 pound mashed potatoes (about 2 cups)
1 pound cooked laver
Pepper
1 tablespoon butter

Preheat the oven to 425°F. Spread a layer of potatoes over the base of a medium-size buttered ovenproof dish and cover with a layer of laver. Repeat these layers, sprinkling with pepper between the layers. Finish with a layer of potato. Dot the top with butter. Heat through in the oven for about 15 to 20 minutes until browned.

Red Seaweed Soup

1 cup of sloke or dulse
2 cups mashed potato
6 cups milk
Salt and pepper to taste
1 tablespoon melted butter
Squeeze of lemon juice

Place the seaweed in a pan with just enough water to cover it. Cover the pan, bring to the boil and simmer for 3 to 4 hours until tender. Drain well and add the mashed potato and the milk. Simmer for 20 minutes. Beat or puree until smooth and season to taste. Add the melted butter and lemon juice and beat the mixture again. Serve hot.

BREADS AND PANCAKES

Morum, moro, panum
(Bread)

The basic ingredients of bread are very simple—flour, yeast salt and water. Bread could be cooked on a hot stone over the dying embers of the campfire, usually covered with a pot to create steam and help the bread to rise.

Wheat is not the only grain used to make bread; barley, buckwheat, maize, oats, and rye are also used. Bread is a basic part of a country's cuisine and the type of grain used reflects the geography and climate of wherever the Roma are based. Western European Roma mostly eat wheat bread, while those in Eastern Europe use rye, barley, and buckwheat to make their bread.

Roma women baked their bread or bought it from a local baker. At harvest time, many Roma worked in the fields to harvest the grain and it's likely that flour formed at least part of their wages.

This traditional bread is one of the simplest; it is made using soft flour and buttermilk, which gives it a distinctive flavor. The use of baking soda rather than yeast means it can be made very quickly, cutting out the need for kneading or proofing time and making up for the fact that this bread doesn't keep fresh for very long. The raising agents are baking soda and cream of tartar, which react with the acids in the buttermilk. The secret of really good soda bread is to work quickly, handling the dough gently, followed by baking in a hot oven.

2 cups all-purpose flour, plus extra for sprinkling
1 teaspoon baking soda
1 teaspoon salt
1/2 teaspoon cream of tartar
2 tablespoons butter
Cooked bacon, chopped (optional)
About 1/2 cup buttermilk

Preheat the oven to 400°F. Sift the flour, baking soda, salt, and cream of tartar into a large mixing bowl and rub in the butter until well dispersed. Stir in the bacon if using. Make a well in the center and pour in the buttermilk, mixing quickly with a broad bladed knife, until the mixture forms a dough. Turn out onto a floured board and knead lightly. Press or roll the dough into a round about 1 1/2 inches thick and lay on a lightly greased baking sheet. Mark the top into 4 sections and bake for 20 minutes, until just colored and it sounds hollow when tapped. Cool on a wire rack.

Grease two to three new 5- to 7-inch clay flowerpots well with lard or oil and bake empty in a 400°F oven for 30 minutes before use, to avoid cracking later.

2 cups wholemeal bread flour
1 1/2 cups strong white bread flour
2 teaspoons salt
2 tablespoons lard or shortening
1/2 ounce fresh yeast
1 teaspoon unrefined milled golden cane sugar
1 1/2 cups warm water
1 tablespoon chopped fresh herbs (optional)
1 egg, beaten
Fennel seeds (optional)

Put the flours and salt into a large mixing bowl and rub in the lard. Cream the yeast with the sugar and add the water, mixing well. Pour into the flour mixture and mix to a soft dough. Add the fresh herbs, if using. Knead until smooth, shape into a ball, and place in a bowl. Cover with oiled plastic wrap and leave to rise for about 1 hour until doubled in size. Knead the dough again and divide in half. Place each piece into a well-greased flowerpot. Cover and leave to rise for 30 to 40 minutes until risen and puffy. Preheat the oven to 400°F. Brush the tops with beaten egg and sprinkle with fennel seeds, if desired. Stand the prepared flowerpots on a baking sheet and bake for about 35 minutes. Turn out carefully onto a wire rack to cool.

Pumpkin Bread

2 pounds peeled pumpkin, cut into chunks
4¹/₂ cups strong white bread flour
1 tablespoon salt
1 ounce fresh yeast

Bring a large pan of salted water to the boil and add the pumpkin. Simmer gently for about 20 minutes or until the pumpkin is tender. Drain well, reserving the liquid. Sieve the pumpkin into a bowl and beat to a puree. Cool until just warm, and then mix with the flour and salt. Dissolve the yeast in 6 tablespoons of the cooking liquid and leave in a warm place for about 10 minutes until frothy. Pour into the flour mixture and mix well to form a firm dough. If the mixture is too dry add a little more cooking liquid. Knead well until smooth, place the dough in an oiled bowl, cover with a damp tea towel or plastic wrap, and leave in a warm place until doubled in size, about 2 hours. Knock back the dough, knead lightly, and shape into a ball. Cover with lightly oiled plastic wrap and leave for about 1 hour until well risen. Preheat the oven to 425°F. Using a sharp knife make a circular incision around the top of the ball about 2 inches from the edge. Place on a baking tray and cook for 45 to 50 minutes until deep golden and cooked through.

MAKES 6 TO 8 SERVINGS

Caraway is a very popular ingredient of German rye breads and adds an unmistakable flavor. Sourdough bread has a characteristic sweet-sour flavor, a thick crust and spongy crumb. It's particularly delicious with cheese and smoked sausage. You need to make the sourdough starter thirty-six hours before you start to make the bread.

SOURDOUGH STARTER
3/4 cup rye flour
Scant 1/2 cup warm water
Pinch of caraway seeds

DOUGH
1/2 ounce fresh yeast
1 1/4 cups lukewarm water
2 1/4 cups rye flour
1 generous cup strong wholemeal bread flour
1 generous cup strong white bread flour
2 teaspoons salt
2 tablespoons caraway seeds

Prepare the starter 36 hours ahead: Mix the rye flour, warm water, and caraway in a large bowl, using your fingertips to make a soft paste. Cover with a damp cloth and leave in a warm place for 36 hours, stirring after 24 hours. **To prepare the dough:** Blend the yeast and water in a measuring cup, then add it to the starter, mixing well. Put the flours, salt, and caraway seeds into a large mixing bowl and make a well in the center. Pour in the yeast mixture and gradually stir in the surrounding flour to make a smooth dough. Turn out onto a lightly floured surface and knead for about 10 minutes, until smooth and elastic. Place the dough into a lightly oiled bowl, cover with lightly oiled plastic wrap, and leave to rise for about 1 1/2 hours until almost doubled in size. Turn out onto a lightly floured surface and knead gently. Shape into a round and place on a greased baking sheet. Cover with lightly oiled clear plastic wrap and rise in a warm place for 2 to 3 hours, by which time it will be risen and puffy. Preheat the oven to 400°F. Remove the clear plastic wrap and bake the loaf for 35 to 40 minutes. Cool on a wire rack.

Campfire Bread

A very basic and easy bread. The dough can be patted into a round and cooked on a hot greased griddle for 5 to 7 minutes on each side until cooked through.

8 cups flour
2 tablespoons baking powder
2 teaspoons salt
4 tablespoons butter or shortening
I cup milk

Combine the flour, baking powder, and salt and rub in the butter until the mixture resembles bread crumbs. Add in the milk gradually to form a stiff dough—you may need to add a little water or more milk. Wind the dough around a clean branch or stick and suspend the branch over the dying embers of the fire, turning frequently until browned and crisp. Pull off the stick and the bread is ready to eat.

Gloucestershire Suet Pancakes

MAKES 4 TO 5 SERVINGS

These fritter type pancakes have a different texture than ordinary pancakes and are delicious eaten alongside eggs and bacon or with a sweet filling. The recipe is believed to have originated in Gloucestershire in England.

6 tablespoons cold butter or shortening, diced
I $^{1}/_{2}$ cups all-purpose flour
I teaspoon baking powder
Pinch of salt
2 eggs
2 to 3 tablespoons milk
Oil for frying

Rub the butter into the flour, baking powder, and salt, until the mixture resembles bread crumbs. Beat the eggs with the milk, stir into the flour mixture and mix to a stiff dough. Roll out the dough on a floured board to a thickness of $^{1}/_{4}$ inch and cut into ten 2-inch rounds. Fry the pancakes in shallow hot oil, turning once during cooking, until golden brown on both sides. Serve immediately.

These delicious little cakes have a close texture and rich flavor and often contain fruit and spices.

2 cups self-rising flour
Pinch of salt
Pinch of ground mixed/pumpkin spices
4 tablespoons butter
4 tablespoons shortening or lard
3 tablespoons unrefined light brown muscovado sugar
4 tablespoons currants
1 tablespoon grated lemon peel
1 egg
1/2 cup milk
Sugar for sprinkling

Sift the flour, salt, and spices into a mixing bowl and rub in the butter and shortening until the mixture resembles bread crumbs. Add the sugar, currants, and lemon peel. Beat the egg and milk together and add to the dry ingredients to form a soft dough. Roll out lightly on a floured surface about 1/4-inch-thick and cut into 2-inch rounds. Cook on a hot floured griddle or heavy frying pan until golden on both sides. Sprinkle with sugar and serve hot and fresh.

Economical Cake

This cake costs very little to make as it needs no eggs or milk.

1 1/2 cups unrefined milled golden cane sugar
1 to 2 teaspoons mixed ground/pumpkin spices (optional)
1 to 2 cups mixed dried fruit, e.g. currants, raisins, apricots, etc.
3 cups flour
1 teaspoon baking soda

Preheat the oven to 325°F. Mix the sugar, spices, and fruit with 2 cups water and bring slowly to the boil. Boil for 1 minute then cool. Stir in the flour and baking soda and put into a greased 8-inch round cake or 9 x 5-inch loaf pan. Bake for about 1 hour until cooked through.

Quick Biscuits

4 cups flour
1 cup sour milk

Put the flour into a bowl and quickly mix in the sour milk. Knead briefly on a floured surface and pat out into a thick round or square. Cut into rounds or squares. Cook on both sides on a hot floured griddle or heavy frying pan until cooked through. Alternatively place on a floured tray and bake for 10 to 15 minutes at 425°F.

RITES OF PASSAGE

Gadje Gadjensa, Rom Romensa
(Gadje with Gadje, Rom with Rom)

Traditional Roma religion was not Christianity, but bore some striking similarities to Judaism; for instance Roma generally were monotheistic, with a belief in one male deity called Del and the devil or Beng, but they never made images of their god. They also practiced circumcision and adhered to strict anticruelty laws. There were also similarities with Hinduism, however, as they frequently practiced numerology. Religion and faith were a way of life, much like keeping *dharma* is for people in India, in that it determines how a person should act their whole lives. The aim of Hindu Dharma is "to reach peace of spirit and harmony in the material life." Roma call this set of requirements and prohibitions *romipen*—"That which gives life order." Good luck charms, amulets, and talismans were, and often still are, common among Roma, (as explained on page 9).

Catholic and Orthodox Christian Roma celebrated the feast days of various saints with music, processions, and feasting. The most important of these was the feast of Saint Sara, the patron saint of Gypsies everywhere.

A large percentage of the Roma are Catholic, both in the United States and in Europe. A more recent candidate for sainthood is Ceferino Jiménez Malla, a Gitano, or Spanish Gypsy, a respected horse-dealer, who converted to Catholicism as an adult and became the first Gypsy to be beatified (the precursor to sainthood) on May 4, 1997 by Pope John Paul II. (In 1936, Spain was about to undergo a civil war and the party associated with the new Spanish Republic persecuted the Catholic faith harshly. One day Ceferino went to the defense of a young priest and cried out to Our Lady to protect the cleric from his enemies. He and a dozen others were arrested and imprisoned in a 16 by 16-foot cell and later transferred to another prison. In both places, the 75-year-old Gypsy led the rest in reciting the Rosary to keep up their morale, but he died in prison on July 17, 1936. His captors stripped his body, took it to the cemetery at night, and buried it in quicklime, his rosary still in his hand. Only after the war was Ceferino re-interred next to his wife. Besides the rosary, he left only one other thing, a set of stable keys. Both his rosary and keys have become precious relics.

Ceremonial events such as christenings, marriages, and religious festivals were (and usually still are) occasions for community activity and sharing. Enormous quantities of food and drink were consumed during these celebrations, which required lengthy preparations and everyone joined in with huge enthusiasm. Beer, wine, and other spirits were often served instead of water on such special occasions.

Birth, baptism, and marriage were all rites of passage and joyous events that were believed to increase luck. When a child was born into Romany society, it was a sign of good luck and God's blessing to the family. During the first six weeks of life, the baby was considered to be ritually impure and in danger of illness and so was given special care. Baptism was a rite that removed the child's impurity. Marriage signified the extension and continuation of the family and was accompanied by great celebrations. It was also believed that good fortune was bestowed on whoever attended any of these events, even if they were not related to the family concerned.

BIRTH

Nane chave, nane bacht
(If there are no children, it is bad luck)

Childlessness was regarded as a great misfortune, as family had an important role in the life of the Roma and was consolidated by the number of children born. The more children, the greater the family's luck would be. The number of boys also improved the standing of the family, or as the Romany proverb says, *O chave hin zor*—"In boys is strength." For their firstborn, the young couple would wish for a boy. Each additional child was warmly welcomed.

Pregnant women ate oatmeal jelly (jello) and also fed this to their children as it was believed to build strong healthy bones and muscles—a belief that has since been proven correct. Oatmeal is easy to digest and was also recommended to strengthen the nerves. Oatmeal jelly was a smooth gruel that set to a jellylike (jello) consistency when cold.

There was a legend among the Roma that when an old Romany musician was going to die, he or she should sing or play to a pregnant woman. Then, when the child was born, it would inherit the musical gifts. One rite practiced by some Roma involved the untying of certain knots (so that the umbilical cord would not be knotted), including all the knots in the expectant mother's clothing. At other times, the expectant mother's hair was loosened if it was pinned or tied with a ribbon.

For several weeks before and after the birth of a child, the expectant mother was *mochardi*—unclean in the Biblical sense. During this time, she was isolated from the community and mostly looked after by women; she had her own set of crockery and dishes and wasn't allowed to prepare food for others. It was usual to erect a special tent for the birth, which was destroyed a month or so after the child was born. In Hungary, when a mother began to suffer the pangs of childbirth, a fire was lit before her tent and kept up until the infant was baptized, in order to drive away evil spirits.

The quarantine period lasted from two weeks to two months, after which the tent and everything in it was burned. The father wasn't allowed to touch his child until after the baptism because the newborn child was considered impure until he or she was baptized, in the Roma way of baptism.

There are rituals (which vary according to tribe) involving the formal recognition of the infant by its father. In some cases, the child is wrapped in swaddling on which a few drops of paternal blood are placed. Other rituals involve the child being covered by a piece of clothing that belongs to the father. In some tribes, the mother puts the infant on the ground and the father picks up the infant and places a red string around its neck, thereby acknowledging that the child is his (*Patrin Journal*, 1999).

After giving birth the new mother breastfed her child and avoided certain foods such as pickles, tomatoes and green vegetables such as cabbage, while breastfeeding, so the baby wouldn't suffer from colic.

The actual birth was an event from which men were banished, as the mother was regarded as *marimé* until the baby was baptized. When a Romany woman was about to give birth, she would not, if she could help it, leave her tent by full moonshine. If a child was born at the time of a full moon, it was believed that the child would make a happy marriage. There was a strange affinity between Roma and the moon that probably dates back to their origins in India and the many ancient Indian legends associated with the moon. One legend, relates that owing to the misrepresentations of a sorcerer, the gypsy leader, Chen, was forced to marry his sister Guin or Kan, and this brought the curse of wandering upon his people. Hence the Romany are called Chen (the moon) and Guin or Kan or Kam (the sun). The name Chen-Kan, or Zingan is known all over the East. Moon worship is very ancient, and witches and other women worked their spells by the light of the full moon, which is derived from that ancient worship.

Nowadays Romany women have their babies in a hospital with their husbands there just like everyone else. Roma regard *Gaje* as *marimé* and outside their world and so restrict their contact with them but Roma women will often use *Gaje* hospitals to shorten the isolation period after childbirth, since they are able to leave all of the *marimé* articles in connection with the birth in the hospital. When women gave birth on the outskirts of their camp the period of avoidance lasted for several weeks. Hospital births shorten this time to just three days.

The baby was baptized two weeks after the birth. During this time, the mother and child were isolated and it was forbidden to pronounce the baby's name before the baptism. The new mother was virtually in quarantine and in some cases, the mother was not allowed to be seen by any man except her husband before the baptism. The husband also faced restrictions. He was prohibited from going out between sunset and sunrise so that he was kept away from evil spirits, called *tsinvari*, which might have attacked the newborn infant during the night. Polish Roma placed garlic under the baby's pillow to protect him or her from devils and witches. A sleep-inducing herb such as Passionflower (*Passiflora incarnate*), Valerian (*Valeriana officinalis*), Hops (*Humulus lupulus*), or lavender (*Lavandula angustifolia, L. officinalis*), was also frequently placed under the baby's pillow.

A few days after the birth (four to seven days, or even more, depending on the custom of the group) the child had his or her "fire baptism" when he or she was given a Romany name. Before being baptized, his or her name could not be spoken, the child was not allowed to be photographed and, sometimes its face could not be shown in public. The newborn child was never kissed before baptism and was never given the name of a dead person. When the child was baptized, a godmother (*kirivi*) and godfather (*kirivo*) were chosen by the new parents. This was a great honor and the new godparents gave the baby a gift, usually a gold cross. The mother wasn't usually present at the baptism because she was still in a state of uncleanliness after the birth. The child was given three names: the first was a secret one, its only purpose was to confuse demons and supernatural spirits (that may bring harm to the child) by keeping the real identity of the child from them. Tradition has it that the mother, the only one who knew this name whispered it at the time of birth, and it was never used. The second name was a Roma name used only among the Roma and *didikai* (part Gypsy) or Roma friends. The third was a name given if the child was baptized again in a Christian church, but this had little importance and was used only when dealing with non-Roma.

The baby was baptized in running water, and then massaged with oil, and in some cases amulets and/or talismans were used to protect the child from evil spirits. After the purification by water, the baby was formally recognized as a human being and could be called by a name.

The great dread of Gypsy mothers was that the new infant would encounter the *Berufen*, become "enchanted," or subjected to the evil eye. All the windows and doors were kept shut in case the spirit of death should enter and harm the baby. Many and various rituals were carried out by the wise woman to counteract this possibility, which bore a striking similarity to birth rituals in parts of India, where charms served to ward off the evil eye and witches or demons. One ritual involved filling a jar with water from a stream, taken *with*, not against, the current. Seven coals, seven handfuls of meal, and seven cloves of garlic were placed in the jar, which was put over the fire. When the water began to boil it was stirred with a three-forked twig, while the wise woman recited a special rhyme.

As the child grew he or she was raised by the entire tribe and had a special place in the family, cherished by his or her parents. He or she learned from the mother or father, initially by imitating them, and later on by helping them whenever possible until the child gradually absorbed the ways of the Roma.

Feasting was a feature of the celebrations to welcome the new addition to the tribe. Beer, wine, brandy, and splendid foods were enjoyed, followed by singing and dancing and the guests contributed to a collection for the new baby.

In Spain rice and salt were basic foods and a rice dish was prepared for festive occasions. Wild ingredients such as herbs, vegetables, game, poultry, fish, and water from a nearby stream were added to the rice. Paella was a popular dish, cooked in a large pan over an open fire—indeed it was said that true paella could only be prepared over an open fire, where the smoke added to the flavor.

Russian Roma served small *piroshki*, pastry dumplings with various fillings such as meat, seafood, cheese, wild mushrooms, sweet preserves, or soft white cheese that were then baked or fried.

Oatmeal Jelly

This jelly is best eaten as fresh as possible, as it won't keep more than a day or two.

1 cup fine coarse oatmeal
Pinch of salt
Sugar or honey to taste

Soak the oatmeal in 2 cups of cold water for up to 2 hours. Stir and strain the liquid into a pan. Discard the oats. Add the salt and sugar or honey to taste and bring to the boil. Simmer until thick—this may take up to 2 hours. Pour into a bowl and allow to become cold.

Mutton with Onions
KAPAMA

This Bulgarian method of cooking a celebratory young spring lamb could also be used with mutton in winter, when a longer cooking time was needed. In spring, chopped fresh herbs were often added at the end of the cooking. It could also be cooked the day before it was needed.

3 pounds young lamb on the bone or 2 pounds boneless lamb
1 pound scallions, roughly chopped
1 head garlic, roughly chopped
Salt and pepper

Trim any excess fat off the meat and cut into large pieces. Put all the ingredients into a large pot with a little boiling water. Cover and bring to the boil, then reduce the heat and simmer gently for about an hour until the meat is tender. Check the seasoning and serve with boiled potatoes.

MAKES 20 TO 30 SERVINGS

10- to 12-pound uncooked ham
3 to 4 dried or fresh bay leaves
A few whole cloves
A few whole peppercorns
4 cups white wine
1 tablespoon prepared mustard
3 tablespoons unrefined light brown muscovado sugar
2 cups fresh bread crumbs
Prunes and apple rings to garnish

Place the ham in a large pan and cover with boiling water. Add
the bay leaves, cloves, and peppercorns and simmer for 2½
hours. Remove from the heat, drain off the liquid and pour in the
wine. Simmer for another 30 minutes. Remove the pan from the
heat and cool the ham slightly in the liquid. Preheat the oven to
350°F. Remove the ham from the pan and place in a roasting pan,
reserving the liquid. Cut away the skin but leave the fat. Mix the
mustard and sugar and spread over the fat. Press on the bread
crumbs and bake for 45 minutes. Strain the reserved liquid and
boil until thickened and syrupy. Place the cooked ham on a serving plate and decorate with prunes and apple rings. Serve the
thickened stock with the ham.

Chicken Paprika

Hungary is renowned for its plentiful harvest of plump red peppers and its national spice, paprika.

1/2 stick butter
2 tablespoons vegetable oil
8 chicken pieces
2 onions, finely chopped
1 clove garlic, finely chopped
3 red bell peppers, seeds removed and chopped
Salt and pepper
1/2 cup chicken stock
4 tablespoons dry white wine
1/2 cup sour cream
3 to 4 tablespoons natural yogurt
1 tablespoon paprika

Heat the butter and oil in a large pan and fry the chicken pieces for 10 minutes, turning until browned on all sides. Remove from the pan. Add the onions to the pan and cook for 5 minutes, then add the garlic and peppers with the chicken pieces and season with salt and pepper. Stir in the chicken stock and wine and bring to the boil. Cover the pan and simmer gently for about 30 to 40 minutes until the chicken is cooked. Remove from the heat. Combine the sour cream, yogurt, and paprika and stir into the pan. Cover and leave to stand for a few minutes before serving.

Barbecued Spicy Chicken

The word 'barbecue' comes from the Spanish barbacoa, indicating a structure upon which meat could be dried or roasted. Barbecue cooking is popular in the United States, where the climate is more favorable to outdoor cooking.

8 chicken joints, skinned
4 tablespoons dark brown muscovado sugar
2 tablespoons lime juice
4 tablespoons fruit chutney
$^1/_2$ inch piece of ginger, peeled and grated
$^1/_2$ cup chicken stock

Score the chicken joints diagonally with a knife, making shallow cuts. Place in a large dish. Mix the sugar, lime juice, chutney, ginger, and stock together and pour over the chicken. Cover and refrigerate for at least 4 hours or overnight. Barbecue (or grill) the chicken until well browned and cooked through. In the meantime, pour the marinade into a saucepan, bring to the boil and simmer gently until thickened. Serve the chicken with the sauce and boiled rice.

Squash Stuffed with Fruits and Nuts

4 acorn squash, halved with seeds and fibers removed
2 tablespoons oil
I onion, finely chopped
2 cooking apples, peeled, cored and chopped
$1/2$ cup dried pears, chopped
4 tablespoons apple juice or cider
Pinch each of ground cinnamon, cloves and ginger
Generous $1/2$ cup pecans, chopped
Salt and pepper

Preheat the oven to 350°F. Put the squash cut side down in a lightly oiled roasting pan and pour in a little water. Bake for about 30 minutes until just tender. Heat the oil and gently fry the onions until soft but not brown. Stir in the apples, pears, juice, and spices. Season to taste and bring to the boil, stirring. Simmer gently for a few minutes, then remove from the heat and add the pecans. Turn the squash halves over and season the insides with salt and pepper. Spoon some of the filling into each hollow and bake for another 15 to 20 minutes until the filling is hot and bubbling.

A tasty stew that's best made with a robust red wine. Don't stir the stew after adding the onions or they will break up.

3 tablespoons olive oil
1 large onion, chopped
2 cloves garlic, crushed
1 1/2 pounds stewing beef, cubed
2 tablespoons tomato puree
2 tablespoons dark muscovado sugar
1 1/2 cups Greek red wine
1 tablespoon red wine vinegar
2 fresh or dried bay leaves
Pinch ground cumin
1 teaspoon chopped fresh oregano
1 teaspoon salt
Pepper to taste
1/2 stick butter
1 pound small onions (about the size of a golf ball)

Heat the oil in a 5-cup ovenproof casserole and add the onion, garlic, and meat. Cook until the meat is browned on all sides. Add the tomato puree and sugar, stirring to coat the meat. Add the wine and just enough water to cover the meat. Add the vinegar, bay leaves, cumin, oregano, salt and pepper. Stir well, cover and simmer for about 1 1/2 hours until the meat is tender. Heat the butter in a frying pan and brown the onions over medium heat.

Add the onions to the casserole and cook for another 30 minutes until the onions are tender.

Apple and cinnamon are two favorite Swedish flavors and they complement each other deliciously in this moist cake.

4 medium eating apples, grated
2 tablespoons lemon juice
1 stick butter
1 cup unrefined light muscovado sugar
2 eggs
2 cups self-rising flour
$1/2$ teaspoon salt
1 teaspoon ground cinnamon
$1/4$ teaspoon ground cloves
2 tablespoons toasted flaked almonds

Preheat the oven to 350° F. Toss the grated apple in the lemon juice to prevent it from becoming brown. Cream the butter and sugar until light, then beat in the eggs, one at a time. Sift the flour, salt, cinnamon, and cloves into the mixture and fold in gently with the apples.

Spoon into a greased 8-inch round cake pan and sprinkle over the almonds. Bake for about 1 $1/4$ hours until golden brown and cooked through. Cool in the pan for 10 minutes then turn out onto a wire rack to finish cooling.

Flan

This simple but delicious Spanish dessert appears at every special occasion.

Caramel
¹/₃ cup unrefined milled golden cane sugar

Custard
3¹/₂ cups milk
4 eggs
4 egg yolks
²/₃ cup unrefined milled golden cane sugar
2 teaspoons vanilla extract
2 tablespoons confectioners' sugar

Preheat the oven to 325°F. **Prepare the caramel-lined pan:** Heat the sugar in a heavy saucepan until it melts, caramelizes, and turns amber. Immediately pour into a 1¹/₂-quart ring mold, swirling the pan to coat.

For the custard: Scald the milk. Whisk together the eggs and egg yolks until blended and whisk in the remaining sugar, vanilla, and hot milk. Pour into the caramel-lined pan. Place in a pan containing 1 inch of hot water and bake in the oven for 45 minutes to 1 hour, or until the custard is set. Remove from the water bath, let cool, and chill. Loosen the caramel custard with a knife and invert on a serving plate.

MARRIAGE

Baksheesh!
(Good Fortune!)
A Romany blessing and toast

It was customary for all Roma to get married; there were very few old maids or old bachelors! To remain unmarried was a rarity and regarded with pity. It was necessary to obtain the permission of the entire camp before marrying, whether man or woman, and it was accepted without question that the bride-to-be would be *janel zhuzhuipen*, pure.

A Romany woman who married a non-Romany man was no longer regarded as a member of the community, and their children were not considered to be Roma by other Roma. Conversely, a non-Romany woman who married a Rom became part of her new Romany family and their children had the choice of joining the Roma community.

Families often had their own customs and traditions when it came to marriage and they varied widely from family to family, but engagements and marriages were joyous occasions for the whole community and were celebrated with lavish amounts of food and drink together with singing and dancing and everyone dressed in their finery.

Roma did not pay much attention to the actual wedding ceremony in the past. Engagements (*mangavipen*) were usually organized for the young couple. The family of the young boy visited the family of the young girl to show their mutual hospitality.

Traditionally, a young man would give the girl of his choice his neck scarf or *diklo* and if she wore it as a headscarf he knew that she had agreed to his courtship. After a time, the couple would go off and live together for several days in a tent or *bender* (a type of wagon) to see if they were suited. If life together suited them, they returned to their clan and were married in front of their relatives and friends. Sometimes a church or civil wedding followed the Roma ceremony a few days later.

In matters of marriage, the fathers of the boy and girl involved gave their formal consent and settled on a bride price or *darro*. The money exchanged for the girl was thought of as compensation for the loss of a daughter and discussion of the bride price was a lengthy process, with friends sometimes called on as witnesses to the bride's virtue and good qualities. *Cheiz* was the name given to the girl's dowry and its display in her parents' house for a few days before the wedding.

More recently and still practiced today by some Roma, when a couple have agreed on an engagement and obtained parental approval, their engagement is celebrated at a ceremony called a *pliashka*, or *plotchka* (engagement feast) attended by friends and family. The young man's father brings a bottle of good wine or brandy wrapped in a brightly colored silk handkerchief. Attached to the bottle is a necklace of gold coins that the father puts around the neck of his son's prospective wife before embracing her warmly. The necklace is a sign to other men that the girl is spoken for. The father drinks from the bottle and passes it around the assembled guests. When the bottle is empty, it is filled for use at the wedding.

During the wedding ceremony, the young people promised to love each other. The leader of the settlement (čhibalo) bound their wrists together and poured wine into the palms of their hands. He drank from her palms, she drank from his palms, and then they kissed each other and became husband and wife. The shared wine symbolized the sealing of their promises and linked destiny.

When a boy married he became a man, a Rom. Among some Romani it was the custom for the newlyweds to live with the husband's family, where the girl became a lower-status member of the family. The new bride assisted her mother-in-law and who taught her new bori (daughter-in-law) how to cook food the way her son was used to. With the birth of their first child, (but sometimes not until the birth of several children), the young wife was fully accepted as a woman, a Romni and the couple could move into their own home. Only when they were parents could they refer to each other as husband and wife. Before then, they used only their first names with each other or in speaking about each other.

One marriage tradition was called "jumping the broomstick." The couple held hands while jumping over a broom made from flowering gorse or thorn in front of their guests. The origins of this are very old and the significance is likely to be that the broom represents a threshold. Jumping over the broom together probably represented crossing this threshold into new territory. Another marriage rite was the joining of hands in front of witnesses.

The mingling of blood, an ancient manner of sealing a pact or a union, was part of the traditional ceremony for many Romany, but is rarely practiced nowadays. A British Pathe newsreel film of September 1938 showed a double Gypsy wedding at Baildon, Yorkshire, England. Huge crowds watched as the open-air wedding was performed according to the rites of the Zingari. The hands of both brides were cut (one of the brides visibly flinched), followed by those of the grooms. The blood of each bride was mixed with that of her respective groom and their wrists bound together. The two couples then held hands and jumped through a fire. The celebrations included singing and dancing and went on for some time afterwards.

A similar tradition involved mixing the blood of the bride and groom with flour, which was then baked into a cake for the couple to share. In a similar ceremony among certain Native American tribes today, young couples are tied together (hand to hand) in the same kind of ritual and it may be still customary for the bride and groom to eat food mixed with their blood. A circle was formed with children in the front and elders at the back. The bride and groom stood in the middle of the circle and held out their hands towards each other, palms upwards. A member of the tribe made an incision on the fleshy part of the hand at the base of the thumb—on the left hand of the groom and the right hand of the bride. Their two hands were then pressed together and a skein of red silk in which there were seven (an important spiritual number found in astrology and many religions) knots tied was wound tightly round their joined hands and wrists. Those present chanted a *gillie* or bridal song while the skein of silk was cut away. The couple ran hand in hand and jumped over a pile of wood—in the unlikely event of their being unable to clear the pile no luck would come to them. They returned to the circle and the eldest person present gave them a loaf of bread that symbolized a wish for plenty throughout their lives together. Wedding gifts were presented to the groom—silver or copper ornaments for the *vardo* were the most coveted gifts. After the present-giving the bride and groom were pelted with yellow ochre and flour (to symbolize luck) and had to run three times down two lines formed by the crowd. By the time this was over the couple was completely coated with luck! Music followed and the bride and groom then went to their new home in an unknown location.

In Orkney, the Gypsy "king" or chief of the tribe conducted marriages. In an article in *The Orcadian* dated September 30, 1954, Ernest Marwick wrote "He mixed together a handful of oatmeal and beremeal and said to the couple: 'let them who can part that part you.'"

Another custom involved a loaf of bread, which was broken and a drop of blood pricked from the thumbs of the bride and groom. A drop of each one's blood was placed on each half of the bread and each ate the piece with the blood of the other. The remaining bread was crumbled over their heads. This echoed an ancient Roman wedding custom, in which a cake of wheat or barley (*mustaceum*) was broken over the bride's head as a symbol of good fortune after which the wedding guests would gather the crumbs as a token of good luck and the couple ate a few crumbs in a custom known as *confarreatio*, "eating together."

Bread was also the subject of another marriage rite. The seated bride had a small amount of salt and bread placed on her lap. The groom took some of the bread, sprinkled it with salt and ate it. The bride followed suit. This union of salt and bread symbolized a happy future for the newlyweds.

Another marriage ritual called for the new bride to fill a bucket with water from a nearby stream or river and take it to her new husband, who took a cup from his pocket and filled it with water from the bucket. Both drank from it, the man first—the only time they would ever share the same cup. Afterwards the cup was broken.

One marriage custom of Greek Roma was recorded by Rennell Rodd in his book *The Customs and Lore of Modern Greece* (London, 1892): "At the close of ceremony the priest and the newly married couple join hands and solemnly walk three times round the alter, through the incense fumes, while the wedding guests pelt them with sweetmeat, a symbolism which has its origins in antiquity and which among the peasantry takes the form of the smearing of honey on the lintel of the young bride's door."

The wedding festivities often lasted for days. Enormous quantities of food were consumed and one particular favorite dish in Britain was roasted hedgehog. A whole pig was often roasted, too. *Kini* (wine), often made from coltsfoot or dandelions, was drunk. In some tribes, such as those from the Carpatho-Rusyn region, when the celebrations ended, the bride's family unbraided her hair and before the groom could take her home there was a feigned abduction of the bride. This custom had its roots in an older tradition of abducting of the bride (with her consent), the chief reason being that her parents would not agree to the marriage. The couple usually went to stay with relatives or friends in another village, and after several days or weeks, they returned to their parents' homes to get "properly" married—though without the usual wedding feast. This practice was welcomed by some of the poorer parents because it absolved them of financing the costly wedding feast. Her unmarried friends made a wall around her to keep the groom out, but happily, he always broke through! The bride's new mother-in-law helped her knot her headscarf, which she would never again be without in public, as this signified that she was a married woman.

Generally, the preparation of the wedding feast was a communal effort and was as extravagant as funds would permit. It was considered an honor to be asked to help with the festivities and the women prepared and cooked vast quantities of food. Food was sent to anyone unable to attend the wedding feast.

In Eastern Europe, *babka*, a rich buttery yeast cake was the traditional wedding cake and a wedding soup of lamb, potatoes, and paprika was served to strengthen the newlyweds for their wedding night.

A typical Bulgarian Roma wedding feast featured *meze* (a selection of appetizers) followed by roast or baked mutton or lamb. *Rakia* (a strong alcoholic drink made from plums, apples, pears or other similar fruits) was drunk with the *meze*, and wine was served with the mutton or lamb. To close the wedding celebrations *blága rakia* was served—a preparation of hot *rakia* sweetened with sugar and colored red, which was prepared by the bridegroom's mother. If it was discovered that the girl was not a virgin, the drink was not dyed red but wood ash was added instead and the unfortunate girl was ducked in the nearest pond before being returned to her mother.

Slovak Roma served *gója* as the first course at the wedding feast. This consisted of fat pork gut stuffed with grated potatoes, cornstarch, or rice mixed with chopped onion, garlic, and spices. It was either boiled in water or baked, which was tastier.

Swedish Roma killed pigs in the camp for a forthcoming wedding feast as no ready slaughtered animals were permitted for a wedding. The reasons for this custom seem to have been lost and are now unknown.

Foods served at a Swedish Romany wedding included roast goose or turkey accompanied by vegetables, whole baked hams, stewed cabbage with meat, rice, and tomatoes, beet soup, and pork chops with onions, tomatoes, and paprika. *Zborna saljamka* was a dish of cubed meats (veal, pork, hare, goose, chicken, etc.) steamed with vegetables and flavored with tomato puree, paprika, and bell peppers. An enormous bowl of *gulas*—pork, veal, or mutton, stewed with sliced leeks, parsnips, carrots, celery, tomatoes, and paprika was always served. Tomatoes were a favorite and were included in practically every dish and were eaten with almost everything.

An obligatory wedding dish in Sweden was *burindiavo*, although this was not included at more recent wedding feasts. The blood of the wedding pig was heated and stirred in a pot with wheatmeal, lumps of pork, salt, and pepper until cooked. This porridge was an important dish at all special occasions and festivals.

Fruit was rarely served but potatoes and bread were expected, along with vast quantities of wine, spirits, and ales. The feast usually began between midday and 1 p.m. Huge brass and copper trays loaded with food were placed on the table and all the courses were served at the same time. There was plenty of food for everyone and dishes were constantly replenished, as the meal lasted many hours.

Curiously, the bride was not allowed to be present at the feast—she had to remain with a relative, weeping to show her sadness at leaving her parents. It was usual for the bridegroom to remain outside the wedding tent as his father began the feast. Toward the end of the meal the bride and groom were at last invited in and everyone toasted their future happiness. Music and dancing followed and the eating and drinking continued for three days. This strange custom may have its roots in an ancient Jewish wedding tradition, in which the newlyweds stayed alone in their marriage chamber, while their guests enjoyed the feast.

In Spain, a *Gitan* wedding was an expensive and lavish affair, with copious quantities of champagne, whisky, beer, wine, and delicacies to satisfy the great numbers of guests. It was a point of honor for the parents of the bride to provide the best foods they could afford. There were cold prawns, mayonnaise, ham (*jamón Serrano*), and rich sweetmeats of all kinds. Spanish Gypsy weddings were characterized by a great many rich, sweet foods, most notably *yemas*, a spectacularly rich egg yolk sweet made from a secret recipe that involved pouring egg yolks through small holes into boiling syrup. The resultant threads were then gathered into fine strands of "angel hair," twisted, and left to cool. These could be made by the Roma themselves or alternatively could be bought from a local confectioner.

Other typical Spanish sweets included: *Alfajores*, honey, nut, and cinnamon cookies bathed in sugar syrup; *Almendrado*, marzipan and slivered almond sweetmeat (or a crumbly cookie made with ground almonds); *Amarguillo*, egg whites, bitter almonds, and lemon peel whisked into a chewy meringue; *Bienmesabe*, literally "how good it tastes," a moist sugar syrup, egg yolk, and almond dessert; *Bocadito de Angel*, "angel's mouthful," a rich marzipan cookie stuffed with pumpkin jam; *Borrachuelo* or *borracho* meaning drunkard, in Andalusia a small fried syrup-soaked pastry and in Castile a sponge soaked in wine syrup; *Cabello de Angel* or "angel's hair," pumpkin jam; *Membrillo*, quince paste; *Pan de Cádiz*, soft egg-enriched marzipan cake filled with layers of pumpkin jam.

There are many varieties of this famous Russian soup—thick or thin, hot or chilled. This recipe is for a typical Ukrainian-style soup.

7¹/₂ cups vegetable or chicken stock
2 tablespoons vinegar
8 ounces cooked beets, sliced into matchsticks
3 potatoes, peeled and diced
I small cabbage, shredded
2 large tomatoes
I bay leaf
Salt and pepper
2 onions, grated
Sour cream (optional)

In a large pan heat the stock and vinegar and bring to the boil. Add the beets and cook until pale, then add the potatoes. Cook for 10 minutes then add the cabbage and whole tomatoes. Cook until the tomatoes are soft, then remove them from the pan and rub them through a sieve back into the soup. Add the bay leaf and salt and pepper to taste. Stir in the onions and cook for about 20 minutes until the onions are soft. Serve with sour cream, if desired.

An oven-ready frozen goose should be thoroughly thawed slowly in the refrigerator before cooking. Prick the bird all over before roasting to allow the fat to escape and pour off the accumulated fat from time to time during cooking. Cover the bird with foil if it's becoming too brown. Save the fat for pastry, roasting potatoes, and for frying.

6-pound goose
Salt
2 tablespoons chopped fresh mint
3 pounds green apples (about 9 medium)
A few stems fresh thyme
3 large onions, sliced
4 tablespoons butter
Pepper

Preheat the oven to 350°F. Rub the inside of the goose with salt. Rub the outside with the mint and more salt. Peel, core, and roughly chop the apples and use half to stuff the goose with the thyme stems. Seal the goose with skewers and place on a rack in a roasting pan. Cook for about 2 hours, basting occasionally. Allow 20 minutes per pound. Pour off the fat halfway through cooking. Reduce the temperature to 325°F after 90 minutes—the goose is cooked when the juices run pale gold—test with a skewer in the thigh. Add half the onions to the pan with the butter 30 to 40 minutes before the end of the cooking time and season to taste with salt and pepper. Add the remaining onions and apples 20 minutes before the end of cooking time. Place the cooked goose on a heated serving plate and surround with the apples and onions.

In the Czech Republic, traditional Romany goulash stands overnight to improve the flavor.

3 tablespoons oil
2 large onions, sliced
3¹/₂ pounds stewing meat (beef, pork, etc.), cut into cubes
I pound tomatoes, seeds removed and quartered
I to 2 cloves garlic, crushed
I bouquet garni (a selection of fresh or dried herbs tied in a bundle)
Salt and pepper
I tablespoon mild paprika
I to 2 cups stock
2¹/₂ cups boiling water
2 pounds potatoes, peeled and quartered (6 medium)

Heat the oil in a large casserole and add the onions and meat in batches (to avoid stewing the meat) and cook for a few minutes until brown. Add the tomatoes, garlic, bouquet garni, salt and pepper to taste, and paprika with just enough stock to cover the meat. Bring to the boil then reduce the heat, cover the pan, and simmer very gently for 2 hours. Add the boiling water and potatoes and bring to the boil again. Cook until the potatoes are tender. Taste and adjust the seasoning. Serve very hot.

This Polish-Romanian recipe could also be made using young beech, hazelnut, or vine leaves

3 tablespoons oil
2 white onions, chopped
3/4 pound ground pork
3/4 pound ground beef
2 eggs
2 cups long-grain rice
1 tablespoon paprika
2 teaspoons salt
1 large head cabbage
1/2 pound smoked sausage sliced in 1-inch chunks (optional)
1 (16-ounce) jar or pack of sauerkraut (not canned), rinsed in cold water
1/2 teaspoon peppercorns
2 bay leaves

Heat the oil in a skillet and brown the chopped onion. Place in a mixing bowl with the ground meats, eggs, uncooked rice, paprika, and salt. Mix well. Remove the core of the cabbage but leave the head whole. Place the cabbage in a large pan of boiling water to wilt the outer leaves. You will be able to gently pull off whole cabbage leaves. Trim away the thick center vein of the leaves. Place 2 tablespoons of the meat and rice mixture on a leaf (starting at the thick end) and roll it up, tucking in the ends with your fingers. Make as many as you can. Arrange the rolls in cooking pot. Put a few chunks of sausage (if using) here and there between the rolls. Fill the pot two-thirds full of water, partially covering the rolls, arrange rinsed sauerkraut on top, and sprinkle the peppercorns and bay leaves over the top. Cover, and cook slowly for about 1 1/2 hours, or until the rice is tender.

This recipe is from Hungary.

Dough
¹/₄ cup confectioners' sugar
²/₃ ounce fresh yeast
³/₄ cup lukewarm milk
2 sticks butter
4¹/₂ cups all-purpose flour
3 eggs
I egg white
Pinch of salt

Walnut Filling
³/₄ cup unrefined light brown muscovado sugar
3 cups ground walnuts
I cup fine cookie crumbs
¹/₂ teaspoon grated lemon peel
¹/₄ cup raisins

For the dough: Mix I teaspoon of the sugar with the yeast and lukewarm milk. Mix the butter with the flour using your fingers on a large flat surface or pastry board. Whisk 2 of the eggs and add them to the flour mixture. Stir in the yeast mixture, salt, and the remaining sugar. Knead the dough quickly. Cover and leave to rest for 2 hours. Meanwhile *make the nut filling:* Mix I ¹/₄ cups water with the sugar in a pan and cook to a thick syrup. Add the walnuts. Remove from the heat, stir in the cookie crumbs, lemon peel, and raisins. Cool before using. Divide the dough in half and roll each out into ¹/₆-inch thick rectangles. Spread with the nut filling, leaving a ¹/₃-inch margin. Roll up the dough and place it on a baking sheet with the folded end of the dough on the bottom. Brush with a beaten whole egg. Set aside to rise in a warm place for I hour. Brush with egg white and leave in a cool place for 30 minutes. Preheat the oven to 400°F. Prick the sides lightly with a fork to prevent the crust from bursting and bake for 25 to 30 minutes. Cut into slices to serve.

Babka

This traditional breadlike cake originated in Poland. Begin the preparations several hours ahead or even the day before.

$2^{1}/_{2}$ to $3^{1}/_{2}$ cups all-purpose flour
$2^{1}/_{2}$ cups bread flour
3 sticks unsalted butter, softened
2 tablespoons active dry yeast
$^{1}/_{2}$ cup unrefined milled golden cane sugar
1 teaspoon salt
$^{1}/_{2}$ cup warm water
$^{1}/_{2}$ cup warm milk
1 cup sour cream
3 egg yolks
1 cup golden raisins
1 large egg, beaten
1 to 2 tablespoons milk
Confectioners' sugar for dusting

In a large mixing bowl combine $2^{1}/_{2}$ cups all-purpose flour and the bread flour. Using a pastry cutter cut the butter into the flours to create a crumbly mixture. Combine the yeast, cane sugar, salt, water, the $^{1}/_{2}$ cup warm milk, sour cream, and egg yolks in another bowl, then stir into the flour mixture with the golden raisins, adding enough of the remaining 1 cup all-purpose flour to form a soft dough. Knead the dough for several minutes on a lightly floured surface, and then place in a well-greased bowl, turning dough over once, and cover. Refrigerate for a minimum of 4 hours or overnight. Gently deflate dough and place in a well-greased tube pan or brioche mold. Make an egg wash by combining the egg with 1 to 2 tablespoons milk; brush it over the bread. Cover lightly with plastic wrap. Leave to rise until doubled in size, 30 to 40 minutes. Preheat the oven to 350°F. Bake for 50 to 60 minutes, or until cooked through and golden brown. Cool for 10 to 15 minutes in the pan on a wire rack before removing. Cool completely on wire rack. Dust generously with confectioners' sugar before serving.

This is a version of a humble dessert from Catalonia. The name comes from the days when wandering musicians traveled around the Catalan countryside and were paid with food. If they were especially good they were given a dessert of fruits and nuts.

8 ounces pie pastry

Filling
2 cups mixed dried fruit, e.g. prunes, pears, raisins, golden raisins,
  apricots, and/or figs
Scant 1/2 cup apple juice or brandy
1/4 cup unrefined light brown muscovado sugar
2 tablespoons flour
2 egg yolks
2 tablespoons lemon juice

Topping
2 tablespoons pine nuts
2 tablespoons chopped toasted almonds
2 tablespoons halved walnuts
1/4 cup unrefined light brown muscovado sugar

Preheat the oven to 375°F. Roll out the pastry and line a deep 10-inch pan with a removable base. Chill for 15 minutes, and then bake "blind" (line the pastry with foil and fill with beans or rice) for 20 minutes. Meanwhile, *make the filling:* Place the dried fruit, apple juice, and brown sugar in a pan and slowly bring to the boil. Simmer gently until thick and the liquid is absorbed, about 20 minutes. Leave until cold then add the flour, egg yolks, and lemon juice and blend in a food processor or beat well.
Spread the fruit filling in the cooled pastry shell. *For the topping:* Mix the nuts and sugar and sprinkle over the fruit, pressing down lightly with your hand. Bake for 20 to 30 minutes or until golden. Cool in the pan, and then finish cooling on a wire rack.

These meltingly rich, crumbly almond shortbreads are liberally dusted with confectioners' sugar. Replace the aniseed liqueur with rum or brandy if you prefer.

2 cups all-purpose flour
1 cup confectioners' sugar
1 1/2 sticks butter
1/2 cup ground almonds
2 teaspoons ground cinnamon
A little aniseed liqueur
Confectioners' sugar for dusting

Preheat the oven to 400°F. Sift the flour and confectioners' sugar into a large mixing bowl and rub in the butter until the mixture resembles fine bread crumbs. Stir in the ground almonds and cinnamon with just a little liqueur to make a smooth dough. Wrap in plastic wrap and chill for 20 to 30 minutes. Roll out on a floured surface about 1 1/2-inches-thick and cut into 2-inch rounds. Place on a greased baking sheet and bake for 10 to 15 minutes, until light golden brown. Remove from the oven and let cool for a few minutes. Sift a generous amount of confectioners' sugar over the biscuits until well coated. Wrap in greaseproof paper and store in an airtight pan up to a week.

This sticky golden pudding is said to have gotten its name when a nun accidentally left out egg whites from a sweet she was making and declared the result fit only for pigs! Another (perhaps more likely) explanation is that bacon symbolized the fat of the land or good living. It is very rich and sweet and has a smooth silky texture. The custard will firm up as it cools.

Caramel
3 tablespoons unrefined milled golden cane sugar
Juice of ½ lemon

Custard
¾ cup unrefined milled golden cane sugar
Twist of lemon peel
12 large egg yolks

Preheat the oven to 325°F. **For the caramel:** Place the sugar, 2 teaspoons water, and the lemon juice in a pan and heat over a low heat until the sugar has dissolved, but do not stir. Increase the heat and, without stirring, boil until a rich golden color. Immediately remove from the heat and pour into an 8-inch square baking pan or dish, tilting the dish to coat the base.

    For the custard: Put the sugar, lemon peel, and ¾ cups water into a pan over a low heat, stirring until the sugar is dissolved. Increase the heat to medium and boil for several minutes, until the mixture is syrupy. Remove from the heat and set aside to cool for 5 minutes. Discard the lemon peel. Whisk the egg yolks thoroughly in a large bowl, then pour on the cooled syrup, whisking all the time. Strain through a metal sieve into the prepared pan. Place the baking pan in a roasting pan and pour hot water into the outer pan to come halfway up the sides of the baking pan. Cover the whole roasting pan with foil. Cook for 25 to 30 minutes until just firm. Remove from the oven and leave to cool. Chill in the refrigerator and cut into squares to serve.

MAKES 4 TO 6 SERVINGS

These sticky squares get their name from the wine and sherry in the ingredients.

3 eggs, separated
1 cup unrefined milled golden cane sugar
1 cup all-purpose flour
1/2 cup sweet white wine
1/2 cup dry sherry
Ground cinnamon

Preheat the oven to 350°F. Beat the egg yolks with 1/4 cup of the sugar until the mixture is pale and thick. Whip the egg whites until stiff and fold into the egg yolk mixture with the sifted flour. Pour the mixture into a shallow 8 x 12-inch baking pan lined with nonstick baking paper. Bake for 20 minutes until firm and beginning to brown. Remove from the oven and leave to cool. Meanwhile *make a syrup:* Combine the remaining 3/4 cup sugar with the wine, sherry, and 1/4 cup water in a pan over a low heat until the sugar is dissolved completely. Increase the heat and bring to the boil, then cool. Cut the cake into squares in the pan and pour on the cooled syrup. Sprinkle with cinnamon and leave until the cake has absorbed all the syrup.

This classic Spanish recipe for a rolled filled sponge cake literally means 'Gypsy's Arm.' Perhaps it refers to the shape.

Cake

3 eggs, separated
$^1/_2$ cup unrefined milled golden cane sugar
Grated peel of 1 lemon
$^1/_2$ cup flour
Ground cinnamon
Confectioners' sugar

Filling

1 cup milk
1 stick cinnamon, broken into three pieces
1 teaspoon grated lemon peel
$^3/_4$ cup unrefined milled golden cane sugar
Pinch of salt
$^1/_4$ cup flour
2 tablespoons butter
4 egg yolks

Preheat the oven to 375°F. *Make the cake:* Beat the egg yolks until thick and pale. Gradually beat in the cane sugar and grated peel. Beat the egg whites until stiff, but not dry. Carefully fold half the egg whites into the egg yolk mixture. Sift in half the flour, followed by the rest of the egg whites. Gently fold in the rest of the flour. Pour into a greased 13 x 9-inch pan and bake for about 25 minutes Remove from the oven and turn out on to a sheet of waxed paper sprinkled with the cinnamon. Trim the edges and roll up like a jellyroll with the paper inside; cool. Meanwhile, *make the filling:* Put the milk, cinnamon stick, and lemon peel into a pan and heat gently until just boiling. Remove from the heat and strain into a cup. Combine the sugar, salt, and flour in a bowl and gradually add the milk. Pour back into the pan and cook gently, stirring constantly until the mixture has thickened. Remove from the heat and beat in the butter and egg yolks. Return to the heat and cook very gently for a minute or two. Cool before using. Unroll the cooled cake and spread with the filling. Sift some confectioners' sugar over the cake before serving.

FUNERALS

Akana mukav tut le Devlesa.
(I now leave you to God)

Roma belief in the supernatural, and fears about death had a significant role in the rites and customs related to dying and death. There was a strong belief in ghosts, a transitional and negative form of the dead person that was also *marimé*. Ideally, people should not die in their habitual place, home, or dwelling so it was customary to move the deathbed in front of the tent or *vardo*, usually under an improvised canopy, or to the outskirts of the camp. The *muló* or ghost of a Romany man or woman in possession of a corpse at certain hours of the day and night risked the possible revenge of the *muló*, against those who remained in the world of the living. Later hospitals were used for deaths; the function of the *Gaje* hospital thus replaced that of the outskirts of the camp.

When a person was about to die, many rituals were initiated. It was essential that relatives were present at the moment of death and via an elaborate communications system, they arrived from near and far. When the person was near death, a candle was brought into the room and at the moment of death the candle was lit and a window opened. It was believed that the candle lit the way to heaven for the soul of the deceased. The body was rubbed  with holy oil, and the tears and lamentations of the family were publicly displayed. In some settlements everyone came to say farewell to the departed. They placed a hand on the body of the deceased and asked him or her for forgiveness.

Touching the body of the deceased was discouraged, for fear of *marimé*. For this reason the dying person was washed and dressed, in the finest clothes, immediately before death. Funeral arrangements were generally covered by the *marimé* system and for many Roma it was taboo to touch the corpse, so this task was given to a non-Roma. If the death was sudden and unexpected and this had not been possible, a non-Roma, (such as an undertaker) was usually called in to perform these tasks immediately following the death. Sometimes, the deceased's nostrils were plugged with wax so that evil spirits could not enter and occupy the body. The surviving relatives greatly feared that the dead might return in a supernatural form to haunt them and for that reason the name of the deceased was not mentioned, the body was never touched, and all objects belonging to the dead person were destroyed.

All Roma had to grieve for three days by remaining in the presence of the deceased. The threeness or triad, (one of the oldest of Indian symbols) signified the unity of body, mind and spirit. During this time they were not permitted to bathe, shave, wear jewelry, change clothes, or prepare food, but were allowed to drink coffee, brandy, or other liquors. Mirrors were covered to prevent the spirit from becoming trapped there and vessels containing water were emptied. Close relatives of the deceased wore mourning clothes for a full year. It was believed that after one year the deceased soul entered heaven.

While the deceased lay pending burial, no cooking was done in their presence, no proper meals were eaten, and no attempt was made to sleep. Several families had a taboo on eating red meat and others would neither cook nor eat hot food— just bread and water or tea without sugar and milk. Children though were not expected to take part in the fast and it was customary for someone outside the inner circle of mourners to look after them. Some families practically shut themselves in with the deceased, while others wouldn't stay under the same roof. Feasting and drinking in the presence of the deceased were however a feature of wakes in parts of the United Kingdom, namely the North Country and Scotland. The Scottish travelers were descended from nomads who were on the roads before the Romany arrived in Britain and kept their own unique customs and traditions.

In Sweden, when a person died all the doors and windows were thrown open and all the water was thrown away, as there was a belief that the dead person washed in this water. The deceased was buried on the fourth day after death and after the funeral when everyone returned to the camp, the dead man's wife or another woman would pour water over the hands of each mourner with a dipper. After this the feast began.

There were certain rules of behavior to follow during this period: the mourners played cards and told stories from the life of the deceased, but they couldn't sing, dance, or make toasts with their glasses. Before drinking their first drink, each person would spill a little out onto the ground in memory of the deceased.

Any food found in the *vardo* or tent after death was held to have become contaminated and was buried. Anything not buried was destroyed. Crockery and cooking utensils were burned, smashed, and mutilated, and the deceased's caravan or tent was set alight and burned to ashes.

But it seems the *vardo* was not always burned. A report of the burial in April 1933 of Urania (Reni) Boswell, aged eighty-one, stated that in accordance with her wishes, her vardo was not burned but was left to stand until it and all its contents rotted away, although there is no record of whether or not this was allowed to happen.

The personal belongings of the deceased were placed in the coffin alongside the body, including valuable items such as jewelry and watches. Other items might include violins, guitars, pipes, cigarettes, glasses, bottles of alcohol, cards, and sometimes prayer books and rosary beads. The family put money into the hand or pocket of the deceased (usually small coins that would be useful to the deceased during the journey from life). The Vlach Roma in Hungary placed money into the pockets of the deceased so that he or she could pay the customs in the other world. Many Vlach Roma still put the favorite objects of the dead in the grave: pipes or knives for a man and shawls or purses for women.

The Hampshire Roma were unique in that they buried food with their dead. Bread and grain are recorded as being placed in the coffin and were believed to offer protection against witches, ghosts, and other malevolent forces. Common Romany expressions of the past were "the dear God's grain and the dear God's bread."

Some Romany believed that the soul of the dead person was still present, so on the day of the funeral as the coffin was carried out it was hit off the threshold three times, so that the soul of the dead would depart for good. Generally English Roma buried their dead in consecrated ground, but some who wanted no contact with *Gajos*, buried the body secretly, fully clothed but without a coffin in unfrequented places such as a lonely heath or a quiet spot in the countryside. In some cases, women guarded the grave during the day immediately after the funeral and the men guarded it all through the night.

On the day of the funeral, it was once common for the mourners to wear an item of red-colored clothing, as the color red was a safeguard against the "evil eye." A small band was sometimes hired to play ahead of the coffin. The widow or widower together with mourning relatives and friends followed this band. As the procession entered the cemetery, the loud lamentations of the mourners increased and reached their peak as the coffin was lowered into the ground. The mourners frequently threw coins as well as handfuls of earth into the grave.

The Hungarian Roma did not sing during either the wake or the funeral. An orchestra accompanied the deceased to the grave, playing his or her favorite song as the coffin was interred in the ground. Family members were not allowed to play in this orchestra. In some places, the musical instrument of the dead was put into the grave, while in other communities it was passed on to the son. The grieving, sobbing family followed the orchestra to the grave.

The burial customs of the Beash Roma, a small group from Southeast Hungary who spoke an archaic dialect of Romanian, included elements of other significant Roma groups in Hungary. Like all Roma, they held a wake, which in this group lasted until the day preceding the funeral. During these wakes it was forbidden to sing and the men and the women sat separately. When some of the drink was poured on the ground, they asked God to "take the deceased to His country." The deceased's favorite objects and tools were placed next to him or her, but no money or jewelry.

Some time after the funeral, the relatives had to go and visit the grave, to tell the deceased how satisfied they had been with the funeral. Various signs, sounds, and appearances in dreams revealed the presence of the dead.

In the traditional Roma cultures in Hungary, the belief in the other world was (and often still is) very strong. This belief was a factor of everyday life as well as their feasts and influenced their way of life for hundreds of years. The Vlach Roma talked about the deceased as though he or she was still alive, often asking for their help if they were ill or in trouble. They believed that the dead lived in the other world in much the same way as they did in this world; they ate, drank, smoked, and generally carried on as they had in life. A person who was lame when alive would remain so, and those whose body parts had been surgically removed would be disabled in the other world. This is the reason why Vlach Roma tend to protest against the dissection of their dead. Women who had passed on though didn't bear children in the afterlife.

After the funeral all material ties with the dead were destroyed, although it was also common practice (in cases of possible hardship to the deceased's family) to sell these objects. They were sold only to non-Roma and for a modest sum, as the family should not profit enormously from the dead; this would be seen as a form of *marimé*. The exceptions to the rule of disposing of the departed's possessions were family heirlooms or *sumadji*, which might have included a woman's dowry and her jewelry, for instance. Sometimes animals that belonged to the dead were killed, the only exceptions being horses. No trace of the deceased was allowed to remain in the camp or household. Even the use of his or her name was avoided, unless absolutely necessary.

The after-funeral feast was held in honor of the dead person and food was prepared by some Roma in units of three, which was, as previously explained, a sacred number (three chickens, three pots of potatoes, etc.). It was generally taboo to indulge in the deceased's favorite food and drink at the funeral feast. American Roma often held their funeral feast in the same room in which the body lay. The food was laid out on a long table and usually included fish and meat. Another feast was also laid on the ground near the grave just after it had been filled in. Wine was poured as the grave was filled and the graveside feast usually consisted of cold turkey, legs of lamb, and hams for those who were prosperous and cold cuts for those who were less well off. If the weather was bad, the feast was served in a tent.

Even today, funeral feasts are usually held on a Sunday, the ritual day for feasts. Bread, fresh fruit, nuts, and meat are usually eaten but there is no dancing or singing. Lighted candles are placed on the tables and after the meal the afternoon is spent drinking and talking. It's bad luck to speak of the departed at night, unless one knocks on an object a few times after. There was a great fear among the survivors that the dead might return in some supernatural form to haunt the living and for that reason the name of the dead was not mentioned.

In Sweden, it was customary to serve a whole roast pig, at the funeral feast but a whole ham later replaced this. Other foods for the feast were roast goose and turkey, beet soup, bread, potatoes, and goulash. Copious amounts of beer, wine, and spirits were also served. Leftover food was never thrown away or saved but cast into running water.

Three days after the funeral, the Feast of the Third Day took place, when strangers and company were offered tea and coffee. If there were no callers the mourners were allowed to go out and invite anyone but the recipients were not permitted to thank their hosts.

Nine days after the funeral, another feast was held—usually at the first meal of the day. During the first six weeks after the death, custom dictated that the deceased man's wife, eldest son or daughter must offer coffee, tea, or wine with bread and cakes to a non-relative, preferably a non-Roma and someone in need. The guest had previously been warned not to offer thanks for the refreshment.

Six weeks after the funeral, a very important feast was held. Even if the other feasts were left out for some reason, all the mourners had to attend this feast. It was believed that the deceased finished his wanderings and came for the last time to eat and drink with his surviving relatives. A chair was placed at the table for him and a place set with a knife, fork, plate, and a piece of bread. Wine was poured onto ground on which no one had trodden. Food and drink were served and it was a sorrowful occasion.

Other feasts followed six months after the death and again on the twelve-month anniversary of the death.

Remembering the deceased with love and gifts was believed essential to safeguard the family's good luck. Several times during the first year after death, special feasts of commemoration or *pomeni* took place. The *pomána* was the funeral banquet held on the anniversary of a person's death. The abundance of food and drink expressed wishes of peace and happiness for the deceased. Families usually made an annual pilgrimage to the grave with offerings such as tobacco and sugar.

Christmas in particular was a time when many families visited the grave of a near relative and ceremonial drinking often took place along with an offering such as a Christmas pudding. A description of a Romany grave by an unknown author was reprinted in the *Church of England Magazine* in 1843 with the title "The Gypsy's Grave." The author visited an English churchyard, where Gypsies had traditionally celebrated Christmas for many years, but the practice had been banned on the grounds that it was too festive. In retaliation the angry Gypsies had refused to help with the harvest and withheld their labor. But the new curate made peace with them and allowed the Gypsies to meet in the churchyard at Christmas on condition that it was no longer a festive occasion. Instead the Roma brought flowers to their deceased's graves and quietly sang solemn songs.

Roma regarded All Souls' Day (November 1) as an occasion for communal rites that varied according to the different groups of Roma. They visited the graves of their relatives, greeted the deceased, and kissed the grave-post. The dead person's favorite dishes were placed on the grave and cigarettes and drinks were offered to the deceased. The lit cigarette was placed on the grave, and some of the drink was poured on the ground before the relatives shared it.

Beash Roma lit candles in the cemetery and a single candle at home for the souls of all their dead. The Hungarian or "musician" Roma, the largest group in Hungary, brought flowers to the graves and lit candles on All Souls' Day. Afterward, back home they "entertained" the deceased with a dinner, which usually included placing drinks, salt, and water on the table to commemorate the dead person.

In Spain, the feast of All Souls revolves around the same tradition of remembering the dead. There are many traditions connected with this time of year, which is known as *La Castañada*.

In the old days, *La Castañada* was celebrated after the family evening meal, a distant echo of the ancient funeral meals. After the usual family supper, chestnuts, *panellets* (small, tasty almond cakes), and other sweet tidbits were eaten, and accompanied by a sweet, white wine. The chestnuts were roasted on the open hearth and placed on the table where everyone was able to eat their fill. Godfathers offered *panellets* to their godchildren; these are believed to have their origins in the offerings placed in the graves with the dead. Although the cakes could be bought from shops, they were usually homemade.

Hungarian Pancakes with Veal Filling — *PALACSINTA PORKOLT*

MAKES 6 TO 8 SERVINGS

Pancakes
3 cups flour
1 teaspoon salt
6 eggs
1 1/2 cups milk
1 1/2 cups carbonated water

Veal Filling
2 tablespoons oil
2 cups chopped onion
1 tablespoon paprika
1 pound veal, cubed
1 large bell pepper, seeds removed and sliced
3 tomatoes, chopped
Veal or chicken stock or water
Salt and pepper
1/2 cup sour cream

Finishing
1 egg, beaten
Bread crumbs
Oil for frying

To make the pancakes: Sift the flour and salt into a large mixing bowl. Beat in the eggs and milk a little at a time until smooth. At this stage the batter can be covered and left for up to 24 hours. Just before cooking stir in the carbonated water. Heat an omelet pan and brush with a little butter or oil. Heat until the oil begins to smoke and pour in about 3 tablespoons batter, tilting the pan so it coats the pan evenly. Cool until lightly browned on one side then flip the pancake over and cook the other side. The pancakes should be thin but firm enough to hold a filling.

To make the filling: Heat the oil and cook the onions slowly until golden and soft. Remove from the heat and stir in the paprika and 3 tablespoons water. Add the veal and cover the pan. Simmer gently for 10 minutes, then add the bell peppers, tomatoes, and a little stock if necessary. Cook gently, stirring from time to time until the veal is tender. Season to taste with salt and pepper and remove from the heat. Remove the veal, chop it, and return to the pan. Pour in the sour cream and reheat gently.

To finish: Put a spoonful of the filling on each pancake and roll up. Dip the pancakes in the beaten egg then in the crumbs and fry in hot oil until brown and crisp.

Spanish-style Rice with Rabbit, Rosemary, and Snails

Arros Caldos de Muntanya

1 rabbit, cut into pieces
1 to 2 teaspoons salt
1 teaspoon pepper
2 tablespoons olive oil
1 pound mushrooms, sliced
1 to 2 pound tomatoes, peeled and chopped
2 to 3 garlic cloves, crushed
1 teaspoon chopped rosemary
2 cups short-grain rice
About 20 fresh snails in shells (optional)
7 1/2 cups boiling water or stock

Season the rabbit pieces with a little salt and pepper. Heat the oil in a shallow pan and fry the rabbit until golden on both sides. Remove the meat from the pan. Add the mushrooms to the pan and cook for 5 minutes. Add the tomatoes and garlic and cook over a high heat until the mixture is dry. Stir in the rosemary and the remaining salt and pepper. Add the rice and snails (if using) with the rabbit pieces. Pour in the boiling water or stock and return to the boil, stirring. Reduce the heat and cook gently for 20 minutes—the rice will be underdone. Cover the pan and leave to stand for 5 minutes by which time the rice will be tender. Serve at once.

Souvla is the Greek word for skewer or spit and *souvlakia* is the Greek term for skewered meat—a favorite dish throughout Greece for thousands of years. Homer described Achilles preparing the dish for visiting envoys from Troy. The grill must be oiled and very hot before you start cooking.

1 tablespoon unrefined dark brown muscovado sugar
1 tablespoon olive oil
1 tablespoon white wine vinegar
Finely grated peel and juice of 1/2 a lime or lemon
1/2 teaspoon ground coriander
1 teaspoon chopped fresh cilantro or parsley
Salt and freshly ground black pepper
4 skinless, boneless chicken breasts, cut into chunks
Slices of lime or lemon and sprigs of fresh cilantro or parsley
  to garnish
Boiled rice to serve

In a shallow bowl, mix together the dark brown muscovado sugar, olive oil, vinegar, lime peel and juice, ground and chopped cilantro or parsley. Season with a little salt and pepper and stir well. Put the chicken into the bowl and mix with the marinade. Cover and refrigerate for at least 30 minutes, if you have time, so that the chicken absorbs the flavors. Thread the chicken onto metal skewers or wooden sticks* and cook on a preheated hot grill for 10 to 15 minutes. Baste the kebabs with the remaining marinade and turn them often, basting each time until cooked and golden brown. Serve the kebabs on a bed of rice garnished with lime or lemon slices and sprigs of fresh cilantro or parsley.

*If using wooden sticks soak them first in warm water to avoid burning.

This delicately flavored dish of salmon marinated with dill is a specialty of Sweden and other Scandinavian countries.

1 1/2 pound middle cut of salmon, filleted with the central bone removed and skin left on
1 small bunch fresh dill

Curing Mixture
2 tablespoons coarse sea salt
2 tablespoons unrefined light brown muscovado sugar
2 teaspoons cracked peppercorns
1 tablespoon schnapps

Mustard and Dill Sauce
2 tablespoons white wine vinegar
2 tablespoons Swedish or honey mustard
Salt and freshly ground black pepper
1 1/2 cup grapeseed oil
3 tablespoons chopped dill

Rinse the salmon fillets and pat dry with paper towels. Remove any remaining small bones. Separate the dill sprigs and twist off the coarse stalks. Combine the sea salt, sugar, cracked pepper, and schnapps for the curing mixture. Place one half of the fish, skin side down, in a shallow dish. Sprinkle with half the curing mixture and rub into the flesh. Top with a good layer of dill sprigs. Rub the other half of the fish with the remaining mixture and place it, skin side up, on the first fillet forming a sandwich. Cover with a plate and a heavy weight. Refrigerate for 3 days, turning the fish every 24 hours. Lots of juices form during the curing time, and the flesh of the salmon is compressed and deepens to the color of smoked salmon. Scrape off any curing mixture, and slice at a low diagonal very thinly.

To prepare the sauce: combine the vinegar, mustard, salt and pepper, and mix well. Stir in the grapeseed oil and chopped dill. Serve with the gravlax.

Broiled Sardines

Very easy and quick, this simple Spanish method of cooking brings out all the flavor of these tasty fish. Light the grill before you start so it becomes really hot.

12 small sardines, cleaned and heads removed
Salt
1 tablespoon flour
Juice of 1 lemon
Pepper
1 heaped tablespoon fresh chopped parsley
1 to 2 cloves garlic, finely chopped
1 tablespoon olive oil

Rinse the sardines and dry on paper towels, then sprinkle with salt and flour. Place the fish in a shallow baking dish and place them under the broiler, about 2 inches from the heat, for 2 to 5 minutes. The time needed depends on the size of the sardines. Carefully, using 2 spatulas turn the fish and cook on the other side for 2 to 5 minutes. Place on a warm serving plate and sprinkle with lemon juice, salt and pepper, parsley, garlic, and oil.

The peppers that grow around Asti in the Piedmont region of Italy are highly prized for their plumpness and intense flavor, and are used in this classic antipasto dish throughout the region. I've added some toasted pumpkin seeds for extra flavor and crunch. The simple rustic ingredients produce a nutritious and colorful starter to a meal.

2 tablespoons pumpkin seeds
Salt
7 tablespoons olive oil
2 cloves garlic, sliced
6 plump bell peppers, preferably red and yellow, halved,
*   cored and quartered*
2 tablespoons tomato puree mixed with 5 tablespoons water

Preheat the oven to 350°F. Toss the pumpkin seeds in a little salt and put into a roasting pan with a tablespoon of the oil. Roast for about 25 minutes. Remove from the oven, drain on paper towels and leave to cool. Heat the oil and fry the garlic gently until soft, then add the peppers. Pour over the diluted tomato puree and season to taste with salt. Stir, cover and simmer for 15 to 25 minutes, or until the peppers are soft. Cover and leave to stand until ready to serve. Arrange the peppers on a serving plate. Sprinkle with the pumpkin seeds. Serve at room temperature or cold with bread and a green salad.

2 cups ground almonds
1 cup unrefined milled golden cane sugar
Grated peel of ½ a lemon
1 egg white, beaten
3 tablespoons confectioners' sugar

Preheat the oven to 400°F. Put 1½ cups ground almonds in a pan, make a hollow in the center and mix in 1 tablespoon of water with the sugar. Add the grated lemon peel and stir the mixture over a low heat until it forms a fine paste. Shape the paste into small balls, brush them with beaten egg white and roll them in the remaining ground almonds. Bake the balls for 7 to 10 minutes until lightly browned. Sift over the confectioners' sugar and leave to cool.

Glassoor Mode
(Fun and dance songs)

Annual festivals, such as religious feasts were, and indeed often remain, great social occasions for the Roma and formal religion often goes hand in hand with supernatural beliefs, omens, and curses. Good luck is very important to the Roma and many items, such as talismans, situations, and food are considered lucky or *baxt*. Serving foods associated with *baxt* is mandatory on saints' days and other celebrations and celebrating religious feasts itself brings luck. Auspicious foods include green leaves, fresh fruit, and bottles of alcohol.

Feast days of various saints were celebrated with music, processions, and feasting. The most important of these was the feast of Saint Sara, the patron saint of Gypsies everywhere.

The great horse fairs in England were an annual event for hundreds of years and were not just occasions for Roma to buy and sell horses, but a chance to meet up with family and friends and exchange news and gossip. Such fairs have now practically died out, and only two survive, namely the horse fairs at Appleby in Cumbria and Stow–on the Wold in Gloucestershire, which have become traditional stopping places for Roma to congregate every year. Appleby Horse Fair has taken place every year since 1685 and Roma set up camp in traditional *vardos* (caravans), wagons, and modern trailers and tents for a week.

Although horses are still traded, there are also stalls selling fine china, ornaments, glass, gold jewelry, and other items including beautiful silk flowers, which have largely replaced the hand-carved wooden flowers, once a traditional Romany craft. Children's clothes stalls are much in evidence—selling predominantly ornate clothes of velvet, satin, and lace. It is also possible to buy traditional cast-iron cooking pots, along with the cooking irons to hang them on and to watch Roma working at their traditional crafts of peg making, carving flowers from elder wood, and painting the vardos and carts.

The *paciva* was a ceremonial feast with singing and dancing that celebrated a meeting with a previously unknown or long lost relative. This joyous event was an occasion for women to bedeck themselves with their gold jewelry, for family stories to be told, and an opportunity to catch up on news. Every woman made a specific dish for the feast and there were many dishes, as it was important that no one was made to feel left out or neglected. Typical foods included roast beef, chicken, and suckling pig roasted over an enormous fire.

Spring was a time of fertility festivals with parties and the lighting of bonfires. The fire was significant as it was the mainstay of life and was needed to boil water and cook food. Spring was the favorite time of year for betrothals and courting and small fires were lit and blessed, ready for prospective couples to jump over them. It was also the traditional time for "spring cleaning"—cleaning out cupboards and wearing something new for good health and prosperity.

At Easter time (*Patragi*), many Roma took green branches and flowers into their houses, caravans, or tents and girls also wore them to stress their close ties to nature. Throughout the Easter season, they sang, danced, ate, and drank and it was customary for some Roma to exchange Easter eggs.

A fortnight after Easter, Seville in Spain is the scene of the annual *Feria*, the Spring Fair. It is a dazzling combination of fair, dance, festival, and equestrian displays. Important bullfights take place in the Plaza de la Maestranza in the afternoons. Everyone from all walks of life attends the *feria* and people meet in *casetas* (entertainment booths) to drink and dance *sevillanas* all night. The presence of the Spanish Romany remains the main attraction today. The women in their beautiful vividly colored dresses and the splendidly dressed horse riders are a magnificent spectacle, while the skilled horsemanship of the Roma causes the crowds to burst into applause. Flamenco was created by the Gypsies together with the Arab Moors of Andalusia and has been danced at the country's fairs and religious festivals ever since Charles III granted the Gypsies their freedom in the eighteenth century. Flamenco was the dance of the poor and dispossessed peoples and its themes are of jealousy, pain, and unrequited love. The dancers are accompanied by guitar music, castanets, stamping feet, and hand clapping.

The singing, dancing, and drinking goes on and on until late into the night, as the spirit takes over the throats of the *cantaores* (flamenco singers) and the agile limbs of the *bailaoras* (dancers), and the Real de la Feria blazes, lit by paper lanterns from the multicolored tents.

Gazpacho, the famous cold vegetable soup, is perfect for eating in the heat of a Spanish summer. Originally made using stale bread, garlic, oil, vinegar, and water (the name comes from the word *caspa*, meaning leftovers) in a deep cooking pot called a *gazpachero*, vegetables were gradually added to make it more substantial. Other traditional dishes included *pescaito frito*, fish tossed in flour and fried in olive-oil, and *huevos a la flamenca*, a fried egg in a tomato sauce.

One celebration that all Roma have in common is *Herdeljes*, which means "Summer Announcement." The beginning of summer, with warm weather and a more plentiful supply of food was a cause for much celebration. It was customary for Roma in Yugoslavia to celebrate the season with their families and hold a large picnic with lots of food and *mastika*, a liquor made from mastic, to drink.

Roma picked herbs such as lavender, meadowsweet, tansy, vervain, bergamot, peppermint, basil, parsley, and dill for good health, good luck, and prosperity and bought lambs to sacrifice for a good year and to avert misfortune. Afterward the lamb was shared, eaten by the families and given to anyone who had nothing to eat. The next morning everyone arose before dawn, and met to light a big fire ready to roast more lambs. Everyone danced and sang and there was good food and drink to celebrate the coming of summer. The whole celebration lasted for eight days.

The Feast of Life was celebrated from September to October and was a month-long succession of parties to celebrate a successful harvest and the abundance of life. Roma frequently helped local villages to gather in the harvest and in return were given some of the harvested grain and fruits. The first loaves of the harvest were eaten at these feasts.

In wine producing countries such as France, Austria, Hungary, and Spain, Roma helped to harvest the grapes and along with the other workers were rewarded with a feast to celebrate a successful harvest. *Choucroute* (sauerkraut, often cooked with wine, sausages, pork, and juniper berries), was a favorite dish of Hungarian Roma.

Gazpacho

MAKES 4 SERVINGS

2 to 3 slices rustic bread
1 pound ripe tomatoes, peeled, seeded, and chopped
2 to 3 cloves garlic
$1/2$ cup olive oil
2 to 3 tablespoons wine or sherry vinegar
1 tablespoon salt

Soak the bread in 3 tablespoons cold water for at least 30 minutes. Blend all the ingredients plus 1 tablespoon water in a mortar and pestle, food processor, or blender until smooth. If the mixture is too thick add more cold water. Leave in the refrigerator for 2 hours before serving. Serve with more bread, diced ham, onion, etc. for each person to mix into their bowl of soup.

Sevillian Kebabs

PINCHITOS MORUNOS

MAKES 4 SERVINGS

¹/₂ cup olive oil
3 to 4 tablespoons dry sherry
1 teaspooon paprika
¹/₂ teaspoon ground cumin
1 pound lamb or pork fillet cut into 1-inch pieces

Combine oil, sherry, paprika, and cumin in a bowl. Add the meat, turning the pieces to coat them in the marinade. Cover and let stand for at least 3 hours. Thread the meat onto kebab skewers and cook on a grill over medium heat for 10 to 15 minutes, turning occasionally.

Fish in Salt Crust

PESCADO A LA SAL

MAKES 4 TO 6 SERVINGS

2- to 2¹/₂-pound whole fish, cleaned and gutted
Salt and white pepper
Lemon juice
A few stems fresh herbs, e.g. parsley, rosemary, and thyme
8 cups coarse salt
Oil

Preheat the oven to 400°F. Season the inside of the fish with salt and pepper and a squeeze of lemon juice. Lay the herbs inside the fish. Put a third of the salt in an oiled baking pan and lay the fish on top. Cover with the rest of the salt. Cook for 30 minutes. Remove from the oven and carefully crack open the salt crust. Remove the skin from the fish and lift the fillet off the bones. Remove the main bones and take off the remaining flesh. Serve immediately.

Shrimp Cakes

½ cup flour
2 eggs
1 bunch scallions, finely chopped
2 tablespoons finely chopped fresh parsley
8 ounces shelled small shrimp
Salt and pepper
Paprika
Olive oil

Mix the flour and the eggs in a bowl. Add 5 tablespoons water and stir into a smooth batter. Add scallions, parsley, and shrimp. Season with salt, pepper, and paprika to taste. Let stand for 30 minutes or more. Heat olive oil in a frying pan. Spoon in about 2 tablespoons of batter at a time; flatten with the back of the spoon into a thin pancake. Fry on each side until golden. Serve immediately.

Gypsy Mazurek

Mazurek is a flat cake, traditionally eaten at Easter.

6 eggs, separated
½ cup unrefined milled golden cane sugar
1 teaspoon vanilla extract
1 cup chopped figs
1 cup chopped dates
1 cup raisins
Peel of 1 large orange
1¾ cups crushed walnuts
3 tablespoons grated lemon peel
6 tablespoons cornstarch

Preheat the oven to 325°F. Beat the egg whites until they form soft peaks, then gradually add the sugar, whisking all the time until the meringue forms firm peaks. Fold in the lightly beaten yolks and vanilla. Combine the figs, dates, raisins, orange rind, walnuts, orange peel, and cornstarch. Gently add the fruit mixture to the egg white mixture. Shape into a 12-inch circle on a greased and floured cookie sheet and bake for 30 minutes.

Grape and Fennel Flat Bread

This sweet flat bread was served warm as part of the celebratory feast for the grape harvest in October.

3 cups white bread flour
$^1/2$ teaspoon salt
$^1/2$ ounce fresh yeast
Scant 1 cup lukewarm water
Pinch of sugar
3 tablespoons olive oil
1 pound seedless black grapes, cut in half
1 teaspoon fennel seeds
2 tablespoons unrefined milled golden cane sugar

Sift the flour and salt into a large bowl and make a well in the center. Cream the yeast with half the water and a pinch of sugar. Pour into the center of the flour with the olive oil and the remaining water. Mix to a soft dough and turn out onto a lightly floured surface and knead for 10 minutes until smooth and elastic. Put into an oiled bowl, cover with lightly oiled plastic wrap, and leave in a warm place to rise for about 1 hour until doubled in size. While the dough is rising put the halved grapes, fennel seeds, and sugar into a bowl and set aside. Punch down the dough and turn out onto a lightly floured surface and knead gently. Roll out half the dough to a rectangle about 11 x 10 inches and place on an oiled baking sheet. Top with three quarters of the grape mixture to within $^1/2$ inch of the edge. Roll out the remaining dough and cover the grape mixture, dampening and sealing the edges well. Spoon the rest of the grape mixture over the bread and leave in a warm place for about 20 minutes until risen. Preheat the oven to 400°F. Bake for 30 to 40 minutes until well browned. Serve warm.

THE BLACK VIRGIN—
LA VIERGE NOIRE

patshiv
(A Gypsy celebration)

Every year on May 24, Gypsies from all around the world but especially the Gitans, Roma, Sinti, and Manouches of France make a pilgrimage to the south of France, to the village of Saintes-Maries-de-la-Mer in the Camargue to pay their respects to their patron saint Sara-la-Kâli, or Sara the Black. The pilgrimages date back to the Middle Ages. For days before the feast, Gypsies from Spain, Italy, Hungary, and Rumania flock to the area.

This celebration is connected with an event purported to have taken place in A.D. 42 when St. Mary Jacobé and St. Mary Salomé are said to have landed in this part of the Mediterranean coast, having drifted from the Holy Land in a tiny boat without oars or sail. With them was a swarthy "Egyptian" serving girl, Sara. Black Sara is believed to have followed the three Marys after Christ's Crucifixion and was baptized by Mary Salomé and Mary Jacobé. An apocryphal text from the eleventh century shows Sara discovering, with Martha and the two Marys, the empty tomb of Jesus, and leaving to announce with the apostles the news of the resurrection of the Christ.

An ancient Provençal tradition describes how, a boat was launched from Jerusalem, without sail, oars, or supplies, and drifted across the Mediterranean until it landed in Saintes-Maries-de-la-Mer, in about the year A.D. 40. The refugees in the boat were Mary Jacobé, the mother of James and the sister of the Virgin; Mary Salomé, the mother of the apostles James Major and John; Lazarus and his two sisters, Mary Magdalene and Martha; St Maximinus; Cedonius, who was born blind and cured; and Sara, the servant of the two Marys.

After landing safely, the group built a small oratory to the Virgin. The disciples went off their separate ways; Mary Magdalene went to Ste-Baume; Martha went to Tarascon; and Mary Salomé, Mary Jacobé, and Sara remained in the Camargue, and were later buried in the oratory. The tomb of these three saints became a shrine and has attracted pilgrimages for almost two thousand years. They were reburied beneath the chancel during the Barbarian invasions, and then removed and enshrined in the present fortified church in 1448 by Good King René.

An early mention of Sara is in a poem by Jean de Ventte in 1357 as a servant of St. Martha and Mary Magdalene. Another tradition, ascribed to by Roma, holds that Sara was a *Gitane*, living on the Provençales banks, rescuing the Saintes-Marys from a storm at sea.

Another story relates that Sara was an Egyptian, abbess of a large convent in Libya. Yet another says that Sara figured prominently among a group of Persian martyrs, with the two Marys and Martha, who arrived in Gaul by ship.

For reasons that have become lost with the passing of time, the local chapel of Saintes-Maries-de-la-Mer adopted the legend of Sara, although the Catholic Church never canonized her as a saint. The first historical mention of Sara is found in a text of Vincent Philippon written in 1521, *The Legend of the Saintes-Maries*, and whose handwritten pages are now located in the Arles library. According to the legend, Sara lived and traveled through the Camargue begging for alms for the needs of a small Christian community. This provided early writers with a reason to make Sara a *Gitane*. To *Gitanes*, she is *Sara-la-Kâli*, a Gypsy word that means both Sara the *Gitane* and Sara the Black.

Saintes-Maries-de-la-Mer is reached by following a solitary road from Arles through the Camargue, past grazing lands and horse farms, where the landscape merges into the sea. The Gypsies of the Camargue consider St. Sara their patron saint and in May and September there are processions of *gardianes*, Camargue cowboys, who drive the bulls through the streets to the bullring for nonlethal bull-fighting or to a pool for a strange sport called *taureau piscine* where amateur bull-fighters dodge the bulls in the water-filled pools.

Gitans have never doubted Sara's authenticity. Sara is regarded as being a wise woman, imparting secret knowledge. Gypsy women are especially known to have access to secret visions and Sara represents this gift. In the week preceding the celebration, *Gitans* arrive and as the dancers and musicians throng the bars, restaurants, campsites, and streets, the town resounds to the distinctive Gypsy music of violins and guitars.

During the pilgrimage the catechism is taught in caravans and many *Gitans* use the pilgrimage as an opportunity to baptize their children in the church of Saintes-Maries-de-la-Mer.

The altar to the saint contains her relics in a casket on the altar and is situated in the crypt. At night Gitans and other Romany visit the ancient crypt of Saint Sara, where her statue stands in the dark, illuminated by the golden glow of hundreds of candles. She is depicted crowned, robed in blue and white, and is dressed in real outfits that are frequently changed. She stands on a black rock, often swathed with tapestry at normal height to make it easy for her devotees to kiss her face. A small carved, wooden shrine beside her statue holds letters and small shoes attesting to her miracles. Children's crutches and metal braces are laid behind her on the rock wall—testaments to her healing powers. She is worshipped with fire (candles) and water.

The Gypsies patiently wait their turn to pay homage to Saint Sara. They kiss their palms, before touching them to Sara's forehead and small children are hoisted up to kiss her face. A large central candle is lit in the chapel, among a multitude of smaller candles that each person holds high in their hands and everyone adds a candle to the blazing mass that quickly spreads in the crypt. Touching handwritten notes are placed near the statue of *Sara-la-Kâli*, along with children's clothes, messages, and even jewelry. The crowds wait all night, saying prayers and attending services. The sick wait patiently to touch the holy relics.

The ceremony involves lowering the casket containing the relics of the two Marys from the window of the upper chapel to the crowds below, and is then left in front of the altar. Afterward, the Gypsies carry the statue of Sara through the town, along the coast, and into the sea. The narrow streets of Saintes-Maries-de-la-Mer are thronged with crowds and thousands follow in solemn procession.

During the passage, children are lifted up, so that they may place their hands and lips to the statues. The Gypsies pay respect to a wooden statue of Sara by touching or rubbing her cloth garments, which they believe will bring them good luck. Camargue *gardians* dressed in black velvet coats and tight-fitting trousers, and seated on white horses accompany the statues of the Saintes-Maries and Sara into the sea. The statues are carried by specially chosen men. *Arlésiennes* honor the escort as well, but it is the *Gitans* that sing hymns ceaselessly and shout, "*Vive Saint Sara!*" Thousands of pilgrims wade fully clothed into the sea, as the statues appear to float above them. Local horsemen stand among the waves with pikes and flags held aloft. They will flank the Gypsy procession and fend off any media intrusion.

After the statues of the two Marys have been carried out to sea, the pilgrimage ends with bullfights. Later that night everyone returns to the church for prayers, reciting the Rosary, benediction, and hymns all through the night.

An account by Walter Starkie of the Gypsies' pilgrimage in 1938 (*Journal of the Gypsy Lore Society*, 1957) stated that the Gypsies arrived by horses and mules, caravans, motor caravans, and cars and that they camped around the ninth-century church. As part of the ceremonies, water was drawn from an ancient well in the center of the church. The atmosphere today is bustling and noisy with people selling from booths and stalls and there are clouds of dust. The arrival of the Marys and Lazarus is commemorated by the *navette*, a small cookie baked in the shape of the boat (*navette*) they arrived in.

This French seaside town has a wide variety of fish and shellfish dishes. *Tellines à la Provençale* is made with the local tiny but tasty clam-like shellfish, which are harvested in the Mediterranean and on the Camargue coast. There's a Spanish influence here, too, and good paellas are a specialty.

May 25 is the feast of St. Mary Jacobé, the patron saint of the village of Saintes-Maries-de-la-Mer, and the mother of St. James the Less.

The Camargue, a desolate, marshy wilderness, is sandwiched between Montpellier and Marseille, from Arles to the Mediterranean. The southern part is made up of inland lakes, lagoons, and low flat plains once covered by the Mediterranean Sea, which has since receded, while the northern part is dry. The Camargue is best known for its elegant pink flamingos and its wild horses. The small Camargue horses are born brown, but gradually turn white. Just as famous are the cowboys who herd these horses, as well as sheep and the bulls that are raised to fight in the *cocardes* at Nîmes, Arles, and other places.

Camargue is sometimes called the Texas of France, due to the raising of the black bulls (*taureaux*). The bulls of the Camargue have been bred in the wetlands here since medieval times. The small black bulls were recently given an Appellation d'Origine Contrôlée for their tender tasty meat. These bulls however have a very different fate from that of the Spanish bulls, which pay with their lives in the bull-fights. A Camargue bull has a *cocarde* (a cord with two tassels) tied between its horns and enters the arena to be approached by *razteurs*—men usually dressed in white who try to snatch the cockade from the bull by means of a special hook. The contest lasts for fifteen minutes and if the *razteurs* are successful they win a prize of money, but if the bull can outwit the *razteurs* and keep its cockade, it returns to the owner's truck and afterwards it is released into its field until the next contest. The bulls live an almost wild life on the pastures and usually end their career in a *gardiane*, or bull stew, a famous local specialty. The *Gardiane de Taureau à l'Ancienne* is the local version of a beef stew, similar to the Provençal *daube*.

The Camargue is the most northerly rice-growing area of Europe. The farmers had little success growing the wild red rice indigenous to the region (the stalk sheds its grains when ripe, making it difficult to harvest), until 1980. It was then that René Griotto discovered that the native wild rice had cross-pollinated successfully with the cultivated short-grain white variety he had been growing and *riz rouge de Camargue* was created. Camargue red rice, now commercially successful, has a slightly sweet, earthy flavor and a pleasant chewy texture, which makes it a popular choice as a base for pilafs and stuffing mixtures. Its delicious nutty flavor also makes it an excellent side dish or part of a main course. Cook the rice in plenty of boiling salted water for 30 to 40 minutes until tender. Drain well and mix with good olive oil, salt, pepper, and some chopped fresh herbs. It is eaten as an accompaniment to the famous *Taureau Sauvage à la Gardianel* (see page 171).

This rich dish of braised meat from the Camargue of Provençe is known as *Gardiane de Taureau*, *Boeuf à la Gardiane*, or simply *la Gardiane*. Some people also make *gardiane* with lamb.

¹/4 cup extra-virgin olive oil
4 pounds oxtail (with bone) or 3 pounds beef shank, cubed
1 tablespoon shortening, butter, or oil
4 onions, chopped
1 pound potatoes, peeled and diced
2 cups beef stock or broth
1 cup robust red wine
A few stems each of thyme, tarragon, and parsley
Peel of 1 orange
1 whole onion stuck with 4 cloves
2 fresh or dried bay leaves
2 to 3 cloves garlic, crushed
2 tablespoons tomato puree
¹/4 cup chopped pitted black olives
¹/4 cup chopped pitted green olives
Salt and pepper

In a large heavy casserole heat the olive oil over medium-high heat, then brown the oxtail or shank pieces on all sides, about 5 minutes. Remove the oxtails from the casserole and set aside, keeping them warm. In the same casserole, melt the shortening over medium-high heat, and then cook the chopped onions and potatoes until the onions are golden, about 8 minutes, stirring frequently and adding small amounts of water to scrape the browned bits off bottom of the casserole if necessary. Return the meat to the casserole. Pour in the beef broth and wine along with the herbs, orange peel, clove-studded onion, bay leaves, garlic, tomato puree, and chopped olives. Season with salt and pepper to taste. Reduce the heat to low and simmer, uncovered, until the sauce is thick and the meat tender and falling off the bone, about 4 hours. Remove and discard the orange peel, herb stems, whole onion, and bay leaf. Serve immediately.

MAKES ABOUT 20 COOKIES

The arrival of the Marys and Lazarus is commemorated by these small cookies, baked in the shape of the boat (*navette*) in which they arrived.

3 cups all-purpose flour
2 tablespoons butter
³/4 cup unrefined golden milled cane sugar
Grated peel of 1 small lemon
1 tablespoon orange blossom water
1 egg

Sift the flour into a mixing bowl and make a well in the center. Add the butter, sugar, lemon peel, orange water, egg, and about ¹/2 cup of water to make a soft dough. Roll out the dough to a ¹/4-inch thickness on a floured work surface and cut out boat shapes pointed at either end or cut out 2-inch rounds with a cookie cutter. Place the cookies on a greased baking sheet and leave to rest for 1 to 2 hours. Preheat the oven to 400°F. Bake for about 15 minutes. Cool the baked cookies on a wire rack and keep in an airtight tin up to a week.

ST GEORGE'S DAY - SLAVA

Baxt hai sastimos tiri patragi
(A wish for luck and good health on St George's Day)

Patshivaki Djili
(Friendship songs)

This saint's day heralded spring and new life and Serbian Roma in particular celebrated the day (*Djurdjev Dan*) with vast amounts of food and drink. Seasonal foods included tomatoes (*patlidžaja*), nettles (*ciknida*), vegetables (*šsturo*), bell peppers (*pipera*), onions (*puruma*), beans (*thavali*), and new potatoes (*terne kolompira*).

Obligatory Slav objects—a tall candle (in order to drive evil spirits away) and a sprig of dried basil (a symbol of love and fertility)—are the icons of the saint and were present at the feast. There were also ritual dishes: *slavsko zito* (boiled wheat grains) and *slavski kolac* (slava loaf), a specially adorned ritual bread blessed by the priest before the main meal, which was accompanied by toasts and singing.

St. George's Day was also the festival of cattle breeders and shepherds. Traditionally, on this day shepherds would take a lamb with a wreath on its little horns to the churchyard. The priest would intone a solemn prayer for the health of both humans and animals, and for a successful harvest. It was customary to have roasted lamb or some other lamb dish on the St. George's Day table.

In Bulgaria on St. George's Day, the women stuck green branches into the fountains and the wells and dropped nettles into the water cauldrons for good health.

Everyone ate outside; indeed in warm weather everything including bedding was moved outdoors. Women prepared colorful salads of tomatoes, onions, and bread that would last each family the entire day, together with a nourishing nettle soup and some fried new potatoes.

The day before the feast, the women baked special cakes (*kolac*) while the men fetched supplies of wine and *rakija* (plum brandy). The Serbs have a saying "we are born, with *rakija* we marry, and with *rakija* we bury."

In the evening, bonfires were lit and the adults drank *rakija* and sang and danced to the accompaniment of violins and tambourines, while the children ran around excitedly. Every family killed a sheep or lamb for the feast. The chosen animal's horns were decorated with a garland of flowers and small lighted candles on the eve of St. George's Day. The head of the family prayed for prosperity and waited for the candles to go out, and then the sheep or lamb was left alone. Early next morning before sunrise the head of the household placed a willow garland on the animal's head and candles decorated with garlands of coins were fixed on its horns. Incense was burned, the candles were lit and prayers were said for the health of the family.

The animal's head was tapped three times with a bag of money—to ensure prosperity for the coming year, then the candles were extinguished, the garland removed, and the sheep was killed by the head of the family. Afterward, the blood was collected and thrown into a river or running water. The willow garland was hung in the room and the sheep or lamb was skinned—but the horns were left intact.

A fire was laid in a pre-dug hole and the lamb or sheep was put on a spit, a green branch was put into its mouth, and it was roasted slowly over the hot coals. When the meat was cooked, the women removed the lungs, which were cut up, salted, and fried. Each member of the family had a taste, then it was offered to neighbors, who each took a piece.

Dinner was served at noon for non-Romany friends from a nearby village or town. At three o'clock the Roma brought their sheep, lambs, and other food and drink and sat down together to share the meal. A branch from a pear tree was stuck in the ground where each family sat, to symbolize fruitfulness, and an Easter egg and candle were attached to it. The candle was lit and burned throughout the meal. The sheep's head was left to be eaten the next day. A great number of magic rituals were connected with sheep and St. George and a number of these highly secret magic formulas were passed from one generation to another.

St. George is also the patron saint of Catalonia and his feast day has remained a time of celebration in and around Catalonia since 1436. The saint's feast also coincides with the Fair of the Book and the Rose. On this day every man offers a rose to his wife or fiancée and she gives him a book in return. The book is in memory of Cervantes (author of *Don Quixote*) as the custom was started in 1926, to commemorate Cervantes' death.

Barcelona, too, holds a Book and Rose Fair. The St. James Square and main streets are lined with stalls selling books of all kinds. There is also an exhibition of roses in the patio of the Palace of the Autonomous Government, as a symbol of the arrival of spring.

In the village of Sant Climent Sescebes the villagers walk in procession to the "magic rock." A local legend holds that there is a magic rock near the village that leads to a huge treasure and the spell may only be broken on the night of St. George's Day. Twelve loaves of bread are blessed before being shared out among the crowd.

St Mary's Day was an important feast in the Pyrenees, known there as *La Fête de Sainte-Marie* and was actually celebrated over two days, August 14 and 15, celebrating the assumption of the Virgin Mary into heaven. The feast began with music, singing, and dancing on the morning of the August 14. Glasses of Armagnac and strong coffee accompanied a dish of braised meat. In the afternoon the feast was held in two tents, where incense was burned. There was a huge choice of dishes arranged around an enormous cake that weighed around 24 pounds and was divided into portions by cutting with a special knife kept solely for this purpose, although the origins of this are known only to the Roma. Each man was allowed to share his allotted wedge of cake as he pleased. The night was sacred to the memory of the dead and songs were sung.

Roma in Canada also celebrated the feast of St. Mary in August, when a ceremonial lamb was served. The roast lamb had an apple in its mouth and cherries on its head.

Another celebration of Roma in the Pyrenees is *La Fête de l'arbre* (The tree feast), which takes place on March 1. A tree is planted in the center of a circle of tents and is decorated with food and drink such as bottles of wine, poultry, and hams. In the afternoon everyone joined hands and danced around the tree. The heavily laden tree was then felled to the ground and the food and drink distributed to everyone present. This custom may have its roots in ancient Indian and Celtic traditions of tree worshipping when trees were believed to harbor spirits.

Chopped Seasoned Lamb in Milk

MAKES 4 SERVINGS

1 pound boneless lamb, cubed
1 cup milk
Salt and pepper

Soak the cubed lamb in the milk for about 2 hours. Drain and thread the cubes onto skewers. Broil under a medium heat. Before serving, season with salt and pepper to taste.

Roast Lamb with Cherries

MAKES 4 TO 6 SERVINGS

2-pound leg of lamb (approximately)
1 teaspoon juniper berries, crushed
1 cup stock or water
$^1/_4$ cup plus 1 tablespoon red wine
1 tablespoon cornstarch
2 teaspoons unrefined dark brown molasses sugar
1 cup sour cherries, pitted

Preheat the oven to 350°F. Rub the lamb with the crushed juniper berries, and place the joint on a rack over a roasting pan. Pour the stock and 1 tablespoon red wine into the pan and roast for 2 to $2^1/_2$ hours, adding hot water to the pan if necessary. Remove the lamb and keep warm. Skim the fat from the pan and deglaze with $^1/_2$ cup water. Combine the cornstarch, sugar, and remaining $^1/_4$ cup wine. Add to the pan along with the cherries and stir the sauce over a medium heat until it boils and thickens. Serve the sauce with the lamb.

This rich Bulgarian bread was prepared for family feasts and celebrations. The name comes from *kolo*, meaning "circle."

6 cups white bread flour
2 teaspoons salt
1 ounce fresh yeast
¹/₂ cup lukewarm milk
1 teaspoon honey
3 eggs, beaten
²/₃ cup natural yogurt
¹/₄ cup butter, melted
Poppy seeds

Sift the flour and salt into a large bowl and make a well in the center. Cream the yeast with the milk and honey and pour into the center of the flour with 2 of the eggs, the yogurt, and melted butter. Mix to a firm dough and turn out on to a lightly floured surface and knead for about 10 minutes until smooth and elastic. Place the dough in a lightly oiled bowl, cover with lightly oiled plastic wrap and leave to rise in a warm place for 1 ½ hours until doubled in size. Punch down the dough and knead gently on a lightly floured surface. Shape into a ball and place, seam side down, on an oiled baking tray. Make a hole in the center using your fingers and gradually enlarge this while turning the dough, to make a 10-inch circle. Cover with lightly oiled plastic wrap and leave to rise in a warm place for 30 to 40 minutes or until doubled in size. Preheat the oven to 400°F. Brush the loaf with the remaining beaten egg and sprinkle with poppy seeds. Bake for about 35 minutes until golden.

JUBILEE DINNER 1938

Kámmoben
(Love and friendship)

The Gypsy Lore Society was founded in May 1888 when David MacRitchie (the Society's first secretary, and later president) sent out a circular that contained the names of the eleven original members. Among the founding members were the explorer Sir Richard F. Burton and Archduke Joseph of Austria-Hungary. The Society was based at the University of Liverpool Library until 1974, when it was dissolved following the death of Dora Yates, the Honorary Secretary. Dora was an intellectual with many Roma friends, whose deep interest and affection for the Roma and the Romany way of life earned her an international reputation.

The Gypsy Lore Society, North American Chapter was founded in the United States in 1977 and since 1989 has continued as the Gypsy Lore Society. Since 1989, it has been headquartered in Maryland. Its aims are the promotion of the study of Gypsy, and other traveling and nomadic cultures worldwide and the dissemination of accurate information aimed at increasing understanding of these cultures. Gypsy Lore Society meetings are held annually and are rotated among different U.S. cities and other countries.

On June 11, 1938, the Gypsy Lore Society held a Jubilee Dinner at Reece's Café in Liverpool to celebrate fifty years of "joyful endeavor in wine and food." The dinner, its planning and organization was the idea of Dora Yates and the occasion was a tremendously exciting and momentous event for everyone concerned.

Augustus John, the president of the Gypsy Lore Society, was unfortunately unable to be present, but he sent a telegram in Romanes, the Gypsy language. The guests, among whom were the author Lady Eleanor Smith, Bernard Gilliat-Smith, the British Consul-General at Bucharest, George Walton from the British Embassy in Moscow and his wife (the former Princess Natalia Galitzin), and Lady Arthur Grosvenor (a champion of the Gypsies) along with university professors and lecturers enjoyed the dinner along with four invited Roma guests.

Annie Lee (the wife of Ithal Lee) greeted the guests. The menu was printed in Romanes. The meal ended at midnight after thanks from Ithal Lee.

Menu

HOBBENESKO LIL

Zumin (Soup)
Goshti (Thick) *korodi* (clear)

Macho (Fish)
Baro Macho (Big Fish—Salmon)
Kerad-kek chordino (Boiled not poached)*

Mas (Meat)
Romani Xeliax (Gypsy Stew)
Ma Puch so si andre lati
Neve Phuvengere (New Potatoes)
Chimerimen Puruma (Braised Onions)

Gudlibena (Sweet)
Durilengi Goi tha Smentena (Bilberry Pudding and Cream)

Vavera
Kial (Cheese)
Chinkerdi (Coffee)

Molengo Lil
Tato Pani (Whisky or Brandy)
Livena or cwrw da (Hard Old Ale)

*Perhaps a play on words, as *chordino* means stolen!

Poached Salmon

Use a large roasting pan or dish to cook the salmon, curving it to fit. The liquid should come halfway up the fish in the pan.

5-pound whole salmon, gutted and cleaned
1 1/2 cups fish stock
1 1/2 cups dry white wine or water
A few peppercorns
A slice of lemon
1 bay leaf
Thinly sliced cucumber for garnish (optional)
Fresh parsley for garnish
Lemon wedges for garnish

Preheat the oven to 325°F. Place the fish in the pan or dish. Mix the fish stock and wine and pour over the fish. Add the peppercorns, lemon, and bay leaf to the pan and cover with buttered foil—don't let the foil touch the fish. Cook for 1 to 1 1/4 hours, basting from time to time, until cooked through. Test the middle part of the salmon to check if it is cooked thoroughly. Cover and cool in the liquid. When the fish is cold lift it very carefully onto a work surface and peel off the skin and discard. Turn over and repeat on the other side. Lift carefully on to a large serving plate. Decorate with wafer thin slices of cucumber if desired, to represent scales. Garnish with fresh parsley and lemon wedges.

This is one of the best ways of cooking onions. They're especially good with roast meats, chops, and steaks, or just on their own.

1 pound small onions, peeled
2 tablespoons butter
Salt and pepper
2 tablespoons unrefined dark brown molasses sugar

Place the onions in a single layer in the base of a large pan. Just cover with water and add the butter, a sprinkling of salt and pepper and the sugar. Cover the pan and bring to the boil. Remove the lid and cook until the liquid has reduced to a rich brown syrup. Shake the pan so that the onions are evenly coated with the glaze. Sprinkle with a little more salt and plenty of pepper.

You can substitute blueberries or blackberries for the bilberries.

1 cup bilberries
Grated peel and juice of 1 orange (optional)
1 to 2 tablespoons honey
1 stick butter
2 cups flour

Preheat the oven to 375°F. If desired, mix the berries with the grated peel and juice of the orange. Stir in the honey. Rub the butter into the flour until the mixture resembles bread crumbs and add just enough cold water to mix to a soft dough. Roll out half the dough and use to line a pie plate or dish. Tip in the fruit mixture and spread evenly in the pastry shell. Roll out the remaining dough and lay over the fruit filling, sealing the edges well. Make 2 slits in the top and bake for 20 to 30 minutes until golden. Alternatively, line a greased 4-cup pudding basin with three quarters of the dough and tip in the fruit mixture. Use the remaining dough to make a lid and seal well. Cover with a lid or a double thickness of greaseproof paper and foil—leaving room for the pudding to expand during cooking. Put the basin in a large pan and pour sufficient boiling water in the outer pan to come halfway up the sides of the basin. Cover the pan and cook for 1½ hours. Top up with boiling water as needed—don't let the pan boil dry! Serve with cream.

CHRISTMAS CELEBRATIONS

Roma penge tele muken.
Roma, kaj save te ulahas rushte, pre Karachonya penge odmuken u aven pale lachhe.
(Roma forgive. Roma, though they are the worst enemies, forgive and are reconciled during Christmas.)

Roma all over the world celebrated Christmas according to their chosen religion. Christmas was, and remains, the main holy day for Catholics and Protestants, while Eastern Orthodox Christians place more emphasis on celebrating Easter or the New Year. Christmas Day was a time when the Roma gathered to feast and exchange best wishes, and to join in the singing of old Romany songs. In Romania, there was a Romany-looking Santa who wore a full-length hooded brown robe and sandals and carried a multicolored patchwork bag.

During Advent in the weeks before Christmas, Roma women prepared by cleaning the home. Roma musicians rehearsed the songs they would play to the farmers on Christmas night under their windows, and Roma boys learned to exchange best wishes for good health and fortune for the coming New Year. At this time of year a good stock of food was ensured, ready for Christmas—one reason why Roma children looked forward to Christmas so much!

Christmas without *szaloncukor* would be unthinkable to Hungarian Roma. *Szaloncukor* was the name of a sweetmeat and also of the occasion itself. Originally, around the nineteenth century, *szaloncukor* was made of sugar and was used as an ornament to decorate the Christmas tree. In the early twentieth century, *szaloncukor* was still usually made of sugar, but in poor households flour was mixed with the sugar to make a dough, which was molded into shapes before baking. Whether pure sugar or dough, the cakes were wrapped in colored paper or foil. Nowadays *szaloncukor* are more sophisticated and are usually made of chocolate and marzipan. After Christmas is over the cakes should be left untouched until the Epiphany on January 6, when they are eaten.

Christmas cake or *chesnytsa* was an essential part of a Serbian Christmas. This cake which was really a type of a flat round bread was usually made early in the morning on Christmas Day. A coin was placed in the dough together with some other items symbolizing various types of skills and accomplishments. Tradition dictated that once the cake was broken and shared, whoever found these items in their piece of cake would achieve particular types of success in their lives. This tradition is very similar to the French *Galette des Rois* or Kings Cake eaten on January 6th, the feast of the Epiphany (an important celebration in France that marks the end of the Christmas festivities). This cake consists of two buttery puff pastry discs with a creamy almond filling. Bakers conceal a *feve* (broad bean) or charm in the filling (to represent the infant Jesus) and decorate the cakes with gold paper crowns. Whoever finds the bean or charm is king or queen of the day's festivities.

Czech and Slovak Roma call Christmas *Karachonya* or *Karachon*, and their celebrations include several elements derived from the respective countries, together with their own Romany traditions, some of which are centuries old.

Among the traditions in which the Romany Christmas differs from a Czech Christmas are those of forgiveness, reconciliation, and remembering deceased relatives. Forgiveness and reconciliation are very important to the Roma, because when they were completely isolated, strong solidarity within the group was vitally important. Roma were entirely dependent on the community in which they lived, so they could not afford to have any discord or dissension amongst themselves. The Christmas season was therefore a good time to strengthen and reinforce the relationships between members of the family or community.

Remembering deceased relatives at Christmas is related to the Roma belief that a person's soul survives and exists in the next world after the body's departure. The Romany word for the souls of their dead ancestors is *mule* and they endeavor to be on good terms with them, since the *mule* can also harm them. At Christmas, dead relatives are placated by gifts of food left on a windowsill or in the corner of a room, so they won't haunt the living. Roma also talk about their deceased relatives and remember them over Christmas.

At Christmas time it was the custom to visit and compliment neighbors, as it was believed that this would bring them good luck. On Christmas Eve (*Vilija*) everyone sat round a table or on the floor and a Romany elder gave a short traditional speech wishing everybody all the best followed by a toast. Afterwards the celebrations began and everyone joined in the dancing and drinking.

As was the custom with Czechs, Roma in that country would also fast on Christmas Eve. The strictness of the fast varied; some families abstained from meat until the evening, while others ate only baked potatoes all day. The mother, with the help of her daughters, always prepared Christmas Eve dinner.

Dinner on Christmas Eve usually consisted of cabbage, beans with plums, potatoes, various types of dumplings, and *boblaky* (buns sprinkled with poppy seeds and soaked in milk). In some areas, Roma went out and about exchanging best wishes immediately after the Christmas Eve dinner; in others they didn't do so until Christmas Day. Romany men and boys went to every house, being careful not to leave anyone out and exchanged their wishes for health and good fortune. During these rounds, Roma would also forgive each other, because as the older Roma say: when Roma stick together, neither hunger, poverty, nor evil can destroy them.

The boys always undertook decorating the Christmas tree. Before dinner the father or oldest member of the family would give a speech, followed by a toast and blessing and a remembrance of the dead. Candles were lit for the departed and food from each course put in a bowl and set on the windowsill or in the corner for them.

In Bulgaria there was plenty of food for the Christmas Eve feast and custom dictated that there had to be an odd number of dishes. Traditional dishes included boiled haricot beans, leaves stuffed with rice or groats, and stewed dried fruit. The Christmas fare also included garlic, walnuts, honey, onions, and preserved summer fruits along with wine and brandy.

Boiled wheat and the *ignazhden* (ring-shaped cake) were also part of the Christmas fare. Boiled wheat was traditional throughout the Balkans and was a very ancient dish. It was served at other special occasions too, such as funerals and harvest festivities. In England a strikingly similar version of boiled wheat known as frumenty, was also eaten at Christmas, although this was made with milk and dried fruits. It's no exaggeration to say that frumenty is England's oldest national dish. The name is derived from early recipes, when it was described as *Furmente of Wheat*. Whole wheat first had to be "creed" or husked. This was done by soaking the wheat in water, then gently warming it in a low oven for about twelve hours until the husks swelled and burst. After beating in a mortar and pestle, the husks could be rinsed away in a sieve, leaving the thick gelatinous wheat. This jelly was slowly cooked with milk, thickened with flour or eggs, and the mixture was then sweetened with honey, sugar, or molasses. Other additions included spices, dried fruits, cream, butter, brandy, or rum.

In some parts of Western Bulgaria, in the regions of Teteven, and Macedonia, unleavened bread with a silver coin concealed inside was baked. The person who got the coin would be healthy and lucky throughout the year. Different objects were placed around the table, such as a bowl of sand, a purse full of money, a sieve full of grains, and a bunch of basil and garlic tied up with red thread. These objects were symbolic—a purse full of money and the sieve full of grains were symbols of a fruitful and prosperous year to come. The basil and garlic tied with red thread drove away evil spirits.

Only family members attended the Christmas Eve supper. The eldest man or woman burned incense at the table and then incensed the rest of the house and its surroundings to ward off evil spirits. A place at the table was set for dead relatives and the table was not cleared for the night because it was believed that the deceased would come to supper. The wheat grains and the remains of the candle burned at the Christmas Eve table were preserved for the following nights.

The year ended on *phuro džives* (an old day) and the New Year began on *nevo berš*.

Boiled Wheat

VARENO ZHITO

MAKES 6 SERVINGS

The prepared wheat needed for the recipe is sold as bulgur, kibbled, or pearled wheat. Look for it at health food stores. Don't be put off by the name—it is a delicious dessert dish, although it is time consuming to prepare.

1 pound bulgur wheat
2 cups all-purpose flour
Salt
Juice of ½ a lemon
3½ cups ground walnuts
2 generous cups confectioners' sugar, sifted
2 to 3 teaspoons ground cinnamon
Grated peel of 1 large lemon

Preheat the oven to 350°F. Wash the wheat and place in a large pan with enough cold water to cover the grains. Let stand overnight but no longer than 12 hours.

The next day heat the wheat and water until boiling then simmer, covered, for 20 minutes. Remove from the heat without removing the lid and leave undisturbed for 24 hours.
Drain the soaked wheat (keep the nutritious liquid to make a dessert) and spread the wheat on a clean folded towel and leave to dry for 12 hours.

Preheat the oven to 375°F. Spread the flour in an even layer on a baking tray and cook until the flour is roasted and golden, 10 to 15 minutes. Remove from the oven and leave to cool. Place the dried wheat on a baking tray and sprinkle with a little salt to taste, then with the lemon juice. Sift the flour over the wheat and shake until every grain is coated with flour. Mix the walnuts with two-thirds of the confectioners' sugar, the cinnamon, and lemon peel. Spoon over the wheat and combine lightly. Transfer the dessert to a large serving dish or tray and spread evenly. Sift the rest of the confectioners' sugar over the wheat just before serving.

English Frumenty

MAKES 2 SERVINGS

This is England's oldest national dish. The name is derived from early recipes, when it was described as "Furmente of Wheat." In Medieval England, it was a savory dish to accompany venison, but as time passed it became a sweet dessert. It became a Christmas specialty in Yorkshire, but had largely disappeared by the beginning of the Twentieth Century.

4 ounces pearled or kibbled wheat
Scant 2 cups whole milk
1 tablespoon currants or raisins
1 teaspoon mixed/pumpkin spices
1 teaspoon ground cinnamon
Honey or unrefined milled golden cane sugar

Soak the wheat overnight in a bowl of water, preferably in a warm place. Drain off the water and place the wheat in a pan with the milk and boil gently for 20 minutes. Add the currants or raisins and simmer gently for another 40 minutes. Beat in the spices and sweeten with sugar to taste. Serve hot with cream or a knob of butter and a dash of rum or brandy.

Rum Butter

Rum butter is eaten at Christmas with Christmas pudding and mince pies in Great Britain, but it's also delicious with any hot sweet tart or steamed pudding (particularly ginger) or as a filling for sponge sandwich cakes. It will keep for several weeks in the refrigerator.

2 sticks unsalted butter
1/2 cup light brown muscovado sugar
Good pinch grated nutmeg
1 to 2 tablespoons dark rum

Cream the butter until soft, then beat in the sugar and nutmeg. Gradually add the rum, beating well until thoroughly incorporated. Spoon into pots or jars and cover with tight fitting lids. Store in the refrigerator.

¹/₃ cup plus 2 tablespoons butter
2 eggs
Salt
2 cups sifted all-purpose flour
2 cups mashed boiled potatoes
12 to 15 plums
Ground cinnamon
¹/₄ cup unrefined milled golden cane sugar, plus extra for sprinkling
1 cup fine bread crumbs

Cream 2 tablespoons of the butter until soft, and then beat in the eggs and salt. Gradually beat in the flour and mashed potatoes. The dough should be sufficiently stiff to knead thoroughly. On a floured surface roll out the dough to ¹/₄-inch-thick, then cut into 3-inch squares. Lay 1 plum on each square, sprinkle with a little cinnamon and sugar and fold the edges over the plum. Shape with your hands into a ball. The wall of dough should be very thin. Drop the dumplings into boiling salted water, cover, and simmer for about 15 minutes.

Melt the ¹/₃ cup butter in a pan and add the bread crumbs until brown. Roll the dumplings in the buttered bread crumbs and sprinkle with more ground cinnamon and sugar.

This cardamom-scented bread is studded with candied fruits.

1 ounce fresh yeast
Scant ¹/₂ cup tepid milk
4¹/₂ cups strong bread flour
2 teaspoons salt
6 tablespoons butter
Seeds from 12 to 15 cardamom pods
1 teaspoon vanilla extract
¹/₄ cup unrefined light brown muscovado sugar
Grated peel of 1 lemon
2 eggs, beaten
1 cup mixed candied fruits, e.g. cherries, pineapple, citrus peels
1 egg white, lightly beaten
1¹/₂ tablespoons unrefined demerara sugar
1 teaspoon ground cinnamon

Cream the yeast with the milk in a small bowl. Sift the flour and salt into a mixing bowl and rub in the butter until the mixture resembles fine bread crumbs. Make a well in the center and pour in the yeast mixture. Stir well, cover, and leave to stand in a warm place for 15 minutes. Crush the cardamom seeds and add to the flour mixture with the vanilla, brown sugar, lemon peel, and eggs. Mix to a soft dough and turn out onto a lightly floured surface. Knead for about 10 minutes until smooth and elastic and place in a lightly oiled bowl. Cover with a damp tea towel or plastic wrap and leave to rise in a warm place for 1 to 1¹/₂ hours until doubled in size.

Turn out and knead the dough, then flatten into a rectangle and sprinkle half of the fruits over the dough. Fold the sides into the middle and fold in half to enclose the fruit. Flatten into a rectangle again and scatter the remaining fruit on top. Fold and knead gently to distribute the fruits evenly. Cover with plastic wrap and leave to rest for 10 minutes.

Roll the dough into a rectangle approximately 14 x 10 inches and, with a short side facing you, fold the bottom third up lengthwise and the top third down, tucking in the sides. Place in a greased 9 x 5-inch loaf pan and rise in a warm place for 1 hour or until the dough reaches the top of the pan.

Preheat the oven to 350°F. Slash the top of the loaf with a sharp knife. Brush the top of the loaf with the egg white and sprinkle with the demerara sugar and cinnamon. Bake for 45 to 55 minutes until risen and browned. If the top of the loaf browns too quickly, cover with foil. Cool on a wire rack.

MAKES 4 TO 6 SERVINGS

Every family has its own recipe for *Mond Kuchen* handed down through generations of women. These cakes probably originated in Austria-Hungary and predated Christianity as the poppy was dedicated to the Moon goddess. Poppy seeds are still called "Moon seeds" in German. Moon cakes began to be made around Christmastime, when all the fancy baking was done. Grind the poppy seeds well in a coffee grinder— it makes a great difference in the texture.

Cake Dough

1 ounce fresh yeast
1 cup lukewarm water
$^1/_4$ cup unrefined milled golden cane sugar
4 cups flour
1 stick butter, softened
2 eggs, lightly beaten
1 teaspoon salt

Poppy Seed Filling

1 pound freshly finely ground poppy seeds
2 cups unrefined milled golden cane sugar
1 cup warm milk
$^1/_4$ cup butter, melted
2 teaspoons grated lemon peel

Preheat the oven to 350°F. **For the cake dough:** Crumble the yeast into a bowl and add the water and sugar stirring until the mixture liquefies. Blend the flour and butter with a pastry blender, or rub the butter into the flour with your fingers, until the mixture resembles bread crumbs. Add the eggs, salt, and yeast mixture and mix to a smooth dough, which leaves the sides of the bowl clean.

To make the filling: Mix together the poppy seeds, sugar, ¾ cup of the milk, butter, and lemon peel. The mixture should be thick but spreadable. If it is too thick add the remaining ¼ cup milk.

Divide the dough into 4 equal pieces and roll each one out in a rectangular shape. Spread each piece with a quarter of the filling and roll up like a jellyroll. Place on greased baking trays and bake immediately for 30 to 45 minutes or until brown.

These rich, crumbly shortbreads from Greece are flavored with
ouzo or brandy, especially for Christmas. Each piece has a clove
on top, to represent the spices brought by Magi to the infant
Jesus.

2 sticks butter
3 heaped tablespoons unrefined milled golden cane sugar
1 egg yolk
2 tablespoons ouzo or brandy
3$\frac{1}{2}$ cups all-purpose flour
Pinch ground cloves
20 to 30 whole cloves
Confectioners' sugar

Preheat the oven to 350°F. Beat the butter and sugar until light.
Gradually beat in the egg yolk and ouzo, then sift in the flour and
ground cloves and mix to a firm dough. Take pieces of the dough
and roll into small balls. Place the balls on a baking tray lined
with non-stick paper and press a clove into the top of each. Bake
for 20 to 25 minutes until light golden. Remove from the oven
and immediately sift with plenty of confectioners' sugar, until
completely coated. When cool, store in an airtight tin lined with
a layer of confectioners' sugar for up to a week.

Marzipan is one of Spain's favorite seasonal delicacies. Freshly made marzipan has a much superior flavor than the commercial variety. You can tint the marzipan by adding a little food coloring powder or paste to the almonds and sugar in the mixing bowl.

2 cups ground almonds
2 cups confectioners' sugar, sifted, plus extra for kneading.
Orange flower water
1 egg yolk, lightly beaten

Place the ground almonds and confectioners' sugar into a mixing bowl and add just enough orange flower water to make a pliable paste. Place the paste in a saucepan and stir over a low heat until it no longer sticks to the sides of the pan. Turn out on to a surface dusted with confectioners' sugar and knead lightly. Pat or roll out and cut out shapes with festive cutters. Cover lightly and leave in a warm place or a very low oven to dry out overnight. Preheat the oven to 450°F. Brush the marzipan with the egg yolk. Bake for about 15 minutes, until golden.

NATURAL HEALING

Drabengro /Drabarni
(Male or female healer)

Wild plants and herbs flourished in woods, meadows, fields, country hedgerows, lanes, and even waste patches of ground. Culinary herbs were called *chitries*, while medicinal herbs known as *drab* were used to prevent or cure various diseases and ailments and herbalism was practiced by both sexes. Recent research by leading drug companies has found that many of these herbs do indeed actually possess medicinal properties. Roma used plants and herbs extensively and their knowledge and range of cures and remedies was astonishing. Their secret recipes were passed on orally through the generations and they rarely consulted a doctor but instead relied on their vast knowledge to treat illnesses. Non-Roma perceived these cures and remedies as magic, even witchcraft.

The Romany knowledge of **poisonous plants** was phenomenal. Some of the most common deadly plants known to the Rom are foxglove (*Digitalis purpurea*) which contains a poison, Monkshood (*Aconitum napellus*), whose flowers resemble a monk's cowl; deadly nightshade; the leaves and berries of yew; and poisonous fungi. Poisonous plants were collectively known as *drab*.

Herbs, flowers, and other wild plants were never collected randomly as it was believed that there were correct harvest times—just as for fruits and vegetables. Plants gathered at the wrong time of year were regarded as lacking the efficacy of those gathered at the correct time. Some plants were gathered after they had flowered while others needed to be collected just before the flower buds had formed. They then had to be dried properly—some required a short drying time while others could take weeks. Certain plants had to be used fresh and were never dried; some needed to be cooked and others could only be eaten raw. Herbs, known collectively as *sastarimaskodrabaró*, were regarded as having a medicinal value in addition to their supernatural qualities.

Adder's Tongue (*Ophioglossum vulgatum*) is a fern that was crushed, cooked in oil, and strained, after which the green oil was used to treat wounds. Water distilled from the plant was used to treat inflamed eyes and the juice of the leaves was drunk as a cure for internal wounds. As its name suggests it was particularly used to treat adder (snake) bites.

Agrimony (*Agrimonia eupatoria*) was also known as cocklebur or sticklewort as the burrs attach themselves to the clothing of anyone passing. It was used to treat eye troubles and as a compress for wounds. Another larger, more fragrant variety *Agrimonia odorata* yielded a yellow dye and the flowers, leaves, and stems were made into a scented tea.

Wild **angelica** (*Angelica sylvestris*), smaller than and not as aromatic as the cultivated variety, has purplish stems and white flowers tinged with purple. The plant grows alongside brooks and streams and produced a yellow dye. The stalks were blanched and eaten with bread and butter and a little of the stem was added to stewed apples or rhubarb to enhance the flavor. The stems when chewed also relieved flatulence. The leaves made an aromatic tonic tea and a piece of the root was placed in the mouth to ward off disease. At one time angelica was cultivated in moist fields around London.

Balm (*Melissa officinalis*) has a very sweet lemon scent and is particularly loved by bees. It was once sold in bunches in London's markets. An infusion of the sweet smelling leaves was used to treat nervous troubles and fevers. Balm has a mild sedative and tranquilizing effect and so made an effective cure for insomnia. Add a handful of leaves to a cup of boiling water and leave to infuse for up to 15 minutes. The juice of the plant was applied to wounds as an aid to healing. The crushed leaves were also applied to wounds and insect bites. A handful of balm leaves was used to polish wood and gave it a good shine as well as a fragrant scent. Balm was also used to treat headaches, depression, menstrual cramps, and queasy stomachs. The essential oil, also known as Melissa, is used in aromatherapy to ease depression.

Basil (*Ocimum basilicum*), native to the Mediterranean, was introduced into England from India in the sixteenth century, but could not survive during the English winter. A small amount ($1/2$ teaspoon) of finely chopped basil leaves added to a cup of hot water was sipped to ease stomach troubles and vomiting. It was also effective for easing migraines. Honey was added to the infusion to make a soothing drink for coughs. The leaves were never chopped, but were cut into strips with a knife or scissors, and were never cooked but always eaten raw.

Bay (*Laurus nobilis*) is an evergreen shrub, not to be confused with the common laurel of the hedgerows (which is inedible). Bay leaves have a strong flavor and exude a wonderful aroma and were placed in dry stores of flour and vegetables to discourage weevils. Their aromatic flavor also encouraged an appetite. The berries yielded green oil when pressed, which was used externally to treat sprains and rheumatism.

Belladonna (*Atropa belladonna*), also known as deadly nightshade, is native to Europe, western Asia, and northern Africa. *Herba bella Dona*, or "herb of the beautiful lady" is well known for its poisonous effects—it increases heartbeat and can lead to death. But like many other plants, when used correctly, it was an important and beneficial remedy. Belladonna contains atropin, which is used in conventional medicine to dilate the pupils for eye examinations and as an anesthetic. Roma used it as a sedative and also to relieve intestinal colic, and to relax distended organs, especially the stomach and intestines.

Bistort (*Polygonum bistorta*) is a powerful astringent and a mild infusion and was used as a gargle for sore throats or applied externally to stop bleeding.

Blackberries (*Rubus fruticosus*) are a rich source of fiber and vitamin C and the juice from the berries was used for various ailments. Tea made from the leaves of the bush was a cure for an upset stomach and was also believed to be beneficial to the mucous membranes—it was drunk hot to soothe a cold, or the warm tea could be gargled to soothe a sore throat. Blackberry tea was also effective for relieving indigestion. Infuse 1 teaspoon fresh or dried blackberry leaves in a cup of boiling water for 5 minutes. Blackberry shoots were boiled into a tea, which was used for mouth irritations—possibly because of its astringent properties. The main chemicals present in blackberries are gallic acid and tannin, which are present in every part of the plant.

Blackthorn's (*Prunus spinosa*) young shoots were boiled in water and the concentrated liquid used as a toothache cure.

Borage (*Borago officinalis*) has emollient properties and was used to bring down temperatures in fevers and also to treat depression. The leaves were cooked like spinach or added to drinks. The bright blue flowers are also edible and were added to wine. The plant has a delightful scent of cucumber and imparts this to liquid when infused. Add a teaspoon of leaves or flowers to a cup of boiling water and infuse for 15 minutes.

Burdock (*Arctium lappa*) is a member of the daisy family. The leaves, flowers, or crushed seeds were made into an infusion to cure rheumatism and some Roma carried the seeds in a little bag around their neck to ward off the disease. The young stems were stripped of their rind and eaten raw to purify the blood. The root of burdock was also used as a blood purifier and as a treatment for the relief of arthritic pain.

Butterbur (*Petasites vulgaris*) was found throughout England growing by the side of rivers and streams. Its huge leaves offered protection from the sun's heat in hot weather. The leaves were used as a tonic and stimulant and also to ward off fevers. The cool refreshing fragrance of the plant was best appreciated in cooling drinks.

Cabbage (*Brassica oleracea capitata*) was regarded very highly and its germ killing and anti-inflammatory properties were well known. Cabbage leaves were used to bind wounds, boils, sores, and abscesses long before sterilized bandages were created. Insect bites and stings were treated with an application of crushed cabbage leaves. A hot leaf was applied to arthritis, muscular aches, menstrual cramps and pains, and rheumatism to bring relief. Hot cabbage leaves were also applied to sore throats. The water that the cabbage was cooked in was sipped (sometimes with a little sage) to treat bowel and stomach infections and curiously to prevent nightmares. Sauerkraut (fermented cabbage), a staple of East European cuisine has the same properties, as the plant's active enzymes are preserved during fermentation.

The greater **celandine** (*Chelidonium majus*) is a member of the poppy family whose roots contain an acrid juice that was rubbed on warts and corns to remove them, although it was widely believed that Gypsy women had the power to simply wish away these afflictions. The juice is effective but should be used sparingly and mixed with a little vinegar first.

Centaury (*Erythraea centaureum*) has tender but very bitter tasting leaves that were made into a tisane to treat jaundice, stimulate the appetite, and as a general tonic and digestive. It is a strong antiseptic and was also used as a mouthwash and applied to scratches and cuts.

Chamomile or camomile (*Anthemis nobilis*) has strong antiseptic properties and a curious aromatic perfume, which strangely is offensive to bees. The peculiar scent comes from the oil contained in the plant, which intensifies if the plant is trodden on. Roma used an infusion of the flowers as a general tonic, digestive, and a cure for flatulence. It also relieved nausea and diarrhea and was helpful for babies with colic and teething pain but as it is an effective sedative, chamomile tea should not be drunk to excess. Applied externally, the infusion deterred biting insects. The flowers were pounded into a paste and used to treat skin irritations such as ulcers, infections, rashes, and burns. Chamomile tobacco was smoked for asthma. The flowers contain the essential oil of the plant (which is bright blue but turns yellow when exposed to the air) that was used to make hair lotions. In the early nineteenth century, farmers in Mitcham and Tooting employed hundreds of people to gather the flowers in July and August, which no doubt was a source of employment for many Roma.

Chervil (*Anthriscus cerefolium*) is a member of the carrot family and had a reputation for possessing restorative powers as well as being digestive, expectorant, and diuretic. Only the young green leaves were used—as the plant matures the older leaves lose their pungent flavor, which is reminiscent of aniseed. In the past it was used along with watercress and dandelion in spring tonics to provide a powerful combination of vitamins and minerals after the cold, dark days of winter. Chervil was never chopped but cut into fine strips with a sharp knife. The flavor is lost by too much heat so it was added at the end of cooking or served raw. Its powerful flavor is excellent with eggs, fish, and chicken and in herb butters, sauces, and dressings.

Chestnut leaves were used in a tincture that was applied externally to relieve chilblains, eczema, and rheumatism. Chestnuts were boiled in water and the resultant "essence" was added to a bath to soothe skin troubles. The wood was used to make fences, stakes, and wine casks and the hoops that went round them, as it doesn't rot if stored in damp conditions.

Chickweed (*Stellaria media*) was an immensely valuable plant and was used both internally and externally. The stems were cooked and given to undernourished children who then gained strength quickly. It was also a potent medicine for rheumatism and cramps, but was never taken in large doses as it sometimes resulted in temporary mild paralysis.

Chicory (*Cicorium intybus*) native to Europe has been cultivated through the ages. Made into a tea or extract, chicory root was a bitter digestive tonic that also increased bile flow and eased inflammation. Its roasted root was and still is commonly used as a coffee substitute. Chicory is an excellent tonic for the liver and digestive tract. The root is therapeutically similar to dandelion root and was good for the action of the stomach and liver and cleansing the urinary tract. Chicory was also taken for rheumatic conditions and gout, and as a mild laxative, particularly suitable for children. An infusion of the leaves and flowers also aided digestion.

Clary sage (*Salvia sclarea*) yielded seeds that were used to treat eye problems, and so was known as "clear eye." It was also used as a tonic to relieve menstrual pain and premenstrual problems. An antispasmodic and aromatic plant, clary sage is used today mainly to treat digestive problems such as wind and indigestion.

Clematis (*Clematis vitapounda*) also called traveler's joy had a country name of "Gypsy bacca" because the Gypsies smoked the hollow stems. **The leaves and flowers are acrid and the whole plant is poisonous.**

Clover (*Trifolium pratense*) bears honey-scented red or purple flowers and an old country name for them was beebread, as bees love the sweet smelling flowers. The dried flowers were infused in boiling water to make a pleasant tonic which was also a cure for indigestion, headache, nausea, neuralgia, and bronchitis. The infusion was also a sedative and used to treat nervous complaints. The dried flowers were mixed with coltsfoot leaves to make an herbal tobacco. Clover poultices were used to heal ulcers and sores.

Colewort (*Brassica campestris*) is just one of several varieties of wild cabbage. The roots were crushed in a little boiling water and were useful as cure for diarrhea and sore throats.

Coltsfoot (*Tussilago farfara*) flowers in February and March and the leaves were not gathered until all the flowers had disappeared. The dried leaves were used to treat colds and bronchitis. Curiously the Latin name of the plant means "cough plant" and the ancient Romans used it as a remedy for asthma and bronchitis as well as coughs and colds. The leaves were infused with boiling water and honey to relieve asthma and pleurisy. A decoction of the crushed leaves was applied externally to insect bites, ulcers, cuts, and burns. The powdered leaves were used as an herbal snuff and coltsfoot tobacco was used by asthma sufferers who inhaled the fumes of the burning plant through a reed or hollow stem. The tobacco was made from coltsfoot leaves mixed with other leaves such as comfrey, beech, and chestnut. The leaves were dried by hanging in bunches until limp and yellow. They were then packed into a wooden box and left to dry. After pressing under a weight, the tobacco was sliced or cut. Coltsfoot was an ingredient of herbal tobacco and was used as such in ancient times—Discorides mentioned its use by the ancient Greeks. The bitter juice, mixed with brown sugar or molasses, is still used today to make "coltsfoot" or "cough" candy, sucked to soothe a sore throat or cough in England.

Comfrey (*Symphytum officinale*), a large bushy plant with green leaves and small purple or white flowers, was known as *knitbone* or *boneset* and many Roma used it to heal broken bones. The root was lifted in March (when it has a viscous texture and contains a watery juice), then grated and mashed and the warm pulp was used as a poultice to treat all sorts of inflammations such as wounds, insect bites, and sores. When set, the mash was firm and hard, just like a modern plaster cast. It was also excellent when cooked and eaten as a green vegetable.

Cowslip (*Primula veris*), once common in the English countryside, is now, sadly, becoming rare. The pale gold flowers were made into an infusion to reduce a high temperature and relieve convulsions.

The **cuckoo-pint** (*Arum maculatum*) flourished in moist shady places and ditches. The entire plant is acrid and emanates a strong aroma of carrion. It was also known by many other names such as Wake Robin and Lords and Ladies in Britain and as Jack-in-the-Pulpit in the United States. A starch for clothes was made from the roots and was reported to have blistering effects on the hands of those who handled the roots. It could also be used as a substitute for soap—the whole plant had to be soaked and crushed into a paste before it was used for laundry. The leaves and scarlet berries of the plant are poisonous.

Daffodil (*Narcissus pseudo-narcissus*) leaves were boiled and the liquid applied to the scalp to check hair loss and increase its growth.

Dandelion (*Taraxacum officinale*) was regarded as an enormously useful plant by Roma. The young leaves were eaten in the spring to purify and cleanse the blood, the juice from the leaves and roots was used to treat liver and kidney ailments and the white milky juice from the stem was used to treat warts. The edible roots were sliced and eaten with bread and butter or could be dried in the sun, then roasted and ground and made into a "coffee."

Dill (*Anethum graveolens syn. Peucedanum graveolens*) was used as a remedy for the stomach, relieving wind, and calming the digestion. Dill's essential oil relieves intestinal spasms and griping and helps to settle colic, and it is often used in gripe water mixtures. Chewing the seeds improved bad breath. Dill was also used to increase milk production in nursing mothers and helped to prevent colic in their babies.

Dock (*Rumex*) leaves had tonic properties and were placed inside shoes to cool the feet and aid walking.

Elder (*Sambucus nigra*) or in Romany, *Yakori bengeskro* (devil's eye) was sacred to the Roma and a charm was recited before picking the berries, blossoms, or leaves. An old custom among Roma forbade them using the wood to kindle their campfires.

When collecting firewood they would look carefully through the faggots in case a stick of elder should have found its way into the bundle.

Every part of the elder plant had a medicinal use. An infusion of the bark, flowers, or leaves was an effective remedy for internal inflammation and colic. The flowers and berries were made into ointments for the skin to cure and soothe sunburn. The dried flowers were powdered and used as an insecticide, as was an infusion of the flowers, which was dabbed onto exposed skin to deter midges and flies. Elderflower buds were dried and soaked in boiling water and the solution was applied to painful backs and to relieve chest pains. In addition, the tree had a practical use as the twigs were woven into baskets and the leaves of the elder were used as a dye. In contrast to the glorious fragrance of the flowers, the leaves and sap of the tree have a curious dank smell.

The berries and flowers were also made into wine and refreshing nonalcoholic drinks. Elderberry juice sweetened with honey or sugar was drunk hot for winter colds. The flowers, dipped into batter and fried are delicious. To treat colds and chills, Roma also mixed elderberry flowers with yarrow and peppermint, and then steeped the mixture in boiling water for 13 minutes to make a fragrant refreshing tea.

Elder leaves made an antiseptic poultice for external wounds and were excellent as an insect repellent. The leaves were valued for driving mice away from grain stores and moles from their usual haunts. The leaves, when made into an infusion or bruised, could be worn in clothing or rubbed on the skin, prevented flies, mosquitoes, and midges from settling. Pour boiling water over a few fresh leaves and cover tightly. Leave to stand for a few hours until completely cold. **Elder should not be used internally by pregnant or lactating women.**

A hot soothing drink known as a "Rob" was made from the juice of elderberries simmered and thickened with sugar. Modern research has proved that elderberries contain viburnic acid, which induces perspiration, and is especially useful in cases of bronchitis and similar troubles.

The bark of the *older* branches and sometimes the root was an ingredient in black dye. The *berries* dyed blue and purple.

Eyebright (*Euphrasia officinalis*), as the name indicates, was used to treat sore eyes. An infusion of the leaves from this bitter astringent plant was applied externally. The plant was gathered when in flower and was cut off above the root and used to make infusions (a generous teaspoon of the fresh herb in a cup of boiling water) for coughs and colds. It was also an ingredient of Gypsy herbal tobacco frequently mixed with coltsfoot.

Fennel (*Foeniculum vulgare*), a member of the carrot family with very fine feathery green or bronze leaves, is strongly aromatic. The whole plant was used—seeds, leaves, and stems. An infusion of the seeds was used as an aid to sleep, a cure for coughs and sore throats, and an eyewash and to treat parasitic worms. The seeds were chewed as a digestive aid and also to treat flatulence and hiccups. Fennel tea was made by pouring a cup of boiling water onto a teaspoonful of bruised fennel seeds. Syrup was made from fennel juice to treat chronic coughs. Fleas detest the plant, and powdered fennel has the effect of driving away fleas from animals.

Feverfew (*Tanacetum parthenium*) was often used by Roma instead of chamomile. A tincture of the very bitter yellow-green leaves was applied to the skin as relief from insect bites and stings and also as an insect repellent. One or two leaves of the herb were chewed as an effective cure for headaches. An infusion of the herb was often given to new mothers after childbirth, as it was believed to clean the womb and hasten the expulsion of the afterbirth. **Some people have an allergic reaction to feverfew that can cause mouth sores.**

Foxglove (*Digitalis purpurea*) seeds were gathered when the moon was waning and made into a decoction to strengthen the heart and spirit. Modern medicine uses the seeds of the deadly poisonous plant for the valuable heart drug *digitalis*. In Kent, England, the hardened stalks were used to make parasol handles.

Garlic (*Allium sativum*) was greatly valued as a powerful natural antiseptic and has recently been proved to kill bacteria and germs and have a revitalizing effect on the body. Its volatile essential oils are quickly absorbed into the bloodstream and herbalists today recommend garlic as a general tonic, digestive aid, and to prevent infection. Roma had always believed that garlic could increase resistance to infection and many old remedies have had their effectiveness proved by modern research results. Recent tests have shown that garlic has the ability to reduce cholesterol levels in the blood and is also thought to keep the arteries healthy. Garlic has the amazing ability to detoxify the digestive system and is especially beneficial to the heart and blood. Several cloves of raw garlic were taken at night, after fasting all day to expel parasites such as worms from the body. It was also used as a treatment for asthma, whooping cough, arthritis, rheumatism, and sciatica and as an effective remedy for ulcers, skin complaints, and lethargy. In the past, many Roma kept a crock of garlic steeping in vinegar to treat wounds and sores. Men who worked as laborers during the harsh winter months would push a garlic clove into their woolly socks to ward off colds and flu. An old remedy for coughs, colds, catarrh, and bronchitis was chopped garlic mixed with honey; garlic has a strong effect on the mucus membranes in the body, while honey soothes the throat. Young children with a chesty cough had the same mixture rubbed on their chests. Painful sprains as well as rheumatism and arthritis were treated by rubbing in a pungent ointment of lard and garlic.

Wild garlic was chopped and eaten raw as a spring tonic for the blood, together with the leaves of the wild rose, hawthorn, sorrel, clover, and watercress. These young spring leaves would certainly have provided much needed vitamin C and minerals after the monotonous winter diet.

Gentian (*Gentiana campestris*) roots were ground and brewed into an infusion that was sipped to relieve indigestion and vomiting.

Golden rod (*Solidago virgaurea*) was also known as Aaron's rod or woundwort. Its leaves were made into an infusion to treat gravel and stone. The name *Solidago* means "makes whole." An ointment was made from the fresh leaves to heal wounds and sores. The pulped leaves, flowers, and stalks were good for staunching blood. A pleasant, stimulating tea could also be made from the leaves and was a good all-around tonic that prevented morning sickness in pregnancy.

Ground ivy (*Glechoma hederacea*) was once sold by London's street sellers as a popular blood tonic. An ointment was made from the stems mixed with chickweed, which was used to treat sprains. An infusion of the leaves made a powerful tonic with a pleasant spicy flavor and aroma. It was also known as hedgemaid, alehoof, or catsfoot.

Groundsel (*Senecio vulgaris*) was made into a hot infusion and applied to infected wounds to draw out the pus and as a poultice to painful limbs. A decoction of the plant was applied to soothe chapped hands.

Gypsywort (*Lycopus europaeus*) grew wild on riverbeds, and in trenches and marshes. Small white or skin-colored flowers appeared between June and September. The plant was used as a sedative and also produced a very good black dye that was used to give wool and silk a permanent color. Some Roma used it to color their skin.

Holly (*Ilex aquifolium*) was a useful medicine and the bark, leaves, and berries were all used. The bark and leaves were used to knit bones together and put joints back into place. The leaves were used as a tonic and a cure for jaundice. A tea made of holly leaves was given to promote sweating in cases of catarrh, pleurisy, and smallpox, and to relieve fever and rheumatism. If swallowed, the berries caused violent sickness, but powdered they were used externally to stop bleeding. **The berries and seeds are toxic; just two holly berries are sufficient to induce stomach pain, nausea, vomiting, or diarrhea.**

Honey was used for all kinds of ailments. Honey is hygroscopic (it draws out water) and is a natural antiseptic. Honey was applied to cuts, sores, and burns, which then healed quickly and prevented further infection. A treatment for coughs, colds, and sore throats was made by pouring a thick layer of honey on a cut onion, covering it, and leaving it overnight. The resultant thick syrup was taken by the spoonful. A spoonful of horseradish was added to the syrup to treat catarrh.

Sore throats and irritating coughs were soothed with a honey mixture: mix 2 tablespoons honey, 2 tablespoons chopped sage leaves (fresh or dried), and 2 tablespoons cider vinegar with a little hot water. An old cure for insomnia was 2 teaspoons of honey stirred into a cup or mug of hot milk. An old Gypsy recipe for a bedtime drink uses the juice of oranges and lemons mixed with honey and hot water.

Hops (*Humulus lupulus*) were a cure for loss of appetite. The tops and flowers were used to treat jaundice, and liver and kidney complaints. A poultice of the tops was applied to treat sciatica and lumbago, while an infusion of the flowers was given to children to expel internal worms. Hops have both tonic and sedative properties due to their volatile oil that produces sedative and soporif-ic effects. An infusion was given to improve the appetite and digestion. The plant's sedative properties were useful for treating nervousness and hysteria and at bedtime to induce sleep. A pillow of warm hops cured insomnia, relieved toothache and earache, and allayed nervous irritation.

An infusion of ½ ounce of hops to 2 to 3 cups of water was used to treat heart dis-ease, fits, neuralgia, and nervous disorders, besides being a useful tonic in indigestion, jaundice, and stomach and liver affections generally. It quickly eased an irritable bladder. An infusion of the leaves and stalks, taken by the wineglassful two or three times daily in the early spring, was good for sluggish livers. As an external remedy, an infusion of hops was applied as a poultice for swellings, inflammation, neuralgic, rheumatic pains, bruises, and boils, where it eased pain and allayed inflammation quickly. Hops may also be applied as a poultice. Hop juice is a splendid blood tonic.

Horseradish (*Armoracia rusticana*) was used as a spring cleanser to revitalize the whole body. Its antibiotic and germ-killing properties made it an effective tonic that boosted circulation, fought off colds, and reduced fever. The mustard oil in horseradish stimulates the secretion of mucus, which helps clear the bronchial tubes and congested sinuses. Recent studies have discovered that the antibiotic and germ-killing properties of horseradish are due to its content of allyl iosothiocynate which is effective against listeria, E coli, and staphylococcus aureus. Cooking destroys the active ingredients and pungency of the root, so it is never heated. A poultice of horseradish was applied to relive rheumatism and arthritis, but this had to be done carefully or the skin would blister. The pungent juices of the freshly grated root had expectorant qualities and were a remedy for coughs, catarrh, and sinus problems. It was used as a digestive and also to treat kidney disorders and neu-ralgia. The root was grated or sliced into boiling water (1 teaspoon of freshly grat-ed root to a cup of boiling water) and infused for 20 minutes before sipping slowly to reduce fever and ease the symptoms of a cold.

Hyssop (*Hyssopus officinalis*) a hardy shrub with blue, white, or red flowers that exude a sweet scent, was used to treat coughs and sore throats. Add a handful of fresh leaves to a cup of boiling water and infuse for 10 minutes before drinking.

Ivy (*Hedera helix*) was used to make a cure for whooping cough. Holes were cut into the thick stem of the plant and water poured into the holes. A few ivy berries were added and the stem was left to stand a day and a night and was applied exter-nally. The leaves also were made into a pulp and applied as a poultice for rheuma-tism and sciatica to the painful area. **Never take ivy internally as the leaves and berries are toxic.**

Juniper (*Juniperus communis*), a small evergreen shrub, bears berries that are blue-black when ripe. The berries contain a volatile oil that relieves gas in the stomach, stimulates the gastric juices, and eases stomach cramps. The ripe berries were chewed by anyone in contact with sickness and were also given to those who lacked an appetite or suffered from catarrh. Rheumatism was treated with juniper tea, made by infusing a teaspoon of mashed berries in a cup of boiling water for 20 minutes then straining before drinking morning and evening. A liniment for rheumatism and lumbago was made by macerating juniper berries in olive oil for two weeks then rubbing into the affected areas. A few ripe berries added to a cup of boiling water and left to infuse made an excellent germicide and it was used to treat cuts and wounds. Chewing a few berries was a treatment for anyone with a stomach infection. **The berries should be avoided by pregnant women or anyone with a serious kidney disorder.**

Lavender comes in at least fifty species. The most common is *Lavendula angustifolia* or English lavender, with smooth gray leaves and long spikes of purple flowers. Its fragrance is superb and this variety is specially cultivated for its essential oil. Plants labeled *L. spica* are varieties of old English lavender. Less common varieties include pink and the exquisitely scented white lavender—*L. rosea* and *L. officnalis alba* respectively.

The essential oil, distilled from the flowers and leaves, has powerful healing and therapeutic powers and is extensively used in aromatherapy for its calming and tonic effects on such diverse conditions as insomnia, nausea, muscle cramps, headaches, travel sickness, sinus trouble, earache, eczema, ulcers, anxiety, and rheumatism. Long before aromatherapy came into vogue, country medicine recognized these properties and used lavender in poultices, teas, and waters to treat many ailments.

Lavender tea has an exquisite flavor and can be sipped hot or cold as a calming restorative, which will also quickly ease a headache. Infuse 6 lavender flowers in a (nonmetal) teapot with boiling water and let stand for 5 minutes before pouring. You can also add herbs such as mint or orange or lemon rind to vary the flavor. Lavender tea also enjoyed a reputation as a cure for a hangover, and a cure for hiccups was to chew a few lavender leaves.

Lettuce (*Lactuca virosa*), whether wild or cultivated, was valued for its soporific juices and lettuce tea was an effective cure for insomnia. It could be made even more potent by including poppy seeds and chamomile flowers. Tear the leaves of a large head of lettuce into pieces and cover with boiling water. Simmer gently for about 20 minutes, then cut the stem and add to the pan and simmer for another 5 minutes. The milky juices of the plant were used to treat gout, coughs, asthma, menstrual pain, and nervous disorders. The stem and leaves were bruised to release the flow of white juice.

Liquorice (*Glycyrrhiza glabra*) was introduced to Britain in the sixteenth century by monks and was cultivated around London, Surrey, Nottinghamshire, and Yorkshire. A sickly child who wouldn't thrive was treated with a small glass of a tonic made by steeping black liquorice in water with a little lemon juice and linseed. The fresh roots of American liquorice (*G. lepida*) were chewed to relieve toothache and the liquid from the soaked leaves was used as eardrops. **Pregnant women should not use liquorice as it can sometimes lead to high blood pressure with prolonged use.**

Lovage (*Levisticum officinale*) is a member of the carrot family with wide ribbed leaves. Small, pale yellow flowers appear in summer and a pleasant aromatic perfume pervades the whole plant. The seeds were made into an infusion to warm the stomach, and to treat jaundice. Lovage tea was taken for rheumatism. Lovage root eased bloating and flatulence. It was also used with other herbs to counteract colds and flu.

Marigold (*Calendula officinalis*) flowers were made into a drink to relieve depression. In Shakespeare's time the dried flowers were put into broths as they were believed to possess recuperative powers and there was a common belief that marigolds raised the spirits and cheered the heart. Because of this the bright orange petals were added to salads and were also used to flavor vinegar. A poultice of the fresh flowers infused in boiling water was used externally to heal cuts, sores, and chapped skin. Only the Pot Marigolds should be used, not the African or French varieties. The vivid orange flowers were used in the past as a cheaper substitute for expensive saffron and, in fact, the flower was known as "poor man's saffron." The color (calendulin) is soluble in fat and was used extensively in soups and to a lesser extent in butter and cheese. A marigold flower was an effective remedy for the pain and swelling caused by wasp or bee stings when rubbed on the affected part. A lotion made from the flowers was used to treat sprains and wounds, and water distilled from them to treat inflamed and sore eyes.

An infusion of freshly gathered marigold flowers was given to anyone suffering from a fever, as it gently promoted perspiration and dispelled any eruption. Marigold flowers were also useful for children's ailments. The juice from the leaves was sniffed up the nose to induce sneezing and a discharge of mucous from the head. The acrid qualities of the plant made it an excellent treatment for warts. A yellow dye was also extracted by boiling the flowers.

Milk thistle and Mary thistle (*Carduus marianus syn. Silybum marianum*) are native to the Mediterranean and were much used as a remedy for liver problems including hepatitis and cirrhosis. Recent research has confirmed traditional herbal knowledge, proving that the herb has a remarkable ability to protect the liver from damage. In recent years, the active principle in milk thistle has been isolated and identified as a flavonol called silymarin which has been shown to stabilize the membranes of liver cells.

Stinging nettle (*Urtica dica*) leaves were made into a tea to purify the blood and act as a general tonic on the body. An infusion of the leaves was used to treat goiter and an infusion of the seeds was used to treat consumption. Another old remedy was nettle tea. Nettles are rich in iron and the tea was traditionally drunk in the spring as a tonic after the winter months. Use only the young leaves from the tip of the plant and add just enough water to barely cover them. Boil gently for 20 minutes, then strain and sweeten to taste. Young leaves made an excellent vegetable and were made into soups and puddings. Nettle beer was drunk as a remedy for gout and rheumatism. Externally it was used as a compress to treat arthritis and as a hair rinse to treat dandruff and stimulate hair growth.

Oak (*Quercus robur*) bark and leaves were used medicinally for their tonic antiseptic and astringent properties. Powdered bark, sprinkled into the shoes or socks of those who worked with their feet in water helped to harden the skin and protect against chapping. Applied to bleeding wounds it caused the blood to clot and prevent further bleeding. A handful of oak leaves boiled in about 5 cups of water were used to treat abscesses and wounds. The leaves, boiled in water, were placed in the mouth to treat toothache. Oak bark is used to treat diarrhea, dysentery, and bleeding. For external use the bark and/or leaves are boiled and then applied to bruises, swollen tissues, bleeding wounds, and varicose veins. Every part of the oak, but particularly the bark, contains a high amount of tannic acid that has tonic and antiseptic properties. The bark was collected in May and dried. A snuff was made from the finely powdered bark, which was beneficial in the early stages of consumption. An infusion of the bark (2 teaspoons fresh or dried to a cup of cold water brought slowly to the boil and boiled for 10 minutes) was drunk to treat heavy menses and diarrhea. The same infusion was used as a gargle for sore throats and inflamed gums, as a treatment for chilblains and as a hair rinse after washing to improve the growth and quality of hair.

Olive (*Olea europaea*) leaves have been used since time immemorial to clean wounds. Olive leaves also reduce blood pressure and help to improve the function of the circulatory system. They are mildly diuretic and also have some ability to lower blood sugar levels; the leaves have been taken for diabetes. The oil is nourishing and improves the balance of fats within the blood. It was traditionally taken with lemon juice in teaspoonful doses to treat gallstones. The oil has a generally protective action on the digestive tract and is useful for dry skin.

Onions (*Allium cepa*) had many medicinal uses. A hot onion was placed on a boil to bring it quickly to a head. To treat parasitic worms, chopped onions were cooked in milk, strained, and the milk taken each day. Raw onions, too, were valued as a destroyer of parasitic worms and were also considered to strengthen the heart. A poultice of raw onion was applied externally to treat rheumatism and arthritis. Raw onion juice or the water in which onions were cooked was used as a skin wash for the complexion. Onions were given to horses that were prone to thrombosis. Eaten raw, onions are powerful as the volatile oils are not destroyed by cooking, but should not be taken by anyone with a delicate digestion or sensitive stomach as they can cause irritation.

Parsley (*Carum petroselinum*) was used in treatments for jaundice, liver, and kidney complaints. Parsley tea was a remedy for urinary and menstrual disorders and was also used externally to treat insect bites and stings and was applied externally to the scalp to discourage head lice—in which case it was left to stand for several hours beforehand. The same mixture was used as a face wash and as a final hair rinse after shampooing to add gloss to the hair. Poultices of parsley and vinegar were applied to sore breasts of breast-feeding mothers to relieve the pain. An infusion of chopped leaves was boiled in water for a few minutes and left until just warm when it was strained and applied as a compress for sore or infected eyes. **Parsley tea should not be taken for more than a few days at a time and never by pregnant women.**

Parsley piert (*Alchemilla arvensis*), a wild plant unrelated to parsley was used to treat bladder troubles and stones, for which it was known as parsley pierce-stone, corrupted to parsley piert.

Peppermint (*Mentha piperita*) leaves were made into a tea to cure headaches and also to treat indigestion and insomnia. A little of the juice was used to relieve toothache. All varieties of garden mint can be made into a tea that will calm nausea, relieve wind, and fight fatigue. The smell of this fragrant, aromatic herb alone has the power to refresh and revive. Peppermint is particularly good for drinking after a meal for its digestive properties.

Periwinkle (*Vinca minor*) was made into a lotion to soothe inflamed skin, treat wasp stings, and boiled to make a poultice to stop bleeding. It also had a reputation as a magic plant; it was believed to have the ability to ward off evil spirits. **The plant can cause serious side effects such as nausea and hair loss, so no attempt should be made to medicate yourself with periwinkles.**

Plantain (*Plantago major*) was also known as ripple grass or way bread. The earliest name for the plant was *waybrode* or *waybroed*, which meant "bread at the wayside." In America the plant is called snakeweed or ripple seed. Another name common in America is Englishman's foot or white man's foot (the name used by Hiawatha) due to the fact that English emigrants carried the seeds to the New World. Its astringent properties made it an excellent wound healer. The bruised leaves were used to heal cuts and staunch bleeding and would also relieve nettle stings. An infusion of the leaves was good for internal hemorrhages.

Potato (*Solanum tuberosum*) was a veritable medicine chest! Raw potato juice, either on its own or mixed with cabbage juice, was used to heal ulcers and treat ailments of the digestive tract. The juice was also taken internally as a remedy for rheumatism and gout. Half a cup of juice should be sipped after meals, twice a day. If you can't tolerate the neat juice, mix it with another vegetable juice such as carrot. Potato juice is also applied externally to treat cysts and swellings; soothe painful burns, scalds, and sunburn; and is reputed to alleviate the discomfort of eczema and chilblains. Thinly sliced or grated raw potato remains one of the best wonderfully refreshing treatments for puffy, sore eyes.

Poppy (*Papaver rhoeas*), a vivid scarlet flower, thrived in cornfields and waste ground. The dried seeds of poppies were used to send restless babies to sleep.

Raspberry (*Rubus idaeus*) leaves were chopped finely and brewed into a very bitter- tasting tea which was sweetened with honey and given to women about to give birth to induce an easy childbirth. The bitter leaves could also be mixed with other food to mask their flavor and make them more palatable.

Rosemary (*Rosmarinus officinalis*) leaves were chopped and added to "Gypsy tobacco" (see Coltsfoot) to alleviate asthma. The herb is a stimulant and has a tonic effect, hence its reputation as a soother of tense nerves and muscles and its ability to improve circulation and liver function. Honey and rosemary were taken as a heart and nerve tonic. An infusion of the leaves was sipped to treat upset stomachs, regulate the menstrual cycle, ease cramps, and as a cure for indigestion—but not more than once a day. Put a stem of the herb in a cup of boiling water and leave to infuse for 10 minutes before drinking. Rosemary infusion was used externally to treat stings and bites and was also particularly good for the hair when used as the final rinse. The crushed leaves were added to food to prevent food poisoning. Rosemary was also believed to be an effective cure for hangovers.

Sage (*Salvia officinalis*) was regarded as a panacea for most diseases. The herb was infused to drink as a tea, made into wine, added to cheese, and eaten with bread and butter. There are several varieties of the herb and all are wonderfully aromatic. Sage essential oil is antiseptic with antibacterial and antifungal properties. It was used to treat mouth and gum complaints such as gingivitis. Add a handful of chopped fresh leaves to ½ cup of boiling water and let stand for 10 minutes. Strain into a clean cup and use as a mouthwash several times daily. The fresh leaves were also rubbed on the teeth, to cleanse them and strengthen the gums. The dried leaves were smoked in pipes as a remedy for asthma.

Scabious (*Scabiosa arvensis*) was also known as the "Gypsy rose" and was used to treat chest ailments.

Scarlet pimpernel (*Anagallis arvensis*) juice was used to alleviate the pain of insect stings and bites. Raw onion has the same effect.

Sloes (*Prunus insititia*) are perhaps best known today in sloe gin. The tart berries were sucked to ease sore mouths and mouth ulcers, as the dark purple fruits had an astringent effect on the mouth.

St John's Wort (*Hypericum perforatum*) flowers at the time of the summer solstice, and was considered to have powerful magical properties that enabled it to repel evil. It was used to relieve pain and inflammation, particularly the pain of menstrual cramps, sciatica, and arthritis.

Strawberry (*Fragaria vesca*) tea was an excellent blood purifier. Simmer 3 teaspoons of strawberry leaves in 1 cup of water for 5 to 10 minutes. Strain and sweeten if desired. In the past strawberries were highly regarded for their medical value. The berries are mildly astringent and were used to cleanse and tone the skin. The fruit will also relieve mouth ulcers, whiten teeth, and remove tartar—rub a juicy strawberry over the teeth and gums and leave for 5 minutes before rinsing well with warm water. The leaves of the plant also make a pleasant tea that was served as an appetizer and acted as a tonic to the system. Two good handfuls of the washed leaves infused in boiling water were a remedy for diarrhea. The same mixture applied externally is reputed to be good for eczema and styes.

Sunflowers (*Helianthus annuus*), with their tall bright yellow flowers are among nature's most useful plants. The flowers were made into a yellow dye and the seeds were used to cure whooping cough. The leaves were smoked like tobacco and the oil from the seeds could be used for cooking. Sunflower seeds were also regarded as a treatment for coughs and the seeds do have an emollient effect on the mucous membranes.

Tansy (*Tanacetum vulgare*) flowers were made into an infusion to expel worms. Its hard flowers earned it the name of buttons or bachelor's buttons. An old Gypsy belief was that if you wore a stem of tansy in your boots it would ward off fever. A hot fomentation of tansy tea was used to treat sciatica, bruises, and varicose veins. An infusion of the strong spicy-scented flowers and leaves was used as a treatment for gout. A bunch hung near food would keep flies away. The strongly flavored leaves were shredded and added to salads and omelets or made into puddings. Tansy was one of the first plants brought to America by the settlers.

Tarragon (*Artemisia dracunculus*) is sometimes known as *herbe au dragon* in France because of its reputed ability to cure serpent bites. It is widely used as an herb in cooking as it stimulates the digestion. It is also reputed to be mildly sedative and was taken to induce sleep. With its mild menstruation-inducing properties, it was taken if periods were delayed. The root was also applied to painful toothache.

Wild thyme (*Thymus serpyllum*) was regarded as unlucky by some Roma and so was never taken into wagons or tents. But it was used outdoors, boiled in water, and sweetened with honey or sugar to treat whooping cough. Thyme tea was an excellent treatment for all sorts of aches and pains, throat and chest complaints, and indigestion. Pour boiling water over a teaspoon of fresh thyme flowers or a few bruised stems of fresh thyme and leave to infuse for a few minutes. Take 2 tablespoonfuls up to three times a day. The antiseptic properties of thyme have been recognized for centuries—it repelled skin parasites such as lice and was in the past strewn over floors to repel insects and hung in kitchens to keep flies away. Thyme will keep its fresh aromatic fragrance for months. Oil of thymol is an ingredient of commercial mouthwashes and toothpastes.

Tormentil (*Potentilla tormentilla*) was found in pastures and woods and the pretty yellow flowers were used to treat leg swelling and pain in the kidneys. The root was also employed as a gargle for sore and ulcerated throats. A strong decoction made a good wash for inflamed eyes. Two ounces of the bruised root was boiled in 6 cups water until it was reduced by one-third. After straining it was ready for use. A piece of cotton soaked in the decoction was applied to warts to make them disappear.

Valerian (*Valeriana officinalis*) is native to Europe and western Asia. Valerian root was used to relieve nervous tension, insomnia, and headaches. Valerian decreases muscular spasms so was useful in cases of nervous digestion, irritable bowel syndrome, and stomach and menstrual cramps.

Violet (*Viola odorata*) was valued for its sweet smelling leaves. They were made into an infusion to treat internal cancers, while a poultice of the leaves soaked in boiling water was applied to cancerous growths. The leaves have antiseptic properties and were scattered in salad, together with the fragrant flowers. Violet vinegar treated headaches and was used as an external application for gout. Violet flowers possess slightly laxative properties and the petals were widely used in cough medicines.

Walnuts (*Juglans regia*) were reputed to promote strength. They were also used to stain clothes and skin black. Walnut husks were collected while still green and made into an infusion, which when mixed with tobacco, made an excellent hair lotion that killed lice and acted as a tonic for the hair. Diluted walnut oil was used to treat dandruff. A yellow dye was obtained from the young green husks. The juice of the green husks, boiled with honey made an excellent gargle for a sore mouth and inflamed throat, while the distilled water of the green husks was applied to wounds and taken internally as a cooling drink for a fever. Dried and powdered walnut bark, made into a strong infusion, was a useful purgative and a treatment for dysentery and skin diseases. Walnut leaves were collected in June and July when the weather was fine and the leaves were completely dry. After being dried in the shade outdoors to avoid loss of color, they were made into infusions and teas and also applied externally to treat sores, shingles, and skin complaints such as eczema, hives, and boils. Use 2 teaspoons of fresh or dried leaves to 1 cup of boiling water. An ointment for skin troubles was also made from the leaves and green husks. Fresh walnut leaves were rubbed into the skins of domestic animals as a protection against insects. Persistent ulcers were treated with a mixture of walnut leaves and sugar. A strong decoction of walnut leaves was painted around doorways and woodwork to repel ants.

Watercress (*Nasturtium officinale*) mixed with brown sugar and honey was used to treat whooping cough and was also beneficial for cramps and rheumatism. Its high vitamin C content would certainly have benefited those who took it as a tonic. It was used in salads and also made into a delicious soup.

Willow (*Salix alba*) trees grow by rivers and in damp places. Pieces of willow bark were boiled in a pan of water to make *santekash*—a drink that was good for headaches, rheumatism, and for curing a hangover. Applied externally it was used to cleanse and heal infected or inflamed eyes. The bark is an astringent and tonic and today is sold by herbalists. Willow contains salicylic acid, which is the principal ingredient of modern aspirin and is very safe to use, mild on the stomach, and has no side effects.

Witch hazel (*Hamamelis virginiana*) trees thrive in damp woods and were regarded as mysterious because water diviners used their branches. Both the leaves and bark were made into a poultice for inflammations and also into a lotion to treat stings. When dried and powdered the mixture was sniffed to stop a nosebleed. Witch hazel is both tonic and sedative and also a natural astringent that was used externally to soothe insect bites, burns, and bleeding wounds. Taken internally, it helped to stop internal organs from bleeding and treated bronchitis, the flu, and coughs. It was often used as a mouthwash for ulcerous conditions of the mouth and throat and bleeding gums.

Angelica Tea

MAKES 2 CUPS

3 teaspoons chopped fresh angelica leaves
2 cups boiling water

Put the angelica leaves into a cup and pour on the boiling water. Cover and leave to infuse for 5 minutes, then strain and drink while hot.

Lavender Cordial

MAKES ABOUT 1 CUP

Lavender cordial is a pleasantly refreshing, lightly scented drink with an exquisite taste. It makes a calming restorative drink and will also ease a headache. It's ideal on a hot summer's day, diluted with sparkling mineral water. Make sure the lavender has not been sprayed with insecticides and rinse gently under cold running water (to dislodge any insects) before use. Alternatively, you can buy culinary lavender from herbalists.

¹/₂ cup sugar
50 lavender flowers

Put 1 cup water and the sugar into a pan and heat gently until the sugar has dissolved completely. Add the lavender flowers and bring to the boil. Remove from the heat; cover the pan and leave to infuse for 30 to 45 minutes. Strain the liquid into a pan and reheat, stirring all the time, until the mixture is syrupy. Cool completely. Pour into sterilized bottles, seal tightly, and cool. Store in the refrigerator for up to 2 months. Drink within 2 to 3 days of opening.

Elderberry Cordial

6 cups washed fresh ripe elderberries, crushed
1 cup unrefined milled golden cane sugar

Put the berries into a pan with 10 cups of water. Heat gently until boiling. Simmer for about 15 minutes or until the fruit is pulpy. Remove from the heat and cool slightly. Pour the liquid through a muslin-lined sieve placed over a large bowl. Let drip slowly for 2 hours to extract as much juice as possible but do not squeeze or push the mixture through the sieve. Return the liquid to the pan and add the sugar. Heat gently until the sugar has dissolved completely, remove from the heat, and cool. Pour into clean sterilized bottles, cover, and keep in the refrigerator for up to 2 weeks. Dilute with water or soda and serve with plenty of ice to make a refreshing drink. Alternatively, 1 or 2 tablespoonfuls mixed with a tumbler of hot water, taken at night, promotes perspiration, is demulcent to the chest and helps to relieve a cold.

Violet Syrup

4 cups violet flowers
2¹/₂ cups boiling water
2 cups sugar

Infuse the flowers in the boiling water for 12 hours, covered in a warm place (an airing cupboard is ideal). Stir in the sugar and bring to the boil. Simmer gently until thick and syrupy. Store in the refrigerator for up to 2 months. Drink within 2 to 3 days of opening.

Tea Punch

This reviving drink combines the scented bergamot flavor of Earl Grey tea and the cool refreshing taste of mint. Bergamot is related to mint and has a wonderful aroma of bergamot oranges, after which it is named. The liver and digestive system as a whole benefit from mint which eases colic, cramps and indigestion as well as nausea. Mint also has a mild effect on the nervous system and increases vitality.

4¹/₂ cups boiling water
3 Earl Grey tea bags
Sugar to taste
Juice of 4 oranges
1 lemon, sliced thinly
6 sprigs fresh mint
ice cubes

Pour the boiling water over the tea bags and leave to infuse for 5 minutes. Remove the tea bags, and stir in sugar to taste. Add the orange juice, lemon slices and mint sprigs and chill for several hours. Serve in tall glasses, poured over ice cubes.

Borage and Wine Cup

The ancient Greeks and Romans used borage in their wine cups to dispel melancholy, cheer the spirits and impart courage. Borage contains calcium and potassium and acts a diuretic, helping to stimulate the kidneys. The cucumber-scented plant has brilliant blue star-shaped flowers and adds a delicate fragrance and coolness to drinks.

2¹/₂ cups white wine
I lemon, sliced
4 tablespoons chopped borage leaves
I cup orange juice
2¹/₂ cups carbonated mineral water, chilled
4 to 6 sprigs flowering borage to decorate

Add the lemon slices and chopped borage leaves to the wine. Cover and leave to stand for a couple of hours. Strain into a jug and add the orange juice. Chill thoroughly and just before serving, add the mineral water. Pour into long glasses and decorate with borage sprigs.

MAKES 12 TO 14 CUPS

Fruit or flower syrups were drunk to ward off colds and chills. Diluted with water and drunk hot they soothed sore throats and aided sleep.

4 generous cups damsons
2 cups elderberries
8 cups unrefined light brown muscovado sugar
4 whole cloves

Remove the stones from the damsons and crack 12 of them. Pour 4 cups water over the damsons and cracked stones. Cover and leave to stand for 24 hours. Heat the fruit and water until boiling, and then boil for 15 minutes. Remove from the heat and strain the liquid over the elderberries. Cover and leave to stand for 24 hours. Return to a pan and bring to the boiling point. Add the sugar and cloves, simmer for 10 minutes, until the sugar has dissolved. Remove from the heat and leave until completely cold. Pour into sterilized bottles and seal tightly. Dilute to taste with water to serve. Store in the refrigerator for up to 2 months. Drink within 2 to 3 days of opening.

Latcho Drom
Good Journey
(traditional Romany farewell)

BIBLIOGRAPHY

Bercovici, Konrad. *The Story of the Gypsies*. London: Jonathan Cape, 1929.

Borrow, George. *The Zincali: An Account of the Gypsies in Spain*. London: John Murray, 1841.

———, and Romano Lavo Lil. *Word-Book of the Romany or English Gypsy Language*. 1874.

Boswell, Silvester Gordon. *The Book of Boswell: the Autobiography of a Gypsy*. London: Penguin Books, 1973.

Bowness, Charles. *Romany Magic*. Wellingborough: 1973.

Crabb, James. *The Gypsies' Advocate; or observations on the origin, character, manners, and habits, of the English Gypsies: to which are added many interesting anecdotes on the success that has attended the plans of several benevolent individuals who anxiously desire their conversion to God, third edition*. Nisbet, 1832.

Croft-Cooke, Rupert. *A Few Gypsies*. London: Putnam, 1955.

Davies, Jennifer. *Tales of the Old Gypsies*. David and Charles, 1999.

Fraser, Angus. *The Gypsies*. London: Blackwell, 1992.

Gillington, Betty. *Gypsies of the Heath, by "the Romany Rawny."* 1916.

Jones, E. Alan. *Yorkshire Gypsy Fairs: Customs and Caravans 1885-1985*. Hutton Press Ltd., 1986.

Journal of the Gypsy Lore Society. Liverpool: 1888 to 1965.

Leland, Charles G. *The English Gipsies and their Language*. 1874.

Leyel, C.F. *Herbal Delights*. London: Faber and Faber, 1937.

Loewenfeld, Claire. *Britain's Wild Larder, Nuts*. London: Faber & Faber, 1957.

Petulengro, Gipsy. *A Romany Life*. 1936.

Petulengro, Leon. *Romany Boy*. 1979.

Petulengro, Gipsy. *Romany Remedies and Recipes, ninth edition*. 1947.

Sandford, Jeremy. *Gypsies*. Abacus, 1975.

Smith, Gipsy. *Gipsy Smith, his Life and Work, by Himself*. Nd, c.1905.

Vesey-Fitzgerald, Brian. *Gypsies of Britain, 2nd edition*. David and Charles Holdings Ltd., 1973.

Wood, Manfri Frederick. *In the Life of a Romany Gypsy*. London: Routledge and Kegan Paul, 1973.

Also available from
Hippocrene's Cookbook Library...

AFGHAN FOOD & COOKERY
Helen Saberi

This classic book of Afghan cookery is now available in an updated and expanded North American edition! This hearty cuisine includes a tempting variety of offerings, such as Aush (pasta with yogurt, chickpeas, kidney beans, and minced meat), Sikh Kebab (Lamb Kebabs), and Qorma-e-Zardak (Carrot Stew). The author's informative introduction describes traditional Afghan holidays, festivals and celebrations; she also includes a section entitled, "The Afghan Kitchen," that provides essential information regarding utensils, spices, ingredients and cooking methods.

312 pages • 5½ x 8¼ • illustrations • $12.95pb • 0-7818-0807-3 • (510)

BEST OF REGIONAL AFRICAN COOKING
Harva Hachten

A gourmet's tour of Africa, *Best of Regional African Cooking* includes everything from North African specialties, such as Chicken Tajin with Olives and Lemon to Zambian Groundnut Soup and Senegalese Couscous. Take a culinary safari through the continent, sampling other delicacies like Nigerian Jollof Rice, Agala Dzemkple (a Crab Stew from Ghana) or Mchanyanto (Mashed Yams and Pumpkins from Tanzania). With over 240 recipes that deliver the unique and dramatic flavors of each region, this is a comprehensive treasury of African cuisine adapted to the American kitchen. The book also includes a glossary of African terms and a list of substitutions.

274 pages • 5½ x 8½ • ISBN 0-7818-0598-8 • $11.95pb • (684)

CUISINES OF PORTUGUESE ENCOUNTERS
Cherie Hamilton

This fascinating collection of 225 authentic recipes is the first cookbook to encompass the entire Portuguese-speaking world and explain how Portugal and its former colonies influenced each other's culinary traditions. Included are dishes containing Asian, South American, African, and European spices, along with varied ingredients, such as *piripiri* pepper, coconut milk, cilantro, manioc root, bananas, and dried fish. The recipes range from appetizers like Pastel com o Diabo Dentro (Pastry with the Devil Inside from Cape Verde), to main courses such as Frango à Africana (Grilled Chicken African Style from Mozambique) and Cuscuz de Camarão (Shrimp Couscous from Brazil), to desserts like Pudim de Côco (Coconut Pudding from Timor). Menus for religious holidays and festive occasions, a glossary, a section on mail-order sources, a brief history of the cuisines, and a bilingual index assist the home cook in creating meals that celebrate the rich, diverse, and delicious culinary legacy of this old empire.
378 pages • 6 x 9 • drawings • ISBN 0-7818-0831-6 • $24.95hc • (91)

EGYPTIAN COOKING
Samia Abdennour

Originally published in Egypt, this ever-popular guide to Egyptian cooking has been revised for a North American audience. Egyptian cuisine has been influenced by several Mediterranean culinary traditions, including Turkish, Palestinian, Lebanese, Greek and Syrian. These nearly 400 recipes, all adapted for the North American kitchen, represent the best of authentic Egyptian home cooking.

From appetizers to desserts, some recipes included are `Arnabit musa a`a (Moussaka Cauliflower), Samak bi-l-tahina (Fish with tahina sauce), Kosa matbukha bi-l-zabadi (Zucchini stewed in yogurt), and Lahma mu'assaga (Savory Minced Beef). The chapters included are Mezze, Breakfast, Main Courses, Sweets and Desserts, Beverages, Kitchen Utensils, and Spices. This classic cookbook also includes a glossary of Arabic terms for ingredients and useful tips on shopping and using traditional cooking utensils.
199 pages • 5½ x 8½ • 0-7818-0643-7 • $12.95pb • (727)

IMPERIAL MONGOLIAN COOKING :
Recipes from the Kingdoms of Genghis Khan
Marc Cramer

Imperial Mongolian Cooking is the first book to explore the ancient culinary traditions of Genghis Khan's empire, opening a window onto a fascinating culture and a diverse culinary tradition virtually unknown in the West. These 120 easy-to-follow recipes encompass a range of dishes—from Appetizers, Soups and Salads to Main Courses (Poultry & Game, Lamb, Beef, Fish & Seafood), Beverages and Desserts. Among them are Bean and Meatball Soup, Spicy Steamed Chicken Dumplings, Turkish Swordfish Kabobs, and Uzbek Walnut Fritters. The recipes are taken from the four *khanates* (kingdoms) of the empire that include modern day Mongolia, Chinese-controlled Inner Mongolia, China, Bhutan, Tibet, Azerbaijan, Kyrgyzstan, Tajikistan, Turkmenistan, Uzbekistan, Kazakhstan, Georgia, Armenia, Russia, Poland, Ukraine, Hungary, Burma, Vietnam, Iran, Iraq, Afghanistan, Syria and Turkey. The author's insightful introduction, a glossary of spices and ingredients, and list of sample menus assist the home cook in creating meals fit for an emperor!
211 pages • 5½ x 8½ • ISBN 0-7818-0827-8 • $24.95hc • (20)

THE INDIAN SPICE KITCHEN:
Essential Ingredients and Over 200 Authentic Recipes
Monisha Bharadwaj

This richly produced, wonderfully readable cookbook, takes you on an unforgettable culinary journey along the spice routes of India with over 200 authentic recipes and stunning color photographs throughout. Simple step-by-step recipes, all adapted for the North American kitchen, allow cooks to create delicious dishes with precious saffron, aromatic tamarind, delicately fragrant turmeric, mustard and chilies.

The recipes are arranged by featured ingredient in a full range of soups, breads, vegetarian and meat dishes, beverages and desserts. Among those included are Lamb with Apricots, Cauliflower in Coconut and Pepper Sauce, and Nine Jewels Vegetable Curry. This cookbook includes historical and cultural information on each ingredient, facts on storing and preparation, medicinal and ritual uses, and cooking times and serving suggestions for all recipes.
240 pages • 8 x 10¼ • color photographs throughout • ISBN 0-7818-0801-4 • $17.50pb • (513)

TASTE OF ROMANIA
Expanded Edition
Nicolae Klepper

This comprehensive and well organized guide to Romanian cuisine presents the
real taste of both Old World and modern Romanian culture in a unique cookbook combining over 140 traditional recipes with enchanting examples of
Romanian folklore, humor, art, poetry and proverbs. The book includes recipes
for such classic favorites as Lamb Haggis, Mamaliga, Eggplant Salad, Fish
Zacusca, and Mititei Sausages. *Taste of Romania* also includes a section on
Romanian wines and a bilingual Romanian-English index.
335 pages • 6 x 9 • b/w photos and illustrations • 0-7818-0766-2 • $24.95 hardcover • (462)

TASTING CHILE
A Celebration of Authentic Chilean Foods and Wines
Daniel Joelson

In 140 traditional recipes, this book contains a variety of dishes from spicy salsas
and hearty soups to the ubiquitous empanada. *Tasting Chile* contains recipes for
simple dishes including roast chicken and rice, as well as more complex and exotic fare such as rhubarb mousse, blood sausage, and fried frogs' legs. The author
describes the unique experience of dining in Chile and the foods unique to this
South American country, and provides substitutes for items not available in the
United States. In addition to recommendations for pairing Chilean wine and food,
this cookbook includes a special section devoted to Chilean wine.
250 pages • 6 x 9 • ISBN 0-7818-1028-0 • $24.95hc • (556)

All prices subject to change without prior notice. To purchase Hippocrene Books
contact your local bookstore, call (718) 454-2366, or write to: HIPPOCRENE
BOOKS, 171 Madison Avenue, New York, NY 10016. Please enclose check or
money order, adding $5.00 shipping (UPS) for the first book and $.50 for each
additional book.